'An invaluable guidebook for women... their and others' lives happier... positive change for women and...
— Vanessa Ki... to Happier

Happiness.

'Giselle's book boldly defines the dilemma women face, and impressively outlines the possible solutions.'

— Jennifer Cox, *Women are Angry: Why Your Rage is Hiding and How to Let it Out.*

'One of the most thorough explanations I have seen on the challenges women face. This book is an inspiration to working mothers on *how* to keep going.'

— Dr Beth Cabrera, *Beyond Happy: Women, Work and Well-Being.*

'Giselle provides an essential roadmap for mothers – and all people, really – seeking time for meaningful work, love, care and connection, and the leisure time to truly savour a rich and full life. Backed by research, compelling stories, and practical tips, Giselle ultimately paints a vision of a hopeful, enriching, and equitable future that will be better for us all.'

— Brigid Schulte, *Overwhelmed: Work, Love and Play when No One Has the Time* and *Over Work: Transforming the Daily Grind in the Quest for a Better Life.*

'For all working mothers, this book tackles the important topic of how time pressures affect well-being and, importantly, what we can do about it.'

— Professor Cassie Holmes, UCLA, *Happier Hour: How to Spend Your Time for a Happier, More Meaningful Life.*

Can Women Really Have It All?

A Happiness Handbook for Working Mothers

GISELLE GOODWIN PhD

This book is sold subject to the condition that it shall not, by way of trade or otherwise, be lent, re-sold, hired out or otherwise circulated without the publisher's prior consent in any form of binding or cover other than that in which it is published and without a similar condition including this condition being imposed on the subsequent purchaser.

Copyright © Giselle Goodwin 2024

Giselle Goodwin asserts the moral right to be identified as the author of this work in accordance with the Copyright, Designs and Patents Act, 1988.

ISBN 978-1-0687786-1-2

All rights reserved. No part of this publication may be reproduced, stored in a retrieval system, or transmitted, in any form or by any means, electronic, mechanical, photocopying, recording, or otherwise, without the prior permission of the publisher.

AGG Associates Ltd
Manchester
United Kingdom

To my daughters, Alana and Georgina.

If you had been Alan and George, I doubt this book would exist.

Table of Contents

CHAPTER 1 THE SITUATION

Surely it shouldn't be this hard?	1
What this book will do for you	4
My story	7
Herstory	16
What does the research say?	21
The situation: in a nutshell	29

CHAPTER 2 WHY WOMEN STILL CAN'T HAVE IT ALL

What is 'it all'?	33
Women's new contract: how did we get here?	39
What *do* women want?	44
Can men have it all?	51
It's not destiny	59
The 'F' word	65
Why women can't have it all: in a nutshell	71

CHAPTER 3 HAPPINESS

What is happiness?	73
Happy genes	77
Happy circumstances	78
Happy habits	88
Four significant things women need for happiness	107
Happiness: in a nutshell	117

CHAPTER 4 WOMEN'S WORK: PAID AND UNPAID

Over(under)whelmed	119
Work, choice and happiness	124
Work challenges	131
Caregiving challenges	137
Does part-time work, work?	145
What works for *you*?	149
Women's paid and unpaid work: in a nutshell	157

CHAPTER 5 WOMEN'S WORK: OUR FEMALE BODIES

Women's third job	159
Nature versus nurture	161
Biology matters	169
Beauty standards and body bashing	176
Safety and the water we swim in	180
Sex *is* work	187
The work of being female: in a nutshell	195

CHAPTER 6 THE SOLUTION

Striving for more	197
Should we tell our daughters to become doctors?	198
Things can only get better!	204
Societal solutions	207
Individual solutions	221
The solution: in a nutshell	233

EPILOGUE	235
ACKNOWLEDGEMENTS	237
FURTHER READING	239
NOTES ON REFERENCES	245
INDEX	277

Chapter 1

The Situation

Surely it shouldn't be this hard?

I love my children in a deep, visceral kind of way. You know the feeling, like you could just gobble them up? That irresistible urge to squeeze their chubby cheeks just a smidgen too hard! I would launch myself in front of a moving vehicle to save them and take a bullet for them before breakfast. So, why would I ever choose to leave their company to go out to work?

'Well,' you might say, 'for financial reasons. For independence. And perhaps, on a day when the job's going well, for a sense of personal fulfilment and achievement.' But on the flip side, there's the perpetual struggle to strike a balance between work and family – the compromises we make to prioritise either work over family or family over work. Is it worth it? Which path leads to happier outcomes for women (as well as for our partners and children)? How do we decide?

About ten years ago, my fabulous friend Fran brought this problem into sharp focus for me. We were sitting at my kitchen table, drinking wine and putting the world to rights. At the time, our small and still squeezable children were busy creating some kind of festering tea party under the table, armed with biscuits and cartons of juice, and merrily scrabbling about on the floor with the dust bunnies. We got onto the subject of children, time management and Fran's friend who works as a hospital doctor. Fran took a slug of wine and eyeballed me. I could feel something controversial hanging in the air. She spat it out: 'Well, it's all bollocks as far as I'm concerned! Life is just too busy, and I would never tell my daughter to become a doctor. By the time she gets to be a consultant, her eggs will have dried up and she will have missed the boat family-wise.'

I spluttered a bit and choked on my Pinot. 'Really?' I said, 'I thought the whole point of buying the kids Fisher-Price medical kits was to encourage them to live the dream?'

'Nope,' Fran said, 'feminism is over-rated. We've been sold a lie. Everyone is stressed out and we've realised we don't really want to *have it all*, after all.'

I remember thinking: *Seriously? Is she right? 100 years since getting the vote and forging ahead with feminist victories, and now we're just too exhausted to be bothered? Perhaps there's nothing to prove anymore; we just want an uncomplicated life and time with our kids, thanks very much. Maybe we are coming full circle, and I should start prepping my girls for a happy life where they marry rich and spend time cultivating useful hobbies. Or advise them to get a part-time job because the stress just isn't worth it.*

It was this conversation that made me start thinking properly about what I should tell my daughters. Was having a career worthwhile or should I tell them to navigate a different, less stressful path?

Trad wife is now trending on TikTok and part of me understands how this has happened. Over the years, I have watched numerous friends grapple with decisions after they have children: whether to stay home or to go back to work, how many days to work and how to juggle it all with their marriage, social life and waxing appointments. No one seems to have the answer, and whichever path they choose women are left feeling uneasy about the road *not* taken.

A common refrain from women I know is that they rarely feel like they are getting it 'right'. We blame ourselves and wonder: *How did I get this wrong? Why am I exhausted, stressed out and losing my mind? Why am I failing to simultaneously be a sex siren for my partner, a Madonna for my children (the religious one – not the sex siren) and Oprah at work?!*

For the majority of mothers, financial circumstances make their choices for them. Two salaries are needed to pay the bills, and ironically, childcare is often the largest bill. Talk about a rock and a hard place. Even mothers with more choice about working outside the home still agonise over the decisions they make about work-family balance. The idea of prioritising our *own* happiness on top of our multiple responsibilities? For most of us, that's pretty laughable.

Yet happiness matters! When questioned, happiness is the thing parents say they want most for their children. Therefore, surely we women need to understand fully what this looks like for us? According to the Greek philosopher Aristotle, 'Happiness is the meaning and purpose in life, the whole aim and end of human existence.' The whole *point* of life is to be happy.

So what should today's women do? What do I say to my daughters? Thirty years after my childhood, will they have an easier time juggling work and family? These are the questions that inspired me to research and write this book. Because working mums need *answers*, even more than we need a long, hot soak in the bath without interruptions.

What this book will do for you

This book will solve all your problems... Just kidding, although I wish I wasn't. What it will do is help you navigate the thorny path of motherhood and work, armed with the latest research on women's happiness. I delve into the specific relationship between happiness and working mothers, aiming to enhance your well-being and that of your children.

Are women generally happier pursuing careers or staying home with their children? Does part-time employment offer a solution? What exactly is happiness, and is it achievable for women who aspire to 'have it all'? Drawing on recent data, this book explores these questions and more, shedding light on why women's life choices often differ from men's despite the progress of feminism. Crucially, I propose what we can do to improve things. My sincere hope is that this book will reassure other women who, like me, have found the juggling act impossible: it is not us – it's society!

Who this book is for

This is a book for *all* working mothers. However, before I start my story I would like to acknowledge the privilege I hold as a middle-class, White, married, heterosexual, able-bodied woman who was born in one of the richest countries in the world and has had the benefit of a free education. Although I try to recognise different realities throughout, I am aware I will not be able to do justice to all voices. Women's issues are broad and deep: they include child marriage (640 million women worldwide), female genital mutilation (230 million women worldwide), not being able to get an education (129 million girls worldwide), domestic abuse (25% of women in the UK)[1], sexual harassment (70% of women in the UK) and the gender pay gap (currently at 15% in the UK).

Women's problems are substantially compounded by ethnicity, sexuality, socio-economic status and disability. If you wish to explore these topics further, I have included a list of reading materials at the end of this book which dig deeper and do more justice to intersectional voices.

In addition, I am cognisant that I mainly speak from the perspective of a heterosexual nuclear family when there are many other kinds of family units. Approximately 1% of families are same-sex couples. Additionally, around 15% of families in the UK are headed by single parents. 85% of single parents are mothers – 70% of single mothers work outside the home and they all deserve a gold medal. My single-mum friends are my heroes – one of my best friends laments 'It kills me that I have to be the mum and the dad.' As if mothering wasn't hard enough, to carry its weight without a partner who finds the unique creatures you have created (with his goggle eyes and your gnarly toes) as loveable and maddening as you do is a doubly heavy load.

Also, to be clear, this is *not* a book about working fathers. As I will explain later, life is still different for them. This doesn't mean that men don't have problems or face challenges in our society. Men's paths are often fraught with a constant need for performance and measurement on a metaphorical ladder. It is not a positive state of affairs for fathers when they feel valued primarily for their money, miss significant parts of their children's childhoods due to over-

---

[1] Domestic abuse happens primarily behind closed doors, and the UK's Women's Aid charity is clear that this is a gender-based crime which predominantly affects women. Abuse can be physical or emotional; coercive control was made a criminal offence in the UK in 2015. See this NHS link to identify the signs of abuse and be signposted for help: nhs.uk/live-well/getting-help-for-domestic-violence/

work and are likely to be given the swivel-eye when they do turn up to playgroup.

Finally, I would like to ask for some empathy – and humour – around this topic. It has taken me many years of research and a fair amount of soul-searching to write this book. I limited my previous writing to safe topics – I wrote a book about my daughter's allergies about ten years ago. I was subsequently trolled on social media by a man who seemed incensed that I was knowledgeable about allergies and nutrition. I had retweeted a statistic from a well-known professor about the health dangers of eating processed meat and what a daily bacon sandwich would do to your lifespan. This bit of information sufficiently infuriated the man – who was clearly a fan of bacon – that he systematically went through all my social media accounts and called me every name under the sun. This kept me off social media for a while but led me to the conclusion that if I was going to be shut down over my opinion on a bacon sandwich then I better start speaking out about things that truly matter to me.

My intention with this book is to share my own experience with you and to impart what I have learned from years of study about women, work and happiness. It tours numerous issues which impact the lives of working mothers today. Of course, I have not been able to cover every subject from every angle. The more I learn, the more I realise that there seem to be about as many diverse opinions on what women *should* be doing as there are shoes in Barbie's wardrobe. Nonetheless, I feel I will have done my job if I can help just one person gain some comfort from understanding that what we working mums are up against is not personal failure, but *systemic* failure. And bah humbug to the trolls!

How to use it

In terms of how to use this book, feel free to read straight from start to finish! I have tried to make it a combination of easy-reading research and practical self-help with a few anecdotes thrown in. Equally, if you are a skimmer or a picker like me, I have provided summaries at the end of each chapter if you prefer to simply absorb the main points and jump to the parts which resonate most with you. We working mums have enough to do without reading the detailed footnotes! Although, I did try to make those interesting too. For those interested in the data sources, I have included a comprehensive list of references.

Suggestions for solutions to the problem of working mothers' happiness can be found in Chapter 3 and Chapter 6. Chapter 3 summarises the current science on well-being and provides ten tips for personal behaviours to improve women's happiness. Chapter 6 offers happiness strategies specific to working mothers and provides both societal and individual solutions to our unique problems. Not all of the suggestions will be right for you. My advice is to look for the one or two nuggets which personally resonate and to give those a go first.

My story

Before I delve specifically into what research says about the happiness of working mothers, I will share a little of my own story to both provide the context of my own experiences and the standpoint from which I approach the data.

The following snippets are my Generation X take on growing up in the 1980s as the eldest of three girls. My parents were kind to us and to each other, which is like winning the lottery as far as childhoods go. They were teachers who (mortifyingly) taught at both my junior and senior school. As a child, I had no traumatic run-ins with boys or specific events which directly led me to believe that life was harder for women. Despite this, I still managed to find myself confused and unsettled by gender politics from quite an early age. I noticed small things. Of course, small things compound over time and end up feeling like big things. But somehow, I didn't feel like I had the right to feel them. I was lucky. I shouldn't make a fuss. Other people just brushed things off. Why couldn't I? In fact, by the time I got to adulting, I was spending quite a bit of time being bothered that I was bothered. I didn't know why gender politics got under my skin so much. Or that so many other women felt that way too. Until now.

What's it all about?

Ever since I can remember I have been fascinated by the subject matter of women, work and happiness. Even as a child (and possibly because I was the rule-governed eldest), I was preoccupied with figuring out the *right* thing to do, where my place was in the world as a woman and how to navigate both a *good* and a *happy* life.

I was born in 1976, and the feminism of the 1980s seemed to make it clear that equality barriers for women had been broken down and my job was simply to get in the game. Tie-dyed T-shirts proclaimed that *Girls Can Do Anything*, and political rhetoric from Reagan and Thatcher reinforced the message that the right thing for a woman to do was to put on her big-girl knickers and make her financial way in the world rather than relying on a man to do it for her.

Set against a backdrop of big perms, fluorescent leg warmers, Melanie Griffiths in *Working Girl* and Julia Roberts in *Pretty Woman*, I learned that I had to work hard and do well in a job, but beauty and sex appeal still mattered for women – and I mean *really* mattered.

Teenage angst

I was subtly aware throughout my childhood and adolescence that womanhood was a puzzle to be solved and a tightrope to be walked. I absorbed many of society's conflicting messages, and despite being told I could *definitely* do anything that boys could do (or perhaps because of being told that!) I carried a subtle, subconscious feeling that somehow figuring life out was a tad trickier for women.

A confirmed geek, I bought my first self-help book on a family holiday to Florida when I was 13. I remember seeing the red cover of *Life's Little Instruction Book* in a gift shop and thinking, *Finally! Someone will explain everything to me!* The book was written by H. Jackson Brown Jr. as father-to-son advice and although many of the instructions were useful – 'Be brave. Even if you're not, pretend to be as no one can tell the difference.' – others were not quite as helpful. For instance, 'Don't trust a woman who doesn't close her eyes when you kiss her.' That was pretty confusing. How was I meant to see what was going on? H. Jackson Brown Jr. didn't help me out as much as I had hoped.

As a teenage girl, my burning questions were more along the lines of:

- Was it more important to be sexy or smart? Should I try to be both or was it better to choose one?
- Were girls meant to behave in *all* the same ways as boys? For example, was it good for girls to be tough?
- Was anyone else worried about VPL (visible panty line)? And how could I get my mum to buy me a thong?!

Girls behaving like boys seemed to be good in some ways but not in others. I knew that a woman's place was now in the world of work, but by the time I was a teenager I had also absorbed the following nuances about my gender:

- Be sexy and attractive but *don't* be 'loose'. When I was 15 and had my first boyfriend, my mum and dad sat me down to explain that boys were like ten-ton trucks at the top of a hill, and it was *my* job to apply the brakes before something awful happened. The inference, of course, was not only that the crashing at the bottom of the metaphorical hill might result in pregnancy but that my flower was not something to be given away to anyone lightly. This chat was accompanied by an actual sketch of said ten-ton truck and an excited, sweaty, adolescent boy firmly positioned in the driving seat.
- Be clever and capable but *don't* show off. Of course, boys don't find girls who are more clever than them attractive. This was obvious. A boy who sat behind me the whole of year eight used to be kind or horrible to me depending on whether I got better or worse test scores.
- Be confident but *don't* be bossy. Or mean. Ever. The message that girls must be good, kind and think of others seemed to float in the ether and I absorbed it as if by osmosis. For sure, I knew that the worst thing a girl could be was a bitch. And of course, the worst thing a boy could be was a pussy – in other words, a girl. Pah!

Out of the cocoon

Despite these messages I received as a teenager about confidence and sexuality, I was pretty sure things were now on a level playing field when it came to school and work. I became more settled and secure about my place in the world in my late teens and early twenties. In high school, it was common knowledge that girls could do just as well on tests as boys. At university I gained a degree in pharmacy and therefore got a job in a field with a fairly equitable gender split – I rarely felt out of place at work.[2]

So my personal experience was that gender inequality didn't overly affect me in the workplace. Lucky me, I know! But gender inequality was about to slap me around the face. Step aside the gender pay gap and make room for the motherhood gap, the yawning chasm between mothers and the rest of the population. My first real experience of this inequality came at the age of thirty-one after having my first child and it was an almighty shock to both me and my husband.

Reality bites

In 2004, my husband and I started a business together recruiting pharmacists. By the time our daughter was born, we had been working together for nearly 3 years and had a great relationship; we fit together like two pieces of a puzzle. Full of naïve optimism, we had no idea what having a baby would mean, but thought we would just figure it out as we went along. After all, we had started a business together; how hard could managing a baby between us be?

After a traumatic labour, we decided it made sense for me to spend the first few weeks at home cracking the enigmatic baby code for sleeping and feeding. After that, the idea was to split the workweek between us on a needs basis. Easy, right? I can hear you laughing now.

Being self-employed, we had no parental leave pay or work-cover, so our daughter was only 11 weeks old when we both knew I had to start going back into the office. The overwhelming feelings I had that cold and blustery January

---

[2] Today, 77% of the current National Health Service workforce in the UK is female. It is interesting to reflect that in 1963 only 10% of women were doctors compared with 47% today. Top management and surgical jobs still primarily go to men, but women are now well-represented in middle and lower-tiered positions.

day are forever etched in my mind. I remember seeming to leak from everywhere: eyes, boobs and brain. On the other hand, my husband seemed confident – almost nonchalant – in waving me out of the door. Although he didn't say it, he positively oozed *how hard can this be?* I can still picture him in our kitchen that morning; as his coffee percolated, he expertly propped our daughter in her bouncy chair and prepared to froth the milk for his cappuccino while he waited for his laptop to fire up. The plan was for him to balance his work-life from home by looking after the baby and carrying on with his emails and phone calls. Ready for business!

I, on the other hand, despite my bright-red power dress and clippy-cloppy high-heels, was not ready for business. It was with a heavy heart that I gathered my briefcase and my breast pump and left for the office. I gave myself a pep talk on the way and rallied sufficiently to wade through the treacle of my baby-brain fog and conduct the morning sales meeting. I was desperate to be in control and acting in overdrive, trying to convince not only myself but everyone else that it was business as usual.

At 4 pm my husband burst through the office door accompanied by the requisite full-to-bursting baby bag and bedraggled appearance that comes as standard when caring for a small infant. His eyes were wild: the baby's hair was wilder. Despite the sleeting rain and wind outside, she was simply sporting a grimace and paper-thin pyjamas with the interesting addition of baby snow boots to her ensemble. Clearly, footwear is important for an 11-week-old baby, but given the choice, I would have preferred to see her in her winter coat.

'I've not had a coffee all day,' my husband announced. 'I've not even looked at my emails. She won't let me put her down.' He handed her to me. 'Will you have a go?'

What the hell?

Birth and breastfeeding are biological facts. But what about nurture? Are women just naturally more nurturing than men? Are we born with an instinct which means we know inherently what to do with a crying baby or do we just put more hours in upfront and therefore end up figuring it out more quickly?

When it came to the biological reality of pregnancy, I must admit I was pretty ambivalent about the whole thing. I would have outsourced that part in an instant if I could; vomiting every hour, on the hour, for 9 months was not my best look. And even though I did recognise that the pregnancy and breastfeeding bits were on me, I had no idea of the weight or force of societal expectations on the role of mother versus the role of father until our babies were born. The idea that this baby stuff – and how to juggle work stuff with it – ended up being primarily my issue to navigate whacked me around the head sufficiently to leave me feeling like I could do with a bit more gas and air.

We know today that fathers are enormously important in the upbringing of their children. Girls and boys with present and caring fathers have higher levels of academic success, and in particular girls with close relationships with their fathers have higher confidence and self-esteem. Without question, fathers are just as important as mothers in the raising of their children. Studies find that women's oxytocin (the love hormone) increases as they spend time with their children. Interestingly, men's oxytocin *also* increases when they bond with their children – and their testosterone decreases. There really is nothing biological that prevents men from being excellent caregivers.

But as my husband and I figured out despite our best intentions, when it comes to parenting, men today still often end up in the role of assistant or backup parent. This starts day one in the hospital, is reinforced by society, compounded by breasts and biology and poses problems for women's equal participation in the workforce.

Adulting

In my personal experience, parenting has been a wonderfully rewarding and joyful job and one I would never trade – mainly because I quite like the little beggars! However, it has been in equal measure the hardest, least recognised and worst-paid job I have ever done. (And I've done some doozy jobs including repetitively peeling garlic over an 8-hour restaurant shift at age 14). Never in my working-outside-the-home life have I experienced the distress that accompanies a crying baby and a tantruming toddler when you need a pee, haven't slept straight through the night in 4 years and are doing everything literally one-handed because the baby doesn't like to be put down and you can't bear to hear her cry.

I spent most of my thirties thinking that it was mainly me who found the challenges of balancing work and family so difficult. I thought that I must be overreacting or making up problems as it so often seemed people around me were handling challenges more easily – or at least had made better choices. Why was work and mothering so hard? There was an ongoing narrative in my head about not sweating the small stuff and just cracking on with things. Why was I upset and struggling when I knew I should be grateful? The news told me every day that things were far worse for others in the world. As I subsequently found out, a substantial part of the problem had to do with expectations; both mine and others'.

Growing up, I had genuinely received the message that women could now have it all; I simply needed to be savvy enough to pick a path along the stepping stones of my reproductive options. However, not only did I never find any decent road map to guide me along the way, but as I got older my experiences seemed to tell me that many of the expectations placed on women were set up either in direct conflict with one another or required a ridiculously delicate balancing act. For instance:

- Lean in at work. But not too far or for too long (no one likes a bossy cow, plus you might miss the baby boat).
- Have children to fulfil your destiny as a woman. But make sure to only do this between the ages of 25 and 35 (don't be either a young or geriatric mum – not good for baby).
- Breastfeed your children. But OMG don't do it in public (gross).
- Earn your own money and pay your own way. But don't work when your kids are very little, and make sure you are present when they are teenagers. Really, you should work part-time during these two stages but then flip without a problem to full-time skilled employment both when they are settled at school and when they leave home.
- Be consistently presentable and attractive. But do this with minimal effort and don't be vain or obsessed with your looks. Natural beauty is best.
- Be body-positive and stop fat shaming. But make sure you are healthy (and thin, of course).

At a writing conference in 2017, I met a professor who studies women and work. I was taken with our conversation and remember thinking: *Ahh! Here is someone with answers to the questions on repeat in my head!* She invited me to an interview about my work and business and after the interview with quite a lot of enthusiastic gabbling on my part, she persuaded me to do a PhD on the subject of *Women, Work and Well-being* under her supervision. I dived into the research with the enthusiasm of a toddler in a ball pit and was fascinated to learn other people's stories. I finished my PhD in 2022 and this book is largely the culmination of what

I learned both from my research and that of other academics in the field.

Herstory

Before diving into the research around the happiness of working mothers today, I'd like to broadly contextualise the impact that patriarchy has had on society. How exactly have we arrived here? According to historian Philippa Gregory, throughout history women have pushed boundaries and defied society's expectations. We have always been pretty badass! However, it is salient that it is less than 200 years since our agitation for women's rights has been formalised and gained significant traction. The eminent historian Professor Yuval Noah Harari, author of the widely acclaimed book *Sapiens*, spoke movingly in 2021 about the incredible advancements of the feminist movement in an interview with Natalie Portman for International Women's Day. He commented that these changes have not only happened within a relatively short period of evolutionary time but also, significantly, without the wars or violence which have characterised so much other social or cultural change throughout human history. He questioned the received wisdom that the current predominance of patriarchal societies has to do with men's advantage when it comes to upper body strength, citing examples like politicians or mafia bosses where leadership is primarily predicated on social power rather than physical strength. To my mind, if the social politics at play in the movie *Mean Girls* is anything to go by, women definitely seem able to hold their own in this regard! Professor Harari concludes that we haven't got a good explanation as to *why* the system of patriarchy has been dominant for so long. The whirlwind tour below gives an over-simplified but valuable snapshot of *her*story, if you will.

In the beginning

Science tells us it all started with the Big Bang around 13.5 billion years ago. Fast forward to about 4 billion years ago when organisms emerged from the proverbial soup, and to approximately 6 million years ago when humans and apes evolved from a common ancestor. Early humans, who we picture living in caves and foraging in hunter-gatherer groups, existed around 2 million years ago. Interestingly, in terms of gender relations, anthropological research suggests that these nomadic groups operated on largely egalitarian principles. Mainly because they had to. Comprising a few dozen to a few hundred individuals, these humans relied on cooperation and power-sharing for survival: both their own survival and that of their offspring. This state of affairs carried on for hundreds of thousands of years.

Notably, it was when humans stopped being nomads and started owning things that the patriarchy took off. This hierarchical system with men at the helm is thought to have gained significant traction around 12,000 years ago during the agricultural revolution. Regularly cited as a contributing factor to patriarchy is the invention of the plough, which required male upper-body strength, and which brought with it a societal shift that confined men to the fields and women to the home. Other factors such as the development of private property, the establishment of inheritance practices – down the male line; making women poorer and granting them less power and decision-making in the family – and the influence of religious beliefs consolidated male dominance and the subordination of women in many societies.

To varying degrees, we've been stuck with the patriarchy ever since. The first known legal codes from around 4,000 years ago – the Code of Hammurabi, named for the Babylonian King – made it clear that a woman was the property of her father or her husband and there were strict laws in place to control her sexuality. For example, if a married woman had an affair the punishment was drowning – whereas if her husband had an affair, the wife was entitled to take her dowry and go back home to her father. No punishment for him! The cultures of Ancient Greece and Rome are full of these kinds of deadly double standards too.

In Athens, the birthplace of democracy, only free adult men were able to be citizens and participate in political life; women had limited access to education and were legally under the guardianship of their husbands or fathers.

In Ancient Rome, law was codified in the Twelve Tables and separate spheres were emphasised for men and women with men participating in public life and women in domestic life. A husband had the legal right to kill his wife if she committed adultery. Alternatively, the punishment for Roman husbands who cheated on their wives varied and depended on many things including social status and the circumstances involved. We can imagine how that may have gone – 'She made me do it!'

In England, laws surrounding coverture started to be formalised around 1100. Coverture was a way of saying that wives were *covered* by their husbands. When she married, a woman's legal identity was subsumed into the man's and the woman ceased to be a person in her own right. This meant women could not own property, sue in court, enter into contracts or claim legal custody of their children. Over time, many European laws and patriarchal systems such as these were exported to indigenous cultures through colonialism.

Recent herstory

- **1848** – the first wave of feminism. A women's rights convention in New York calls for women's suffrage, property rights and equal education and employment.
- **1851** – Sojourner Truth gives a landmark speech at a women's rights event asking 'Ain't I a Woman?'

highlighting the intersectional struggles of Black women in America. Slavery was abolished in the USA in 1865, and in the UK, it was abolished in 1833.
- **1882** – The Married Women's Property Act is a significant step along the way to revoking the laws of coverture in England.
- **1893** – New Zealand is the first country in the world to give women the right to vote. Today, New Zealand regularly ranks highly in league tables for both gender equality and well-being.
- **1918** – the UK gives certain women over the age of 30 the right to vote. Essentially the rich ones; those who either owned property or were married to someone who owned property which had a yearly value of at least £5.
- **1920** – the USA gives women the vote. But not Black Americans or Indigenous Peoples, who faced a number of discriminatory practices until the passing of the Voting Rights Act of 1965. More subtle forms of voter suppression such as voter ID laws continue to affect marginalised communities today.
- **1926** – women in the UK can hold and dispose of property on the same terms as men.
- **1928** – the UK gives the vote to all women over the age of 21.
- **1948** – Cambridge University becomes one of the last UK universities to grant women the right to obtain a degree. Oxford University did in 1920, and the University of London, in 1878.
- **1961** – birth control becomes legal for *married* women in the United Kingdom; it is not until 1967 that single women can be prescribed birth control or that abortion is legalised.
- **1962** – Australia grants all Indigenous Peoples the right to vote; White Australian women got the right to vote in 1902.

- **1967** – homosexuality is decriminalised in England and Wales; but not in Scotland until 1980 or Northern Ireland until 1982.
- **1970** – the Equal Pay Act means UK women have the legal right to equal pay for equal work.
- **1971** – Switzerland gives women the vote. Other countries include Finland in 1906, Germany in 1918, France in 1944, Japan in 1945, India in 1950, Zimbabwe in 1978 and Saudi Arabia in 2015.
- **1975** – the UK's Sex Discrimination Act is passed which means an end to the marriage bar. Previously women in certain jobs had to give up their work when they got married. It also means women can get a mortgage and a credit card in their own name. Prior to this, women needed a male co-signatory.
- **1982** – women are legally allowed to buy drinks at the bar in English pubs without being refused service.
- **1991** – rape within marriage becomes illegal in the UK. Prior to this, the repugnant legal presumption was that marriage implied consent to all sex. In addition, the definition of rape was expanded to include oral and anal sex in 2003.
- **1993** – the USA passes a law which requires federally funded medical trials to include women and ethnic minority groups.
- **2014** – same-sex marriage is legalised in England, Wales and Scotland.
- **2018** – women in Saudi Arabia are allowed to drive.
- **2024** – France becomes the first country in the world to explicitly include the right to an abortion in its constitution.

There is always pushback against change. In Afghanistan in 2021, the Taliban rolled back the previous 20 years' progress on women's rights in one fell swoop. Women who had previously enjoyed the benefits of an education are now banned from going to school, working outside the home, and participating in public life. Still today in Russia and parts of eastern Europe there are horrific abuses of freedom for LGBTQ+ communities. In the USA in 2022, the Supreme Court overturned[3] a 1973 ruling meaning that in some states abortion is now illegal at the point of conception.

My intention with this list of dates and facts is to provide a taste of women's progress over time as I believe it gives us important context. While it's a simplified overview primarily from a Global North perspective, it sets the stage for the examination of women's current status in our privileged part of the world. We still have a desperately long way to go even though we're considered the lucky ones with our first-world problems around childcare and arguments over who is doing the dishes. Those of us in the Global North are simply at the thinner end of an extremely large wedge of gender inequality. However, I argue our problems are especially urgent given our relative good fortune, as we are able to use our position to uplift the voices of others who are more marginalised.

What does the research say?

So, what exactly does the research tell us about the happiness of working mothers who live in high-income countries today? The following sections will briefly summarise what the current evidence reveals about women's

---

[3] The overturning of Roe v. Wade by the U.S. Supreme Court came despite polls consistently showing that the majority of Americans support the right to choose abortion – 69% in 2023, and in the UK it was 85%. In April 2024, American women's rights trailblazer Gloria Steinem reiterated in an interview with journalist Emma Barnett just how crucial a women's right to choose is for women's human rights – full stop. Gloria said, 'I am not going to work together with someone who doesn't think that reproductive freedom is a basic right like freedom of speech.'

work, mum-guilt, women's choices, women's expectations, women's happiness and the impact of gender inequality. This overview will be expanded in the chapters which follow. They lay the groundwork for us to understand exactly why so many working mothers feel we spend far too much time on the rack![4]

About women's work

Women today are accountable for both the finances of the family *and* the heavy lifting of parenting. Researchers call this part of women's *new sexual contract*: the idea that women today aren't fulfilled unless they participate in both mothering *and* paid work. This is vastly different from the previously held societal expectations for women.

A hundred years ago, around 25% of women worked outside the home. In the UK today, *76% of mothers work outside the home compared with 92% of fathers.* Around one-third of mothers are now the breadwinners for their families, and a disproportionate number of these are single mothers earning far less on average than their male counterparts. Women have acquired a role in the workplace and are expected to get on with it – after all, we asked for it – *and* the crucial job of parenting at the same time.

To make matters worse, intensive parenting is on the rise; an impossibly high set of expectations which is big on the concept of maternal sacrifice. Think baby yoga, clean-food culture and a head-spinning flurry of after-school activities. And before-school activities. And weekend activities. And, if you are the parent of multiple children who play multiple team sports, you might as well decide to give up your paid job now.

---

[4] For those who haven't visited the Tower of London, the rack is a medieval torture device where your limbs are secured to rollers which pull you in opposite directions. Sound familiar?!

Back in the 1950s, renowned paediatrician and psychoanalyst Donald Winnicott coined the phrase *good enough mother*. He said – and experts stand by this today – that it is good for children when their parents aren't perfect and fail now and again as it teaches the children coping skills. Good enough means it's okay not to be Super-Mum. Yet how we try to be! Research shows that working women today spend *double* the amount of focused one-to-one time with their children than they did in the 1970s. The proportion of time that men spend with children has also increased in recent times but not nearly to the same extent: women's contribution to caregiving duties is still 2.5 times that of men.

Simply put, the current contract mothers have with society is that the joys and rigours of parenting are primarily our responsibility, with significantly less responsibility for parenting placed on either fathers or the state. We know it takes a village to raise a child and yet society today mainly leaves it to mothers to cope on our own and then makes *us* feel guilty when we can't seem to do it all.

Researcher Sarah Blaffer Hrdy's work on alloparenting[5] shows that humans evolved in societies where children benefitted from the input of several carers, not through the single intensive efforts of one mother. It was advantageous from an evolutionary perspective to gain different skills by forming social bonds with multiple caregivers in the community. This is unlike today's society where the emphasis is primarily placed on the nuclear family, and where parents increasingly move away from family support networks to take up job opportunities. Modern-day surveys do find that both mothers and fathers place importance on being a good parent. However, for men good parenting often

---

[5] Alloparenting is any type of parental care performed by someone who is not the child's parent, such as friends, members of the wider community or other family members.

involves financially providing for their children, whereas for women good parenting involves a time-bound, in-person, emotionally nurturing role. Add on doing a day job, and you have a recipe for frustration and exhaustion. It is no wonder many mothers feel we are coming apart at the seams.

About mum-guilt

One of the things which was of great interest to me during the research phase of my PhD was finding that the word guilt came up regularly in relation to working mothers. It wasn't just me! According to a WM People survey, 85% of working mothers feel guilty about their conflicting roles.

The media rarely tells us about societal problems stemming from choices career dads have made and the term working father's guilt is just not in regular usage. However, pick up any newspaper and you will regularly find the phrase working mother's guilt, sometimes alongside an irritating portrayal of how working women are to blame for things such as childhood obesity or the breakdown of the nuclear family.

Mothers I interviewed during my research spoke regularly and at length about feeling guilty trying to juggle two roles. Whereas, when I interviewed working fathers *with children* and working women with *no children*, they didn't mention the word guilt once. I found that women were twice as likely as men to start their own business to be able to work flexibly, and for mothers this was all about managing childcare. By contrast, men primarily start businesses to earn more money. The men I interviewed with children described flexible working as more of a bonus or luxury rather than something necessary to help them cope with childcare.

One man with three young children who ran a business with his wife explained that if he had to work late in the evenings, he would happily come home the next day and 'Snore my way to glory on the sofa at 3 pm watching the cricket.' Any mother reading this will instantly intuit why this man's wife, who also had a job, would never be found snoring in front of the television at 3 pm on a school day! Mothers feel guilty because society tells us we are responsible for two jobs. We regularly end up torn between them and can feel like we are doing neither properly.

About choices that aren't choices

Choice is strongly correlated with happiness. The 20th century brought more choice for women than any time in history. Two world wars meant women's primary place at home was called into question, and the boon of the contraceptive pill in the 1960s meant we had more control than ever before over our bodies. However, researchers today term the choices that women make around work and family *constrained choices* because they are often made from a position of either limited options or difficult trade-offs. Work that either isn't flexible or isn't interesting, and outside childcare that isn't good enough, or home-based childcare that is exhaustive and *all on us*. Sound familiar?

Perversely, women can also find that we suffer from too much choice. A bit like when you go into a restaurant with a 20-page menu. Great, but bamboozling. Women today have ended up with so many overwhelming choices that we sometimes decide not to choose, but instead to do it all. We focus on our looks, our career, our fitness, our homemaking skills, our social credentials and our parenting. #FOMO central. Author Courtney Martin, who wrote *Perfect Girls, Starving Daughters*, says: 'We are the daughters of feminists who said "You can be anything" and we heard "You have to be everything".'

About the cost of comparison

An additional issue that doesn't help women is explained by social identity theory: this is the idea that the groups people belong to create an important source of pride, self-esteem and identity. Being part of the in-group creates a satisfied social identity and the out-group a dissatisfied one: not good for happiness and well-being. Based on decisions we make around work and parenting, women can often find themselves siloed into groups like career mum or stay-at-home mum.

Researcher Shani Orgad, author of *Heading Home*, describes an interaction with what she terms the yummy mummies from her local London school who asked her one morning to join them for coffee. When she explained that she couldn't go because she had to work, one of the mums said, 'Oh dear, poor you.' This kind of passive-aggressive comment is enough to bring us all out in a rash! Even the part-time working mums, who might have been able to make that coffee, can struggle to figure out which camp they belong in. I know this dance all too well. When my kids were little, I found myself in all kinds of chameleon-like contortions trying to keep my fingers in *all* the pies.

Social comparison theory is relevant here too: the idea that we all assess our worth in comparison to others. Because women can belong to several groups, as opposed to men who perform primarily on one work ladder, we end up with several social comparisons to make. Even if we are happy with our performance and place in our own group, we still end up looking over our shoulders at the other groups. Naturally, it is then unsurprisingly easy to assess – with the help of social media – how we don't stack up there. Of course, none of this is a recipe for happiness.

About women's happiness

This part of the research genuinely grabbed me. A comprehensive 2009 study found that *women's happiness has consistently declined both absolutely and in comparison with that of men since the 1970s.* I wasn't crazy; I wasn't alone – and neither are you!

The authors of the study suggested that women's happiness had declined due to the unmet expectations of an incomplete feminist movement. Women are now comparing themselves not only to the woman next door but to the man in the corner office.

My summary of the situation goes like this: women are fed up because we have been led to believe we are now on an equal playing field with men and yet persistently, in both small and large ways, we find ourselves in situations where the goalposts have been changed and the rules aren't equally applied to both teams.

Several academic papers followed this 2009 finding and discussed at length whether women could have it all – all being defined as having both a career and a family. They explored how women face persistent societal pressure around primary caregiving and claimed that women end up unhappier than men in later life as they are less able to achieve their life goals. The 2009 study was validated again in 2024 by another wide-ranging and comprehensive study which confirmed that women today both in Europe and in North America are less happy than men.

About the impact of gender inequality

Quite simply, women have unmet expectations. And that's a problem. Mo Gawdat's book *Solve for Happy,* neatly supports this academic finding. Mo is an incredibly intelligent man with a humbling back story. His son Ali died at the age of 21 during a routine appendectomy. At the time,

Mo was the chief business officer at Google [X], and in the aftermath of the sorrow and anger he experienced losing his son, he quit his job and went on a quest to research happiness. As maths and data were his thing, he decided to summarise his happiness findings into an equation. He found that: 'Happiness is greater than or equal to your perception of the events in your life minus your expectations of how life should behave.'

This equation can be applied to any aspect of life and serves as a brilliant reminder of the importance of perspective. However, happiness research, dovetailing with Mo's philosophical approach to dealing with life's vicissitudes, also tells us that there must be a practical approach. It isn't good enough to tell women to just lower their expectations. Another important research finding is that both women and men are happier when they live in more equal societies. Happiness is highly correlated with equality, and this relates not only to gender but to racism, homophobia and disability discrimination. So, in as much as it is important to find ways to deal with the fact that life isn't fair, it is equally important to champion equality for all. The OECD (Organisation for Economic Co-operation and Development) reports that:

> 'In most developed countries, gender inequality persists in the form of discriminatory social institutions and beliefs about gender roles that undercuts women's opportunities, inhibits their full participation in economic, social and political activities and therefore reduces their quality of life.'

In basic terms, it is not good enough. Not for us and not for our children. No wonder women are seriously naffed off.

The situation: in a nutshell

Without further delay, I would like to let you into a secret. Spoiler alert: as it currently stands, working mothers cannot have it all. We're unhappy with the current setup and have figured out that it is impossible to *do* it all and stay sane at the same time. It is essential to recognise that none of this is because we are personally failing as women and mothers. It's because women's work as currently mandated by society is driving us crazy and no one has found a solution yet. I very much hope this book will help.

On a macro scale, we must look outwards for answers as we desperately need society to change so that mothers have unconstrained choices and proper support. On an individual level, not able to fix society overnight, we must look inward as to what we can personally control and what brings each of us happiness. The following chapters explore mothers' happiness in the context of work; they provide an outline of the societal problems we face and offer some solutions to help us improve both our happiness now and that of our children in the future.

Chapter 2 delves into what *having it all* actually means, and whether this is different for men and women. I explain society's new sexual contract for women which sees us mandated to provide both financial support and caregiving to our families. Surveys find that part-time work is now what society ideally wants women to do. Mothers who stay home with children are shamed for being lazy, and mothers who work full-time are shamed for being bad parents. But what do women want? I explore the furore which was created when Kevin Roberts, then Saatchi & Saatchi Chairman, said in an interview with *Business Insider* that women's ambition was not about climbing the career ladder but instead an intrinsic, circular ambition to be happy. Do women want happiness, or do we want success? And can we have both?

Chapter 3 is all about happiness. I explore the definition of happiness – a combination of both pleasure and purpose – and which life circumstances make people happier. For instance, does money make us happy? Are married people happier? Does parenting make us happy or does moving to a warmer climate give us a happiness boost? The answers to these questions may surprise you. I explain ten behaviours, backed by the latest research in the positive psychology field, which you can implement to improve your own well-being.

Chapter 4 discusses women's work – both paid and unpaid – and answers the question I've been asking myself since I had my children: Are mothers generally happier when they go out to work or when they stay at home? I outline the challenges that mothers face in both arenas; very few of our choices are easy ones. I unpack why it is that we feel we can't do right for doing wrong, and explore whether part-time work is the answer to our problems or if it brings its own challenges. I make some suggestions to help with the intensive juggling act that many of us perform.

Chapter 5 is also about women's work – but this time the work of living in a female body. In addition to mothers fulfilling our new contracts with society by managing jobs both inside and outside of the home, I contend that females have a third job related to our sexed bodies. Throughout history, women's work has been closely tied to *re*production and men's to production. Our lives are different than men's as we deal with different issues. Our *biology* – pregnancy, breastfeeding, periods, contraception, miscarriage, infertility, abortion and menopause. Our *beauty* – we spend far more time and money than men in a multi-billion-dollar beauty industry that plays on our insecurities and keeps us feeling inadequate on purpose. Our *safety* – we are simply physically smaller with less upper body strength than men. And our *sexuality* – which should be fun, but is often complicated by pelvic pain, the proliferation of pornography and the orgasm gap. What can we do about all of this?

Chapter 6 comes full circle and answers the question my friend Fran posed at the beginning of this chapter: Should women become doctors or is it just too hard? I put into clear perspective the progress of working mothers over time to give us hope and to show just how far we have come. I outline four things that society needs to do to improve the happiness of working mothers and, importantly, explore what we can do as individuals. Using the mnemonic EMPOWER LIFE, I detail 11 specific tips working mothers can use today to improve our happiness. My aim is to arm you with information to help you pick your best-fit path through the challenges women face. Of course, the answers will be different for everyone. However, my hope is that the knowledge contained here may give you some small insight which will help both you and your children navigate this path, so the next generation of working mothers doesn't feel quite as frenetic and frazzled as we currently do!

Chapter 2

Why Women Still Can't Have It All

What is 'it all'?

In the 1980s of my childhood, *having it all* became a well-known catchphrase used to describe women balancing their careers with raising a family. The exact origins of the phrase are unknown, but at that time it was popularised by books such as *Having It All* by Helen Gurley Brown and *Superwoman Syndrome* by Marjorie Hansen Shaevitz.

Before we dive into dissecting what having it all is today, I thought it may be useful for me to start by telling you, in my personal experience, what having it all is most definitely *not*:

- It is *not* sprinting in a panic to your child's school play, sweating that you had to cut that business call short, then sliding into the back row of the school hall wracked with guilt that you may have missed your child's starring moment as the singing cat in the school's alternative nativity.

- It is *not* the conversation I had with a friend whilst I was sporting mascaraed panda eyes, scrubby nails and 2-month root regrowth. She confided that one of the reasons she'd decided not to go back to work after having children was that all the mums she knew who did seemed completely worn out. She was right!
- But then *nor* is it giving up your financial independence to be relegated to the position of second-class and underappreciated citizen for the enormously important job of parenting. Researchers find that society '... simultaneously fetishises and trivialises motherhood.' Oh yes! I have been there and own *that* T-shirt. The same friend who pitied my panda eyes also confessed her immense frustration on a family holiday when her husband pulled out the sports section of the newspaper whilst reclining on his sun lounger as she was still prepping lunch and slathering small, wriggly bodies in suncream. Of course, *he's* on holiday but *her* job continues.

For the purposes of this book, the having it all I explore mainly relates to the balancing-career-and-family definition I was raised with. However, I additionally contend that in today's society, having it all is even bigger and more encompassing. When we say we want it all now, we have expectations of having *everything*! Tight buns, wrinkle-free faces, well-mannered children, satisfying careers where we *do good work*, Pinterest-worthy homes and homemade nutrition – a sad goodbye to pot noodles. For many of us, the rapid rise of both social media and the wellness industry has led to us feeling anything but *well* – rather more like we've been harnessed to a treadmill by a sadistic trainer who keeps pushing the uphill incline and faster buttons while we become too out of breath to protest!

Women struggle more than men with this cult of having it all. For starters, women face additional societal pressure to look hot. And, no, I don't mean hot in a sweaty, menopausal kind of way. I mean the extra expectation for women to not only be competent as income providers and caregivers but to also look good whilst doing it. Across everything we do, we're judged on our appearance. We're meant to be sexy in the bedroom. We get looks if, after another sleepless night with the baby, we leave the house sporting sloppy joggers and wild hair. We're enormously judged on the physical image we portray in the workplace, and here is a little statistic to make your blood boil: obese women are paid less and have fewer job opportunities than obese men.

In addition, women are compelled to be society's caregivers. The emotional labour we perform at home and in our communities seems to come as part of the job description. I'm talking about things like remembering birthdays, temperature-checking the children after a tough day at school and looking in on elderly relatives. This glue is the magic stuff which binds people and communities together and this work – and it *is* work – is primarily done by women (with men often complaining about women making a 'fuss' and, in my house, tutting from the sidelines asking, 'Why do we need to buy Christmas presents?!'). Feminism was meant to fix our problems, but by middle age, many working mums get to the point where we feel like we've been sold a lie and it's too late to get our money back.

This chapter will explore these conundrums. I ask why so many of us are running around in circles trying to please everyone except ourselves? Importantly, how did we get here? And why do we feel chronically guilty? I explain why having it all *is* different for men and why it truly doesn't have to be this way for women. I outline why feminism means different things to each of us and why it is so important when women get behind each other as we *all* need a leg up.

All things to all people

Women can invariably be found tying themselves in knots trying to be all things to all people. Contrary to working women's shoulder-pad-wearing, ball-breaking behaviour of the 1980s, researchers find that the working women of today are busy trying to mould themselves into hybrid male/female identities at work. Trouser suits and shouting are *out* and bringing your whole, authentic self to work is *in*. However, I'm not convinced this makes it any easier for women. The current ideal for women at work is this:

- You need to be able to get things done by being the most conscientious person at the table. A female lawyer and mother I interviewed for my research said her boss told her he actually liked to hire mothers – he seemed quite proud of this, like he was being edgy and counter-cultural – as it's well known that mothers experience a hiring penalty because of our caring responsibilities. This guy qualified his reasoning by saying he reckoned he got far more work for far less money out of mums because of mum-guilt. Cheeky sod! His excuse to work us hard and pay us less.
- Regardless of how busy you are, you still need to be perceived by colleagues as supportive and caring. You must never be so 'up yourself' that you won't offer to make the coffee or do a quick whip round to celebrate someone's birthday.
- Crucially, you should look fresh and attractive whilst doing all this. Not too made-up – you mustn't be *that* woman, drawing attention – but wearing the right lip-gloss and attractive, bold-print, power dress. Oh, and the

foot-binding, crippling contraptions known as high-heeled shoes are still in fashion.

In my searing opinion, this requirement for women to be competent, caring, attractive and all things to all people is setting us up for failure. Look at any female news presenter – turn on Fox News or even Selling Sunset, if you can stomach it – and tell me that isn't one of the highest-stake tightrope acts you have ever witnessed.

And it isn't only at work where women are tying themselves in knots. The list below is a small smattering of the jobs that play on the minds and never-ending to-do lists[6] of many working mums I know:

- Family nutrition provider. This includes regularly nattering about eating vegetables. Also making homemade white bean and kale soup once a month that nobody eats.
- Playdate instigator. And friendship finagler. Fun party host is also on the job description along with a requirement to know the latest cool presents by gender and age.
- Queen of the social calendar. Organising who in the family is where, when and how at any given moment.
- Bedtime reader, homework nagger, general educator and/or tutor organiser. Personally, I'm out long before it gets to quadratic equations.
- Partner, spouse, friend, daughter, sister, and listening ear to all.
- Nurturer and caregiver. Wiper of teary snots and kisser of skinned knees.
- Picture taker and memory maker.

---

[6] I reckon 'to-do' lists for mothers would be better termed '*should*-do' lists! All those things that we don't necessarily get around to but spend mental energy feeling guilty that we *should* be doing.

- Wardrobe wrangler and person in charge of pairing missing socks.
- PTA volunteer community organiser and holiday fun-maker – anyone for a visit to a pumpkin patch?
- Relationship manager. Who books the babysitter for Valentine's Day?
- Cleaner. Dusting, brushing, mopping, washing, ironing, wiping, polishing, sewing, scrubbing, folding, sorting and vacuuming.
- Shopper. For flipping everything! Food, toys, clothes, shoes, winter coats, braces, holidays, birthdays, Christmas, Father's Day, Mother's Day, underwear, socks, loo roll and peppercorns – because it isn't the peppercorn fairy who replaces them in the peppermill.
- Personal improvement implementor. Exercise, nutrition, and fashion fads – luckily by middle age, hoarding mums may still have their high-waist jeans from the 80s even if they don't fit.
- Physical appearance co-ordinator. The ridiculously time-consuming work of self-care – hair-drying, waxing, dying, plucking, cleansing, moisturising, accessorising and the list goes on…

Working mothers' lists are crackers! In the majority of relationships, even if there is a relatively even split of the practical jobs, mothers still carry far more of the mental and emotional load than fathers. As a result, working mothers are up to 40% more stressed than women who work full-time without children. This can be measured in biological stress markers. In addition, working mothers are 28% more likely to get burnout than working fathers. Women have been set up with multiple jobs and like 'good girls,' we are trying to do what is expected of us and keep everyone happy. The main person this is not working for is *us*.

Women's new contract: how did we get here?

This societal requirement for women is new. Not the part where we must be the nurturing social glue stick and focus on our looks and sexuality. If the 1960s portrayal of the stone-age family *The Flintstones* is to be believed (and it's not!), Wilma Flintstone was partial to a string of pearls to match her white mini-dress even then. Fast-forward to today, and the expectation now is that women's jobs aren't only to be attractive to men and fulfil our reproductive destinies by becoming mothers; we are also compelled to financially provide for our families.

Since the early noughties, academics have been discussing society's new sexual contract for women: the recent wholesale change from traditional gender roles. Women had thought feminism would give us a full upgrade from our previous crappy terms and conditions, but it turns out there is quite a lot we missed in the fine print. One outcome of our new contract is that society now considers that women can only really achieve fulfilment if we do *both* mothering and paid work.

In the British Social Attitudes (BSA) Survey of 1984, 49% of people agreed that '… a man's job is to earn money; a woman's job is to look after the home and family…' In 2017, just 8% of people agreed with that same statement. Further, in that same 2017 BSA survey, 72% of people agreed that '… both the man and the woman should contribute to the household income…' and only 4% disagreed.

Work for women is now formally approved and sanctioned, which of course is brilliant news for us – when we aren't trying to do everything else too! Research shows that with money comes power in a relationship. So when we are not beholden to the benevolence of our husbands but earn money ourselves, we have more autonomy to make decisions not only for us but for our children. And, crucially, we also get more financial security.

Let's face it, people have always had an opinion on the 'right place for a woman'. Ideally, we should have small feet to get closer to the kitchen sink – cue eye-roll. But this dynamic around work has shifted radically – and relatively quickly. The number of women in the workforce has *tripled* in the last 100 years. Just pause and let that sink in. It is truly a wholescale seismic revolution in an infinitesimally small period of evolutionary time. It gives us hope that even more change is on the horizon for women. We can now stand for parliament, perform brain surgery, own property and *even* credit cards without our fathers or husbands co-signing for us. It is incredible to think that we couldn't do any of these things 100 years ago.[7] Note to the patriarchy: what we'd now like to do is crack on without having to do everything else *at the same time*.

This legitimising of work is additionally a boon for the 17% of UK women who don't have children. Historically, childless women were pitied as barren spinsters; unhappy and unfulfilled for not completing their biological destiny. But in fact, research has now shown that single women without children often top the charts for happiness and well-

---

[7] It was actually a bit more than 100 years ago that the UK got its first female MP – Nancy Astor in 1919. Throughout history, the UK has only had three female Prime Ministers. The first female brain surgeon (or at least the trailblazer in the field) was an African American neurosurgeon, Dr Dorothy Lavinia Brown in 1951.

being. Governments in several affluent countries[8] now have the opposite problem: how to get more women to have babies to sustain the economy as many women have decided they don't quite fancy it under the current terms.

To be clear, it is a *good* thing that women can earn their own money. It is just that the revolution is not yet complete. Let's have a look at how working mothers have got to where we are today: attempting to be jugglers extraordinaire.

Sisters are doing it for themselves!

First things first, let's be clear: women have always worked. Homemaking is *work*. Feeding your family is *work*. Mopping muddy footprints off floors is *work*. Staying up all night with a poorly child is *work*. But what about women working outside of the home?

It wasn't completely unheard of for women to have paid jobs prior to the 1950s. The image many of us hold of the traditional 1950s housewife is largely an idealised notion that became more pronounced after World War II. It romanticised a family dynamic where women stayed home to look after children and men, many returning from war, resumed their 'proper place' as family breadwinners. Before this however, during the Industrial Revolution of the 1800s for instance, it was relatively common for working-class women to work in factories or at home in the sweated industries in order to make ends meet.[9] There has long been

---

[8] In Japan, the declining birthrate is widely reported as being due to the increased education of women but the still traditional gender divide of domestic responsibility in families. The Japanese labour market is so intensive they have a word for working yourself to death: karoshi. These factors combined mean many educated women are choosing not to have children. Japanese women are deciding that something has to give and for many, that something is having children.

[9] Sweated is a term for women doing poorly paid work from their homes whilst caring for children – things like sewing, washing and baking.

a class divide between upper- and middle-class women – whose proper place was considered to be in the home – and working-class women who at times needed to work for money. However, as historian Helen McCarthy points out in her fascinating book *Double Lives: The History of Working Motherhood,* the main constant throughout time is that women consistently have been, and still are, paid less for their work than men.[10]

As well as work relating to reproduction, homemaking and caregiving, throughout history women have also worked in roles such as agricultural labourers, brewers, bakers, midwives, educators, herbalists and in religious roles – such as nuns or priestesses. In medieval Europe, women participated in crafts and trades such as textile production, spinning, weaving and pottery – at times even being associated with guilds such as the glovers, embroiderers or weavers but more often than not in cottage industries where sewing and crafting was done at home. Entrepreneurial women through the ages, from regular market traders to rich widowed merchants' wives, have capitalised on opportunities to earn a living selling goods and services.

Over the course of the last 100 years, however, societal attitudes toward women working to earn money have changed radically. Two world wars at the beginning of the 20th century meant that while men were off fighting, women

---

[10] There are glimmers in history when women's work was paid at the same rate as men's. For instance, in Anglo-Saxon England, women were, at times, paid the same day-rate for the same day's labouring work as men. However, following the Norman conquest, the hierarchical feudal system of medieval England formalised the gendered division of labour and the industrial revolution of the 1800s entrenched systems where women's work in factories was devalued and consistently paid less compared with the equivalent work of men. An interesting small blip for equity in women's wages came around 1400–1425 after the plague and the peasants' revolt when the population was so decimated that women working for pay became necessary for society to function. For a short time, this increased demand gave female workers greater bargaining power.

took on many roles which were previously solely reserved for men: truck drivers, mechanics, electricians and engineers. Increasing numbers of women realised that not only *could* they perform 'men's work' but that they were good at it and rather liked the money![11]

Another influencing factor in the increasing numbers of women working outside the home in the 20th century was the second wave of feminism in the 1960s (the first wave involved women getting the vote). This movement was significantly influenced by a book published in 1963 called *The Feminine Mystique*, by Betty Friedan. Friedan spoke about the problem that has no name and explored women's disillusion with their roles as wives and homemakers. The book was a runaway best-seller. Betty was said to have articulated the voice of a generation of women who wondered whether there was not more to life:

> 'The problem lay buried, unspoken, for many years in the minds of American women. It was a strange stirring, a sense of dissatisfaction, a yearning that women suffered in the middle of the 20th century in the United States. Each suburban housewife struggled with it alone. As she made the beds, shopped for groceries ... she was afraid to ask even of herself the silent question – "Is this all?"'

Spurred on by this feeling of dissatisfaction and an economy in the 1970s suffering a financial recession, women started entering the workforce in ever-increasing numbers. By the 1980s, women were *sisters doing it for*

---

[11] During the war years, policy was to keep women on the same rate of pay as the men had been (although this didn't always happen). The idea to not downgrade pay when women started performing men's work was encouraged through an agreement between the (all-male) government and (all-male) trade unions as this rationale protected the wages for men when they returned from war.

themselves going out and *working 9 to 5* – thank you, Annie, Aretha and Dolly!

It is without question a wonderful thing that women today have the ability to not only achieve financial independence, but to pursue a career that speaks to our talents and interests. Hurrah! However, women entering the workforce has not meant that our domestic and caring roles have become any easier. Oh no! If women want it all, we can jolly well get on with it.

Of course, this is a problem. Women have asked for it all but having got it, we're finding it increasingly hard to manage. So, we must then ask the question, what *do* women really want?

What *do* women want?

Author Tom Robbins says that trying to understand what women want is like trying to smell the colour nine. He might be on to something! Look, I'm not pretending that anyone has this stuff completely figured out; we are all complex individuals with different upbringings and imprints from childhood as to what we think is right. Our formative years and our subsequent experiences of the world shape our opinions, whether we like it or not.

Deborah Frances-White, author of *The Guilty Feminist* and host of the podcast with the same name, explores the conflicts women encounter trying to marry the attitudes from their upbringing to the practical nature of the world we live in, plus just what appeals to us. She describes a type of internal struggle, for instance when the desire to be a strong woman who can take on the world clashes with a sincere wish to wallow on the sofa eating chocolate and reading *Hello* magazine. I get it! I fully confess that my own feminism is cloaked in contradictions and at times doesn't make sense. I want to have my cake and eat it too. For example:

- I want my husband to feed, clothe and care for our children, but only if he does it as well as I do and my children like me best.
- I want a high-flying career and a pay package to match, but I don't want to compromise on time spent with my children.
- I want my husband to open doors, fill the car with petrol and offer to carry heavy bags, but be fully supportive of my independence.
- I want to go out to work and earn my own income, but even though I'm fully supportive of the rights of *anyone* to be a stay-at-home parent, I know I'd feel resentful if my husband didn't work outside the home at all.
- I want to be complimented on looking good, but don't want my appearance to make a difference in how I am treated.
- Wolf whistles make me both hot with shame *and* a weensy bit flattered. (I know!!)

But I am not letting men off the hook when it comes to conflicting expectations. After a reasonable amount of field research, I have observed the following in many men:

- They want their partners to look sexy and attractive, but not to take too long getting ready *or* to spend too much money on the whole charade. Apparently, a natural look is best but unfortunately, most men have nil understanding of the excessive effort required to 'look natural'.
- They want you to work in order to provide income for the family so it isn't all on them, but they don't want to do housework because that's boring – and for girls.

- They want you to earn good money – because otherwise what's the point of them having to do the housework – but not too much money because that's emasculating.

Researchers find that it makes both women and men unhappy when the woman in the relationship earns substantially more than her husband. Women who are killing it at work and bringing home big chunks of the bacon are also likely to do more housework to compensate for the unwitting emasculation and are more likely to have their husbands cheat on them. Charming, eh?

However, the corollary is that men who earn substantially more than their wives are *also* more likely to cheat. So, 'marry rich' isn't necessarily the answer either. Marriages where there is a sole breadwinner get divorced at a rate 14% above the average. It seems that couples are the happiest and most likely to stay together when they earn relatively equal amounts.[12]

More importantly, studies show that when husbands do more housework wives are less depressed, marital conflicts decrease, the risk of divorce halves, and excitingly, in households where men do more housework they *have more sex*. Both men and women who identify as feminists are found to have more frequent and more varied sex. As a wise midwife counselled a friend's husband after they had their first baby: foreplay starts in the kitchen. So, what do women want? More men in Marigolds sounds like a good start!

---

[12] Note that the greater the gender equality of a country, the less people place importance on the financial resources of a partner. So when men complain that women only want them for their money, this should encourage them to fight for gender equality. (Also, with greater gender equality comes less importance placed on chastity and good looks for females). A study that looked at gendered attitudes to attraction between 1939 and 2008 found that what men and women look for in a potential partner is more similar than it ever has been, with men increasingly wanting good financial prospects, education and intelligence in a partner.

Success versus happiness: Where's the joy?

So, share and share-alike with the housework is the way to go – of course, good luck with that, and more on this later. But what about career? Do women *really* want work success in the same way as men? Do women even see ambition in the same way, or are the majority of mothers more content with a job that fits around the children instead of the heart-rending hustle of a crazy corporate world?

The hugely successful advertising company Saatchi & Saatchi was involved in an almighty furore a few years ago after their chairman Kevin Roberts gave an interview to *Business Insider*. When asked to explain the fact that only 11.5% of creative directors within advertising agencies are female despite women making up 46.4% of the workforce, he colourfully claimed that there wasn't a problem, that the '… debate is all over…' and that his firm had never had a problem with sexual discrimination. He then went on to say that the reason more women weren't in senior executive roles was that '… their ambition is not a vertical ambition, it's this intrinsic, circular ambition to be happy…' And according to him, many women were '… very happy…' not getting the higher-level roles. Note that it later came out that the company had settled a sex discrimination lawsuit for 3 million dollars just 2 months before the interview. The media storm was electric. So much so that his position became untenable, and he resigned from his role after 20 years with the company.

But was he right? Do many women decide that they aren't interested in whatever lies at the top of the greasy, corporate pole? *Are* women looking for happiness rather than success? And why aren't equal numbers of men doing the same?

Of course, there is more to life than work, and as Kevin also pointed out, younger generations are no longer driven by those Darwinian urges of wealth and power; millennials and Generation Z often look for connectivity and collaboration, and to do good, meaningful work. He is absolutely right on this point, and as head of an ad agency, he'd know. However, it is more complicated than that.

Kevin also said something which is quite telling about women in business. He explained that in his experience of trying to promote talented women, once they have about 10 years of experience, 2 out of 3 women will turn a promotion down because, in his words, '…(they) don't want to manage a piece of business and people, (they) want to keep doing the work…' So, ten years into working, women turn down promotions. Interesting timing, don't you think? Right about when, with their biological clock ticking loudly, women may well be looking to start a family – or already be knee-deep in baby grows, nappies and *The Wheels on the Bus*. It is not that women don't want success *and* happiness; it is just that we have realised we can't yet have both.

It is an issue for all of us when ambitious mothers give up because they can't do it all. As the campaign name says: women are now Pregnant *Then* Screwed. We absolutely know in our hearts that as things stand, we simply cannot give our all to a full-time, fulfilling career pathway and the crucial, life-affirming job of parenting and do both justice. Something *has* to give: it's either our career, our kids, our health or our sanity.

Guilt and eating the burnt toast

Consequently, guilt is a woman's middle name. Novelist and poet Erica Jong claimed: 'Show me a woman without guilt and I'll show you a man.' Teri Hatcher, actor from the TV series *Desperate Housewives*, calls the habit of women putting themselves last because of this guilt *eating the burnt toast*. You know the scene; a woman rushing around the kitchen in the morning, putting everyone's breakfast on the table, reminding kids to brush their teeth, picking up washed sport kits and packing away homework. The woman's own measly slice of breakfast toast (mind the waistline) gets burned in the bustle, but she eats it anyway while seamlessly emptying the dishwasher, braiding a child's hair (mind the crumbs) and feeding the dog. A viral social media meme reads: 'Motherhood is finally understanding why Daddy's porridge was hot, Mummy's was cold and Baby's was just right.'

I can't tell you how many books and advice columns I've read over the years that suggest it's our fault we're doing it all and we must just stop! We must stop feeling guilty, stop prioritising everyone else and start looking after ourselves. Remember, we're told on an aeroplane you put your *own* oxygen mask on before helping others. It is our own silly fault if we are behaving like martyrs.

The difficulty is, at the very same time, we're given another message: you are not a good mother if your children don't always come first. One morning at the swimming pool when my children were small, another mother I knew wrapped one of my girls up in a towel and handed me my wet, wriggly parcel of legs and arms, saying she couldn't bear to see her cold. I had been busy getting myself dressed first while the children waited, stubbornly shoving *my* wet legs into *my* skinny jeans. As well intentioned as this mum's gesture was, it made me feel shamed and like I shouldn't have dressed myself first. That it wasn't ok for my cold, wet legs to be covered up before the children's were.

Mothers are conditioned to be like this. Guilt and self-sacrifice come with the job description. So, it feels doubly annoying when we are also told to stop being martyrs – like it's our fault for not reading the room and we just need to stop. Mothers are instinctually aware that stopping maternal sacrifice is not currently on the acceptable menu of options. Tiffany Dufu's brilliant book *Drop the Ball* addresses this issue; she tells mothers to expect less from themselves and says we must actively start dropping some balls if we are ever going to allow others to pick them up.

Standards of mothering have now risen beyond what was common even 50 years ago. Women today spend much more time on primary caregiving activities with children than we did in the 1970s: things such as reading, enrichment activities or fully-focussed play. Studies show that working mothers are now spending up to *double* the amount of time on primary caregiving: one study cited 54 minutes a day in 1965 and 104 minutes a day in 2012. The idea that children should play outside, roam around on their bikes and be home in time for dinner is no longer the norm. What is now expected of mothers – and what we expect of ourselves – far exceeds what we used to do.

Somehow, the guilt women have from working has mutated into a compulsive, visceral need to prove our worth as mothers. Stay-at-home mothers aren't let off the hook here either. If anything, they now feel the need to justify their worth even more urgently as they are compared to working mothers: What did you do all day?

What thanks do we get for this trouble? Intensive parenting – sometimes known as helicopter parenting where you hover over your children, pre-emptively solving problems for them – is known to make parents unhappy and children less resilient.

So, instead of telling you to stop feeling guilty, I would like to acknowledge it's not just you and it isn't all in your head! You are feeling guilty because this is how society currently operates: the pink jobs are all-consuming and we are now expected to do blue jobs too. However, society's systems are not fixed, they are in continuous motion. For the sake of our children, *we need change*.

Can men have it all?

Before digging any further into solving women's problems about having it all, I want to drive home the point about why this balance of work and family is still different for women and men. When telling friends I was writing this book, I had several say to me: 'But men can't have it all either, having it all doesn't exist for anyone.' I get this! I genuinely take on board and have empathy with the way our patriarchal culture puts pressure on men too.

Remember the 80s movie *Parenthood*? Steve Martin plays the character of Gil Buckman, an all-American, stand-up dad and family breadwinner. There is a scene where Gil comes home from a gruelling day at the office, having just been demoted by his boss for not being able to put in the same hours as his younger colleague because he always had to get home to his family. He arrives home steaming with frustration to a chaotic house full of kids running riot. Tripping over toys, he rants to his wife as he is changing his clothes and getting ready to take his son to Little League baseball practice. His wife, an easy-going empathetic character and stay-at-home mum, tries to get him to calm down and put things in perspective. She says he doesn't have to go to Little League. Gil responds poignantly that he can't stop or take a break because his whole life is 'have to' and he has his son and a team of kids relying on him.

I don't know anyone who doesn't relate to the idea of their whole life being *have to*. Men especially can feel like they are railroaded down a breadwinner path with very limited socially acceptable choices about staying home to raise a family. Men must often feel that they have *responsibilities* whereas women have *choices*. They are influenced by a society which expects them to be in paid employment and thinks less of them if their wives are breadwinners or if they stay at home full-time with children.

A friend's husband who owns a successful business maintains that the best job in the world is that of the affluent housewife: coffee, shopping, long walks, golf, tennis and ladies lunching. I understand why he would think that. However, full-time mothering regardless of income is rarely that simple. The big jobs all come with flash titles, big pay packets and kudos, but they also come with an enormous amount of stress. Another friend's husband, when promoted to partner with a top accounting firm, was given a prestigious title and handsome pay package alongside a gym membership and personal trainer. The company acknowledged that life expectancy in the job they had just awarded him was shorter and this was their way of keeping him alive a bit longer.

In addition, expectations of men's role at home have been raised substantially. Increasingly, modern-day men are seen carrying cappuccinos while pushing prams or with babies strapped to their chests. Studies do show that men *want* to spend more time with their kids and can lament the time spent at work. According to the National Fatherhood Initiative, 57% of dads and 58% of mums say that parenting is extremely important to their identity. Often quoted as one of the top deathbed regrets: 'I wish I hadn't worked so hard and had spent more time with my loved ones.'

So, men can feel the strain of being the main provider plus the added pressure of modern manhood to step up at home because their wives are working. And even when their wives do stay home with children to relieve family pressure, this dynamic can cause friction and misunderstanding. My friend's husband who works flat-out on a 60-hour-week has been known to come home and pointedly run a finger over the dust on the mantelpiece and ask his wife in a wondrous tone, 'What did you do all day?' Even worse, another sarcastically asked his wife, 'How was your holiday today, darling?'

Without a doubt, there are fathers out there who feel enormously frustrated and trapped in a life dedicated to breadwinning and with limited choice about this. But I argue that it is mothers who feel this frustration of limited choices even more acutely. Being the default carer is a full-time job for life, with limited rest breaks and optional sleep. You can't quit mothering and get a new job, even when your 2-year-old boss rides you like a tyrant. The pay is non-existent, and unfortunately, in today's society money matters. Quite simply, the person in the family who earns it is the person in the family likely to have more power, more agency for decision making and *more choice*.

The other problem for women is that we simply have a greater workload than men when it comes to other elements of having it all. Things like looking good, emotional caregiving and our age-old problems with the domestic load.[13] So even when mothers are breadwinners and have more control over the finances, we often still end up with a raw deal when it comes to equitable leisure time. According to a British Social Attitudes Survey, 70% of men still think that laundry is women's work. Men now do double the amount of housework than they did in 1965, but women are still doing 2.5 times more domestic and caregiving work. I have also yet to see men sign up in droves for highlights, make-up or a fake tan. And as far as things like sending

---

[13] Researcher Arlie Hochschild described women's *second shift* as the domestic load we are responsible for doing after we come home from a day's paid work. Feminist author Naomi Wolf, who wrote *The Beauty Myth*, calls women's work relating to beauty our *third shift*.

birthday cards, I can honestly say I have yet to see one of the male members of my family send one! Studies may find that today's men are keener than their fathers were to play with their children, but they are still pretty resistant to picking lint out of the dryer door or scrubbing the toilet.

Here's the bottom line: men's roles have not changed to the same degree as women's, and gender roles are not equitable. For the vast majority of working heterosexual couples today, there are still entrenched jobs labelled *pink* and *blue* and women can't get out from under the housework. This leads to tension on both sides.[14] Women are now working in both feminine pink and masculine blue zones, whereas men are still predominantly blue because pink is just too emasculating a colour.[15] The problem with this, of course, is that it is paid work and not homemaking that gives us money, and it is *money* that enables us to have both more choice and more power for decision-making in our lives.

---

[14] We can all feel a compunction to behave in gender-appropriate ways. Studies find that women end up making work choices which are not in their financial interests due to a strong social need to be accepted. Researchers call this phenomenon 'gender identity and economics'.

[15] What is an accepted way for women and men to behave varies greatly across societies. In Middle Eastern and North African cultures, for example, it is not uncommon for men to hold hands in public as a sign of friendship and camaraderie. Not a chance my husband would do that with his mates in our leafy suburbs! There are also extensive cultural differences within the UK. A 2023 McKinsey report cites British women with a Black, Bangladeshi or Pakistani heritage as being the furthest behind on pay and labour market participation. British Asian women report substantial cultural pressures to fulfil traditional roles at home which can be amplified by living in multi-generational households where older family members exert pressure for traditional values on the younger generations.

Tall poppy syndrome

Is this all such a big deal? Are ardent feminists making a mountain out of a molehill and do we find that most women are happy earning less money, working part-time and being the primary carer for their children? Do the majority of women *not* want to perform brain surgery, but as my friend Fran put it, just want '… a nice life and time at home with their children, thanks very much.' The answer is complex.

According to our new sexual contract, the vast majority of people now think women should contribute to the family income. The problem with this is that although society has come around to the idea of women working, there is far less acceptance of us being ambitious career women. This is another significant reason why women still cannot have it all in today's world.

Society desperately needs capable women in parliament, policing, law, education, technology and the financial industries to make the world a more equal place. As men climb the corporate ladder, they're doing just fine as dads if they provide well financially for their children and rock up to sports day. The problem is that similarly ambitious women just *cannot* follow suit, and so we lose them. Women cannot be as ambitious and successful in our careers as men and still be considered wonderful parents. The whole issue is baked into the lexicon: we hear incessantly about what working mums should and shouldn't be doing but we never hear talk of working dads and wonder how they are coping with their implied double shift.

When women *do* behave in similarly ambitious ways as men? That's unsettling, to say the least. People twitch and spasm and try to bend their minds around successful women who have opinions. They just can't seem to shake that *Who does she think she is?* feeling. Think about Meghan Markle marrying Prince Harry and daring to put her arm around him rather than the other way around. Or Michelle Obama as the 'angry Black woman' when she talked openly of her frustrations around her husband's job taking him away from his family. There is a general idea that 'women should know their place' and some people become irked when they think women are 'getting above their station' – especially if said woman is from an ethnic minority. It is called Tall Poppy Syndrome – this idea of cutting ambitious people back down to size. Women are subject to it far more than men. A 2023 study found that 60% of women believed they would be penalised if they were perceived to be ambitious at work. And 87% of women across 103 countries had experiences in work where they were attacked, criticised, disliked, resented or cut down because of their achievements or success. Unless we have particularly strong stomachs, it ends up being easier to withdraw. Many women instinctively make themselves smaller in order to be liked and to fit in.

Hillary Clinton talked openly about the challenges she faced in her 2016 campaign for President of the United States. Not only did she lose to a candidate whose main experience had been in entertainment and property development, but she lost to a man who bragged about grabbing women by the pussy and threatened their reproductive rights. This wouldn't happen the other way around. If it was the woman candidate whose companies had gone bankrupt multiple times and who bragged about abusing men, she wouldn't even be in the race. Pundits surmised that the main issue with Hillary was that she failed the likeability test. People couldn't marry her ambition and forthrightness with the warmth they expect in a female. In the 2024 race, Kamala Harris fared no better, despite putting forward a friendly, upbeat persona. Kamala was derided for laughing too much, and people worried about trusting her on the economy. It seems America is just not yet ready for a woman president.

Room at the top?

The mothers who drop out of the workforce tend to be at the very top and very bottom of the income brackets. Of course, our primary concern is for those at the bottom of the income bracket who are just worried about having any of 'it', as these women tend to fare the worst and their children live on the poverty line. However, the opting-out phenomenon of women at the top is also relevant for all women.

A key reason that highly educated mothers drop out of the workforce is the crazy work culture at the top. Their husbands may be city bankers, parliamentarians, corporate lawyers and generally the movers and shakers of the world, but when they become mothers, women can't keep up. They just can't do what their husbands are doing in their careers because someone needs to be there for the children, and according to modern-day gender roles and the structure of nuclear families, that someone is the mum. Breadwinner mothers tell me that even when their partners stay home full-time, the weight of expectation around parenting is still on mum.

The impact of this societal structure matters for *all* women. Until more women are in positions of power, we won't make sufficient progress on any number of issues that affect women. For instance, making laws that protect women regarding stalking, domestic violence, sexual harassment and abortion. Or medical professionals providing much-needed research on women's health issues – where there are gross gender disparities in the research undertaken. We desperately *need* women doctors. It isn't good enough for senior medical careers to be incompatible with mothering, but not fathering, to the extent that women are opting out. I don't know any fathers who say to their sons: 'I'd think twice before studying medicine; you'll never get to school pick-up on time.'

Of the world's millionaires, 90% are men and 10% are women. That's a shockingly big gap. Money is power, and men still hold the vast majority of it. Melinda Gates claims that to move the needle on gender equality, we urgently need more women in technology, politics, media and finance. If we are ever going to solve the big problems of the world, we must not leave 50% of the world's brainpower sitting on the sidelines. From a global perspective, problems like climate change affect women more than men, and politically, women are found to be more interested in solving climate change.[16] It needs to be made easier for women to have a seat at the tables of power as well as at the kitchen table.

Women are understandably backing down because honestly, it *is* too hard. We can't do it alone and we shouldn't have to. The current setup just isn't working:

- Women don't get the same social rewards as men do for their ambition. We regularly feel like we are failing at home and are too often told we need to pipe down at work.
- The big careers often require nonsense hours and/or travel. Nobel prize-winning economist Claudia Goldin calls these *greedy jobs* and cites them as a key contributor to the gender pay gap.
- There is a domestic load gap. Fathers are simply not yet willing in sufficient numbers to take on the role of

---

[16] Globally, charities cite climate change as an issue which disproportionately affects women. Women are likely to have less money than men and are often left home to tend the land and children while men go to urban areas to find work, leaving the women far more impacted by floods and wildfires.

support partner to accommodate mothers who want to work full-time.
- Society heaps pressure on good motherhood much more so than good fatherhood. The UK government does not do enough to support parenting. There is sufficient political will in the UK to fund a free National Health Service, but when it comes to the caregiving work that makes society turn, it is primarily done by women for free.

This is why having it all is different for women. *This* is why we need change.

It's not destiny

I'd like to spend the next few paragraphs debunking some myths about the 'natural order' of things and why it is perfectly possible to change the way society currently functions and make it better for us all. It truly doesn't have to be this way.

The old argument goes something like this. You are going against nature, Darwinism and survival of the fittest if you try and interfere with the inherent order and hierarchy of things: first men, then women and then children. The idea that women are equal to men is a nice idea but wishful thinking: men are bigger and stronger and that is just how it works.

I have listened to this type of pronouncement from men holding beer and grilling steaks on BBQs on more than one occasion. A male friend-of-a-friend pontificates 'It's just natural and has always been that way.' He compares us to apes, lions and a variety of other animals and the hierarchical nature of their social groups. Apparently, this is just the way of the world, and women need to get used to it.

The lion analogy is a popular one: King of the Jungle! But what we should remember is that, in this case, it is the lioness who typically does the hunting while the lion stays home to protect the cubs! In fact, we know that there are several female-led societies in the animal kingdom – see the 2024 National Geographic series *Queens* narrated by Angela Bassett – but somehow we don't seem to talk about them as much. Canadian YouTube star and psychologist Jordan Peterson also tries to make a point about the biological nature of social hierarchies and gender relations by comparing humans to lobsters, and has collected an unnerving number of followers of his theory. Many people are drawn to the argument of the law of the jungle, biology is destiny and a fascination with comparing human behaviour with animals insisting it is natural and can't be messed with. These simple arguments pass the sniff test and are therefore seemingly impossible to refute at a family BBQ.

Well, extra big, hairy bollocks to that. If we are to ever make progress, we need to be able to cut through the noise of what is biology – birth, boobs and bleeding – and what is baloney.

Humans aren't apes

First, it makes no sense to compare humans to animals and project their natures onto human beings to argue that biology is destiny. For instance, I happen to know from first-hand experience that it is natural for hamsters to sometimes eat their young after giving birth. I can tell you this from having had a ringside seat at this particular event not long after bringing our first family pet home when I was 12 years old. Never before or since have I heard my mum scream quite so shrilly as when we observed Betty gobbling up the babies she had just birthed. Humans don't eat their babies, nor do they behave like lobsters or lions. And please, please do *not* compare me to apes!

This comparison is based on the idea that human beings share a large proportion of our DNA with apes – 98.8%.[17] Humans, chimpanzees and bonobo apes are all descended from a common ancestor 6 million years ago. However, if you are insisting on comparing me to an ape, I'll take the bonobo rather than the cheeky chimp every time, thanks very much. For those of you who aren't David Attenborough fans, I will illuminate a little further the lives of our feminist friends the bonobos. Primatologists explain that while chimpanzees use violence to get sex, bonobos use sex to avoid violence. Apparently, not only are bonobos wonderfully promiscuous but they love food, and nothing starts a bonobo orgy faster than a feast. If you give a troop of bonobos food, they will all start having quickie sex before politely sharing the food. There is also a sisterly solidarity among the females, and although they are smaller than the males, if a male gets out of line and harasses a female all the other females gang up on him. This, coupled with lots of sex, tends to keep the males behaving politely towards the females. Scientists have found that, compared to their cousins the chimps who are male-dominant, the quality of life for bonobos where the females assert authority is much greater for *both* sexes.

Primatologist Frances Burton gives us another example of gendered behaviour that doesn't come in standard pink and blue. Burton studies macaque monkeys and found that

---

[17] Scientifically speaking, these DNA comparisons are actually too reductive as there is so much more to human behaviour than diluting it to DNA. Human beings share around 99.9% of our DNA with each other. We also share a pretty sizeable percentage with other animals (about 90% of our DNA with cats and about 60% with fruit flies) and we don't spend nearly as much time comparing our commonalties with them.

despite no differences in testosterone levels throughout different troops of monkeys, the childcare behaviour of the males varied greatly from troop to troop depending on the social patterns in their particular group. Some male monkeys took the lead role in protecting, carrying and grooming 1- and 2-year-old infants and others of the same species took just a partial role or no role at all. Burton argues that if testosterone was the key to the monkey's behaviour around childcare then similar patterns would be seen across all troops, and this was not the case.

I've therefore decided that if reincarnation exists, I'm coming back either as a bonobo for the food and quickie sex, or at least a macaque for a bit more help with childcare. Either of them seem to be having a better time of it than the modern-day homo sapiens with the XX chromosomes.

Oestrogen doesn't make you like pink

It isn't just men who feel strongly about biological determinism.[18] While having a similar conversation with a friend, she pointed out the window to her niece and nephew, 2-year-old twins, who were visiting and playing in her garden. The little boy was busy delving with his blue digger truck and the little girl was head-to-toe in a pink costume, prancing around with fairy wings and a glitter wand. My friend said that even though they were so young, their parents hadn't made them choose those activities; it was surely simply inherent that the little girl was attracted to pink and the little boy to trucks and digging. I knew what she meant!

---

[18] Biological determinism is the idea that human characteristics are passed down genetically at birth and are not shaped by environmental, social or cultural factors (i.e. it is biology which determines destiny).

However, had that little girl been born 100 years earlier, she may have had limited interest in the colour pink as it was considered a boy's colour in the 19th and early 20th centuries. Pink was a muted version of masculine red and conversely, a delicate shade of blue was more popular for girls – like the Virgin Mary or Marie Antoinette, two slightly different role models!

Sociologists now know that it is specifically around the age of my friend's niece and nephew, 2 to 3 years old, that children begin to understand themselves as individuals who are separate from their parents. Gender then becomes one of the important ways they categorise themselves in order to relate to the world. It is specifically around this age that boys shun pink and girls are drawn to it: this is a modern-day, Western phenomenon.

Neuroscientist Melissa Hines and psychologist Wang Wong studied this particular situation of pink-versus-blue alongside toy preferences. They compared how long children who were 20 to 40 months old played with trains and dolls compared with 6 months later. The results were fascinating. As the children got older and more aware of their gender, there were moderate to large differences in the time girls would play with a pink doll and boys with a blue train, but small insignificant amounts of time with a *pink* train and a *blue* doll. The colour pink has developed into such a strong gendered preference in our modern-day culture that a lick of paint made all the difference in what toys children of different genders were drawn to. We become aware of our environment and what is expected of our gender from a very early age.

Now, please don't get me wrong, I am not saying that biology is not impactful or important. It matters enormously, and I will get to that later. What I am saying, however, is that we need to think carefully before absorbing a narrative that says, *It's just the way it is*, because that quickly leads to *There's nothing we can do about it*, and *that* is dangerous territory.[19]

The patriarchy is a social structure

Significant evidence points to the fact that our system of patriarchy and men holding the power has varied throughout history and across different cultures. It is by no means a fait accompli.

Firstly, as discussed in Chapter 1, early human societies of hunter-gatherers are thought to have been organised around egalitarian principles, where power and decision-making were shared among members of the community regardless of gender. In these early nomadic societies, consisting of a few dozen to a few hundred individuals, cooperation was essential for survival. In many hunter-gatherer societies, women played crucial roles in food gathering, social organisation and decision-making. Anthropologists estimate that up to 60%–80% of calories in some hunter-gatherer societies came from food that was gathered by women rather than hunted by primarily men. Of course, at that time, food could be considered currency. And, although it is commonly said that men did all the hunting in those early societies, there is now significant archaeological evidence that women hunted too. Ethnographic studies of modern-day hunter-gatherer groups like the !Kung San

---

[19] There are many things in history considered to be *natural* and *just the way it is* that people have been able to change through social organisation. During the First World War, the death rate in childbirth for American women was so high that it eclipsed the number of male American soldiers who died in the war. When women in the United States got the vote in 1920, this political move proved crucial in keeping women alive during childbirth. Rates of maternal mortality in America plunged between 1920 and 1940, significantly as a result of the political will to prioritise healthcare for women who could now vote. One-half of society making all the decisions won't do. We need equality.

people in Africa and the Aka and Baka tribes in Central Africa also find that women often participate in hunting alongside men. Note that this is not to say that I am recommending winding back the clock to early history – I would miss hot showers too much – but simply to highlight that humans evolved through co-operation.

Secondly, culture is varied. There are many examples throughout history, and today, of matrilineal societies. These are societies which focus on the mother's side as the core unit. For example, in relation to clan or group membership, this is via the mother's ancestry. They also emphasise maternal influence in decision-making, and inheritance (such as property or titles) is passed down the maternal line. Examples include the Navajo Nation in the USA, the Mosuo people of China and the Khasi people in India.

So, it truly isn't destiny. Humans have a myriad of choices around how we organise our societies for the benefit of everyone. Of course, the problem with these types of long-winded explanations is they currently don't go down well at a Sunday afternoon BBQ with men drinking beer around the grill!

The 'F' word

Oof! That awful word, *feminist*. Cue a slight wince and sharp intake of breath. This is where we can all become unstuck. For some reason, many people struggle with this word. Some people think we should come up with another one, possibly equalist.

The definition of feminism is this: the belief that women and men deserve equal rights and opportunities. I think we would *all* agree with this. And yet, only about two-thirds of women say they identify as feminists, which frankly blows my mind. In surveys, women will more often agree they are feminists when they are given the definition alongside the word because unfortunately, in some circles the word feminist has become synonymous with man-hater, and no one wants to be that. Firstly, because we don't hate men. They are lovely and sexy, and we want them in our lives. Secondly, more uncomfortably, we are told feminists are enormously unattractive – hairy armpits and burnt bras etc. – and the irony is that many of us certainly don't want to be *that*! Although, I am told the hairy pit is coming back into fashion – I honestly can't keep up with which bits of myself I am meant to be waxing or not!

Let's start from the premise here that even if you don't identify with the term feminism, you do identify with the prospect of equality for all. For me, this includes feeling passionate about all the things that now protect women by law. For instance, the idea that women can now own property and credit cards, ask for equal pay, assert reproductive choices and simply have the ability to walk into the pub and buy our own gin and tonics, dammit. Women *need* feminism – if only so we can get tiddly on our own terms!

Men and feminism

I find social hierarchies fascinating and complex, and in case anyone is in any doubt after my Darwinian rant earlier, I put them wholeheartedly in a box labelled *socially constructed*. Who gets vilified depends on your place on the totem pole which generally starts with rich, White men at the top and then has those underneath jostling for position in terms of ethnicity, class and gender.

Just to be clear, I am not saying that men have it easy and only women and minorities struggle in society. This is not a competition. We know the patriarchal system does not always work well for men either: they are conditioned to be strong and silent; they don't access healthcare to the same degree; they do the more physically dangerous jobs, spend more hours at work, have fewer friends, see less of their families, die earlier than women and are three times more likely to die of suicide.

Therefore, I can understand why some men struggle with feminism. I imagine it makes them feel like they are being personally blamed when it's not like they haven't got their own schizzle to deal with. However, all the more reason to fight for equality. Studies show repeatedly that *everyone* is happier when we live in more equal societies. To make progress on these issues of equality, we all must get on board. We mustn't dissolve into whataboutery, but instead try to understand *why* and *where* differences arise for both men and women and what we can do to support each other.

Supporting each other

Women can also become divided from one another when it comes to feminism. When we should be building each other up, at times we seem to be locked in competition and battling against the choices we didn't make. Even the women who do believe in equality between the sexes and who do identify as feminists can often disagree on the right approach to take.

Indulge me here in a bit of academic theorising as there are several branches of feminist thought. In my experience, the two which cause women to become most alienated from one another are *liberal* feminism and *cultural* feminism, and the differences between them.

- Liberal feminists champion *equality as same*. They argue that there aren't that many differences between men and women, and we shouldn't be treated differently based on what's beneath our underwear. The idea is that the sexes are generally more alike than not alike. Women are equally as intelligent and competent as men and the fact that male and female sex bits are different shouldn't prevent women from voting, working outside the home or wearing trousers. The concept is that there is a whole mosaic of human behaviour which doesn't neatly divide into 'All men do this.' and 'All women do that.' Essentially, liberal feminists argue that women should be given equal opportunities to men because we *aren't that different*.

- Cultural feminists believe in *equality as difference*. They argue that of course men and women are different, and difference is good! We don't need to merge into a homogenous sludge of behaviour in order to pretend we are something we aren't. Different isn't better or worse, it's simply *different*. They feel there are fundamental differences in both men's and women's roles in society and that each of these roles should be celebrated and valued equally. For example, cultural feminists may refer to women's collaborative leadership style as a benefit which complements men's top-down approach. The idea is that both the masculine and the feminine are valuable and worthwhile. This philosophy pushes back against the idea that women need to assimilate and behave like men to succeed in the world. Cultural feminists argue that women should be given equal opportunities with men because *different is equally as good*.

These two groups of feminists challenge the other's thinking:

- Liberal feminists argue that lumping all men and all women into two categories is limiting to individuals and doesn't account for the enormous variety of personality

attributes and varying interests in the population. They also argue that in a capitalist society cultural feminism may promote social equality, but not financial and power-sharing equality for women if their focus remains in a traditionally feminine, caregiving role.
- Cultural feminists argue that perceiving men and women to be sufficiently the same devalues the feminine and doesn't account for women's biological reality. It's all well and good to say that women can do the same jobs as men, but men can't birth the babies or breastfeed, and females simply don't have as much upper body strength to push that flipping plough.

In a nutshell, we are scuppered either way; neither of these options is the 'one true way' to equality. So the least we can do is to support each other. Academics who spend their lives dissecting and debating these differences have pretty much concluded that both liberal and cultural feminists have the same objectives – i.e. equality of the sexes. Therefore, to my mind, one of the most important things we can do to make progress is simply to acknowledge that what women really need is more *choice* and *support* and to get behind each other on this point.

The whole issue is emotive and complicated, and I know very few women who can put a label on these feelings. We just inherently know what we feel based on our upbringing and experiences of navigating the world. I have friends who feel vehemently defensive over the right of women to be treated as an individual person rather than a female: Who says I can't become an astronaut just because I have a period? And I know women who feel equally strongly that a woman's life course is heavily influenced by her biology. They are both right.

Before I had children, I was definitely more of a liberal feminist; I didn't think that biology was so impactful that it should translate to a woman's primary role being in the home and a man's primary role being the breadwinner. When I was 18, my boyfriend's mum grilled me as to whether I would iron my future husband's shirts. She must have had me pegged from the beginning as a non-ironer – go figure. And she was right! Even at 18, I had somehow already conflated that anything to do with laundry was subordination. It was only after I had children that the pendulum began to swing, and I became much more empathetic to the ideas of cultural feminism. Females are indeed the only ones who can give birth and breastfeed, so women staying home with children for the first few months makes sense – and it would at least have given me a chance to mop up my leaking body parts! And *surely* we can come up with an argument about upper body strength to ensure men are persuaded to do the bins?!

Realistically, we need both liberal and cultural feminists to fight alongside each other for equality for us and our children. We need to support each other and understand that the job of caring for a family is an incredibly difficult and labour-intensive one requiring multiple skill sets, and we must not let anyone denigrate or belittle it. We need to stop shaming women who do go out to work and break those glass ceilings in politics, law, tech and finance, which will impact all women's lives – stop suggesting they aren't sufficiently feminine, or worse, they are crappy mothers. We need to help each other break down the barriers of inequality so our daughters and women of the future can succeed in both careers and parenting in the same way men currently do.

Why women still can't have it all: in a nutshell

- Women now have a new contract with society which means we aren't seen to be fulfilled unless we are participating in *both* mothering and paid employment. Economic need and today's more, more, more culture means it is rarely a choice for mothers not to work and we end up being pulled in competing directions.
- Women are expected to shoulder the main caregiving load and we don't have sufficient support either from fathers or the state. It is now seen as socially acceptable for women to work in paid employment, but it is still not cool for men to stay at home with children. So, women end up running in circles doing pink *and* blue jobs while men still mainly stick in the blue zone.
- Society doesn't accept ambitious women who want a career in the same way it accepts ambitious men. Watching a woman strive makes people twitch. Tall Poppy Syndrome is the phenomenon of cutting those with ambition back down to size. Women experience this disproportionately to men: 'Put her back in her box!'
- In heterosexual couples where both parties are ambitious for their careers, it is most often the mother who takes a back seat when children come along as big jobs often require greedy hours.
- Today's raised expectations of intensive parenting mean that working mothers spend increasing amounts of time in helicopter-parent mode, and there are still double standards around what it means to be a good dad versus what it means to be a good mum.
- Maternal sacrifice seems to be baked into the lexicon. Society tells us that women need to put everyone else before themselves, while at the same time, social media

feeds us an endless narrative around self-care and healthy well-being which makes us feel like we are failing again.
- All this shame and being pulled in different directions leads to chronic levels of guilt and stress for mothers, which leads to women's unhappiness. What working mothers today need is more choice and more support.
- It doesn't have to be like this. It is not that biology doesn't matter, but that patriarchal rules are socially constructed. We desperately need to deconstruct them if we are to improve the situation for working mothers.
- We still have a way to go before we solve world hunger, world peace, climate change and gender and racial equality. However, for context, it is 6 million years since we crawled out of the swamp and while there have been many changes since then, feminism is still in its infancy. It's only about 100 years since women got the vote and about 50 years since we entered the workforce en masse. We're just getting started!
- We're broadly heading in the right evolutionary direction but to make the world a better place we need to work together. As Chimamanda Ngozi Adichie says: 'We should all be feminists.' It is *so* important that we lift each other up.

Chapter 3

Happiness

What is happiness?

When I was 9 years old, I had to write a speech to present to my school classmates about my favourite day. At that age, it was a great exercise in self-awareness and figuring out what I actually liked and what I didn't. I remember my favourite day involved watching *The Sound of Music*, drinking hot chocolate with marshmallows, taking a ride around the block on my bike with my best friend Tara, and having a sleepover in my imaginary treehouse.

Several decades later, my favourite day is highly unlikely to involve a treehouse unless it is one heavily equipped with central heating, a shower and hairdryer. It's much more likely to involve food, sunshine, walking in nature and chats with people I love. Humanity is a mixed bunch, and others will have any number of things that would please them far more and me far less: rollercoasters, running, rain – or worst of all, my idea of purgatory, running in the rain!

Rather like success, the concept of happiness is therefore both relative and subjective. However, the major misconception people often have about happiness is that it is solely about pleasure. Research now confirms that happiness is not only about seeking the good life but also about seeking a meaningful life.

Positive psychology expert, Professor Paul Dolan, defines happiness as *a mixture of pleasure and purpose.*[20] We can find a neat illustration of this balance of pleasure and purpose in the happiness of parents. Studies find that happiness nosedives when people become parents, as pleasurable things like leisure time become rare commodities. However, as children grow up and leave home the more ethereal qualities of meaning and purpose that children bring become apparent. Studies show that while non-parents are generally happier than parents when children are little, parents have more overall happiness in terms of purpose and life satisfaction when children are grown and sleepless nights become a thing of the past.[21]

It is said that happiness is the entire objective of the human experience. Aristotle[22] claimed 'Happiness is the meaning and purpose in life, the whole aim and end of human existence.' In the American Declaration of Independence of 1776, Thomas Jefferson asserted a man's

---

[20] Terminology which academic researchers use is that pleasure well-being is *hedonia* and purposeful well-being is *eudaimonia*. The term eudaimonia comes from Greek philosophy and is actually even more encompassing that just purpose or meaning in life. Eudaimonia is about self-growth, the realisation of one's full potential, autonomy, engagement in life, positive relationships with others and living a life that is true to one's nature, values and virtues.

[21] The happiness dip on becoming parents is found to be worse for both young mothers and highly educated mothers.

[22] Note that Aristotle was quite the sexist: Greek history is full of them. Another little gem of his: 'The female is female by virtue of a certain lack of qualities. We should regard the female nature as afflicted with a natural defectiveness.' Oh, and he also believed that women didn't have souls. Charming.

right to life, liberty and *the pursuit of happiness*.[23] The Dalai Lama XIV said the meaning of life is to be happy and useful. Ultimately, happiness is the thing we say we want most for ourselves and for our children. Why else do people break the bank taking the family to Disneyland, The Happiest Place on Earth?

Before World War II, measurements of happiness and well-being were focused on the absence of disease and disability. Then in 1946, the World Health Organisation (WHO) expanded this definition to describe well-being as '… a state of complete physical, mental, and social well-being and not merely the absence of disease and infirmity.'

In the last 25 years, there has been another big push in this field of research led by Martin Seligman, an American professor known as the father of positive psychology. Scientists study a flourishing definition of happiness where the goal is to understand how humans can function optimally: how do we go from *good* to *great*?

The happiness industry is now prolific and mainstream – countless books and social media posts give generic happiness advice and extol activities such as positive affirmations, diaphragmatic breathing or open-water swimming to name but a few. I have several friends who get an endorphin thrill from a dark, chilly, 6 am dip, but it gives me the horrors. Despite trying it more than once, I have yet to enjoy missing sleep to dip in an ice-cold, black-bottomed lake! The fact that happiness is subjective and you must pick what is right for you, is, of course, one of the lessons.

In this chapter, I have made it my mission to distil the current research on happiness into practical, bite-sized, *working-mother-appropriate* chunks. I describe what makes

---

[23] Of course, Jefferson referring to the rights of 'men' supposedly covered everyone but, in practice, rights for women and ethnic minorities were not considered until much later.

us happy in the context of genetics and detail which circumstances influence our happiness. I explain the science around ten behaviours that leading academics recommend to improve everyone's happiness. Finally, I delve deeper into four important criteria which particularly contribute to *women's* happiness: good relationships with others, money of our own, time for ourselves and gender equality. My aim is to provide food for thought so you can optimise your own happiness. This chapter sets the scene to further explore specific solutions to improve the happiness of *working mothers* in Chapter 6, The Solution.

What makes us happy?

One of the key learnings from the last two decades of research into happiness is what exactly contributes to our happiness:

- **Behaviours:** A large proportion of happiness (researchers think around 40%, depending on the study) is under our individual control and can be changed for the better by adapting our behaviours – doing things like building positive relationships, looking after our bodies and setting goals.
- **Life circumstances:** These account for around 10%–25% of our happiness. Some of these circumstances we can change, for example, whether or not we have a partner, and some are trickier to control, like the impact of age, ill-health or disability on happiness levels.
- **Genetics:** The rest of our happiness (said by different researchers to be between 30% and 50%) is down to genetics and whether we are born with a genetic predisposition to optimism or not. You know who you are!

Read on, because this is the stuff you need to know not just for yourself but for your children too.

Happy genes

My sister has been called out on occasion for her RBF (Resting Bitch Face!). This is the blank and possibly peeved expression she wears when she is concentrating. It is unnerving to those around her, as like many women she has made a lifetime practice of cultivating a personality that is upbeat, accommodating and cheerful. Anyone who happens to come across her while she is concentrating is therefore perturbed by this change in her normally sunny demeanour.

Researchers find that some of us tend to be naturally sunnier than others: we can be genetically predisposed to being a bit more Tigger, or a bit more Eeyore. In fact, studies of fraternal and identical twins find that approximately 30%–50% of our happiness levels are genetically determined. We all have an inbuilt set point of happiness that we return to despite major triumphs or setbacks. Scientists have discovered that people who have inherited the longer variants of the gene 5-HTT report they are significantly more satisfied with life compared with those who have the shorter variants. The 5-HTT gene is responsible for how well nerve cells distribute serotonin throughout the body. Serotonin is the feel-good chemical in our bodies and the antidepressant drug Prozac works on this neurotransmitter too.

However, before you despair or run off to your GP for prescription drugs it is important to note that genes interact with our environment, and biology is not necessarily destiny. A natural predisposition to RBF in no way means you are destined to be miserable! Science very helpfully shows us that we can influence our happiness levels by modifying choices we make about both our *life circumstances* and our *behaviours*.

Happy circumstances

Would winning the lottery make you stupendously happy? Or being a super brainbox? Or being dazzlingly, blindingly, impossibly gorgeous? Which life circumstances lead to the most happiness may not be exactly what you're expecting.

Money

For many people, life circumstances can be fixed and immovable due to financial necessity. Limited funds mean there's no way to change careers, go back to college or move to a new home. There's no free *choice*.

One of my mum's sage nuggets of wisdom over the years has been that money itself doesn't make you happy but it does give you choices. Academic research backs this up and we know that the main reason money buys happiness is specifically related to the autonomy it provides.

Money primarily makes a difference to happiness when income is very low. Every pound spent increasing the fortunes of those who are financially the worst-off increases happiness levels ten times more than that same pound in the hands of someone ten times richer. This is especially relevant to women, who are much more likely than men to live in poverty. I will explore this more later, looking at the pay gap, childcare responsibilities and other reasons for women's financial inequality.

So, money is good, and a baseline of sufficient money is a necessary prerequisite for happiness. However, being ultra-rich does not necessarily make you ultra-happy. For the middle classes, researchers have found there's a saturation point – typically that of professional incomes – after which happiness no longer increases with rising income levels. For example, a 2020 European study examining happiness in relation to income for 26 European countries cited this figure at around £25,000 per year above which happiness was found to increase no further. A 2010 American study put this figure at around £60,000 per year.

Money does matter. Living in poverty or in debt makes you unhappy. But you don't need to be a millionaire to be happy.

Marriage

If we take four categories – married men, single men, married women and single women – we find that married men are the happiest, and single men are the unhappiest. In fact, married men have overwhelmingly better mental health than single men with half the suicide rate, and single men suffer twice as many mental health problems as single women.

Often cited in happiness research is that men benefit health-wise more from marriage than women. Prominent US government demographer Patrick Glick once estimated that being married is about twice as advantageous for men as it is for women. This idea brought to mind my Auntie Caroline who once told me with a good-humoured huff and a twinkle in her eye just how disgraceful it was that my Uncle Bob, aged 67, needed to be given specific instructions on how to open a tin of soup if she went out, otherwise she would find him forlorn and dehydrated on her return. Women tend to be responsible for most of the caring and domestic elements of relationships; there is a protective effect for men when women are around.

In general, marriage is found to make both sexes happier than being single. This is thought to be due to an increased level of security and emotional support. However, bad marriages are highly detrimental to happiness levels and, as I will expand on later, it is the quality of the relationship which makes all the difference. For couples who are unhappy, studies have shown that divorce increases happiness levels, with both women's and men's happiness boosting to similar degrees once the divorce is complete.

Also interesting is that in several recent studies, it is single, educated women with no children who top the happiness league tables. If you want a giggle, look up comedian Chelsea Handler on Instagram for the amusing ways she spends all the extra cash she has from not having children, including a hyperbaric oxygen chamber to keep her young!

Health

As well as happiness, of course, we want health for our children. We have all heard expectant parents claim, 'I don't mind if it's a boy or a girl just as long as the baby is healthy.' This seems to go hand in hand with that other parental claim: 'I just want them to be happy.'

Studies conducted by the UK's New Economics Foundation found that one of the greatest detrimental impacts to happiness is poor health. Why is health important to happiness? Simply due to a person's level of physical comfort and ability to function. Poor physical health itself causes unhappiness, but it can also impact mental health as many physiological diseases actively cause anxiety or depression.

Unfortunately for both sexes, the old adage is true: women get sicker, and men die quicker. A 2024 report by

McKinsey found that women spend 25% more of their life in ill-health than men. We know that women suffer far more from autoimmune diseases, migraines, Alzheimer's disease and issues relating to our reproductive organs.[24] Women report more anxiety and depression and deal with period problems, menopause and numerous health complications resulting from childbirth. In the UK and the USA, women from ethnic minority backgrounds have worse health outcomes than White women, particularly when it comes to maternity services and mental health.

Some studies find that women have a higher range of emotions than men; we have been reported to experience both more negative emotions and considerably more positive emotions, more frequently and more intensely than men do. I relate to this personally: on any given day my husband can rate his mood as either a 7/10 or an 8/10. My mood, in comparison, can shift between a 2/10 to a 12/10! I have rarely seen my husband lower than a 7, although it does happen. But then I don't think I have ever seen him

---

[24] 80% of those with autoimmune disease are women (autoimmune disease includes conditions such as diabetes, thyroid disorders, Crohn's disease, rheumatoid arthritis, multiple sclerosis and more). Women suffer migraines versus men at a ratio of 3:1 and Alzheimer's disease at a ratio of 2:1. Research released in 2024 finds that stress and elevated cortisol are related to Alzheimer's. In 2017, breast, uterus and ovary cancers, accounted for 30.7%, 3.1% and 2.4% of all new cancers. Prostate and testicular cancers accounted for 26.2% and 1% of all cancers. 1 in 10 women suffer from endometriosis and 30 times more women than men suffer from urinary tract infections. This is before we've even started on complications during and after childbirth. How many women do you know who say their bodies have never been the same after they had their kids? In 2022, the UK government produced their first-ever report to tackle the gender health gap. The UK has the largest gender health gap in the G20 and the 12th largest globally. The report says: 'Women live on average for longer than men but spend more of their life in poor health, often limiting their ability to work and participate in day-to-day activities. Closing the gender health gap and supporting women to live well will not only benefit the health and wellbeing of women but the health of the economy.'

ridiculously ecstatic either – unless England is winning in the football!

We're not sure if these differences are primarily to do with the socialisation of women to be more willing to report differences in mood or if women do actively experience a wider range of emotions influenced at times by hormonal factors – hello pre-menstrual tension, post-natal depression and menopause mayhem! Extensive research has been done on the different ways men and women are socialised to express certain emotions like anger (acceptable for men but not for women) and sadness (acceptable for women but not for men) and the impact this can have on well-being for both sexes. Women report more depression, but men are three times more likely to die of suicide.

Age

Generally speaking, scientists say that happiness is smile-shaped in relation to age: highest both when we are young and old and dipping in mid-life. Mid-life crises are well-studied, and the quarter-life crisis is now also a thing.

For working mothers in particular, mid-life often coincides with greater responsibility at work, caregiving responsibility for children and increasing care responsibility for elderly parents – as well as physical and emotional changes around menopause. It is not uncommon for women to end up giving up their jobs – or their sanity – around this time. The good news, however, is that as long as health is on track, happiness starts increasing again after 50.

What, seriously? Yep. Surely getting old is rubbish? Yet this counter-intuitive finding is said to be due to a maturation process that changes our priorities and gives us a more rounded life perspective. Happiness guru, Mo Gawdat, explains that we are all born with a certain number of hours to live and none of us knows how long that will be. He says that the older we get, the wiser we tend to become and more conscious of appreciating the time we have left.

Beauty

According to a study by Ed Diener, well-being psychologist and author of the book *Happiness: Unlocking the Mysteries of Psychological Wealth*, looks matter very little for overall well-being. He finds that although there is some relation between happiness and beauty, this link becomes small when hair, jewellery and clothing are taken into account.

Diener is trying to say that beauty is not the be-all and end-all. For many women, however, it can feel like it is! Several other studies show that beautiful people are given more job opportunities and earn higher incomes than those who are less attractive: this is termed the beauty premium.

Women's relationship with beauty is complex and different than men's. For millennia, women's beauty has been seen as our currency. This sets up a complicated relationship between how we value ourselves, our self-worth, and by implication, our happiness. A billion-dollar beauty industry which keeps women preened, plumped and plucked is a testament to this. However, being beautiful doesn't guarantee happiness as it can also come with challenges such as a loss of beauty and self-worth with ageing – cue visits to the plastic surgeon. One study found that fashion models, who make a living from being beautiful, suffer from low levels of happiness.

I write much more on beauty in Chapter 5, in terms of women's pressure to perform in this area, but for now, it is useful to know that happiness doesn't correlate terribly strongly with being a supermodel.

Intelligence

If you had to choose, what would it be? Beauty or brains? Leading economist and previous happiness advisor to the UK government Richard Layard explains that intelligence does contribute to increased happiness but not substantially, in the sense that other factors such as positive relationships with others are much more important to the big picture of happiness.

The main way intelligence helps happiness is through earning potential. Three things are found to impact our ability to earn money: beauty, intelligence and personality. Therefore, similar to findings for beauty, we know that educated people earn more and it is mainly through this mechanism that those with a higher IQ have greater happiness. [25]

In terms of whether you should pester your kids to go to university, studies show that those with a degree are somewhat happier than those without. Again, primarily to do with earning potential – with the cost of student debt, this is a highly debated issue. Interestingly, those with a PhD are less happy than those with a degree.

A particularly high IQ is not a very good predictor of happiness. People who are very clever may not only suffer from unmet expectations but be prone to worry and rumination about things that can pass others by. A lovely friend of mine from university – a super-clever doctor – told me she was especially prone to worrying about ducks going barefoot. She's amazing at her job but would admit to being far less good at taking things in her stride.

---

[25] People with a higher IQ also have better health. And as we see, good health also contributes in this way to good happiness.

Where you live

John Denver wrote that *Sunshine On My Shoulders* made him happy. However, researchers find that living in a sunnier climate doesn't make as much difference to happiness levels as you might think. They tell us not to bother moving as the change might boost happiness a little in the short term, but the effects decrease when we get used to it.[26] Friends of mine who moved to Australia claimed that after one summer season there they stopped noticing the weather. I'm not sure how much I believe them as I write this from the drizzle of the UK! However, research shows that of all the factors which affect happiness, climate is not found to be hugely influential. Countries which top the charts for happiness and well-being are often the cold countries of Scandinavia, Canada and Iceland. At the bottom of the happiness index are hot countries in Africa and the Middle East. In the USA, a study found that those living in the sunny climes of California were no happier than those braving the rain and wind in the Midwest.

However, we aren't making it up when say we feel fabulous sitting by the beach with a Piña Colada. Sometimes it is simply the change of seasons we end up enjoying – like the sun breaking through the clouds after a rainstorm. Sunshine biologically boosts happiness in the moment by releasing serotonin. Those with Seasonal Affective Disorder (SAD), like me and around 6% of the British population, are prone to physiological reactions to a lack of sunshine which

---

[26] This phenomenon of getting used to something so that it no longer gives you a happiness boost and you return to your baseline of happiness is known as *hedonic adaptation*. Positive psychology researchers find this applies to a number of situations such as buying a new car or even winning the lottery. We get a buzz out of it at first and then it wears off and we go back to our baseline of happiness.

disturb our circadian rhythms, lower serotonin levels and can actively make us depressed.

In terms of whether you are happier living in the city than in the country, studies find that country life does contribute to happiness levels. This is thought to be related to more cohesive social connections and lower rates of crime. So, by all means, if you are looking to improve your happiness, swap city-slicker living for connections in the countryside – but you don't need to upend your life and move to the tropics to make yourself happy.

Work and commuting

People with a job are significantly happier than those without. So yes, as a working mum you may feel harried and tired and like you need to clone yourself to deal with everything on your to-do list, but you still may be happier working than not working.

Unemployment is one of the life circumstances most highly correlated with unhappiness. Researchers have found that people who lose their jobs experience a happiness dip to the same extent as being bereaved or divorced. The effect is slightly less for women than men – on a 7-point scale, men experience a dip in happiness of 0.5 points and women of 0.4 points. The Trade Union Congress reported in 2023 that Black and minority ethnic women are three times more likely than White men to suffer unemployment.

How about getting to work? Unsurprisingly, commuting only a short distance to work improves happiness for both men and women – but more so for women. Why? Well, research shows this is sexism at its finest: less time commuting means more time for women to manage their domestic load at home. I don't know about you, but one of my most stressful memories of when my children were little was being stuck in motorway traffic and trying to get back before the nursery closed.

Flexible work has been found to increase happiness for both men and women. Albeit with several caveats around missing social interaction, blurred boundaries between home and work and feeling more pressure to be continually available. Women request home-working more than men and this is mainly – you guessed it – for reasons of coping with the domestic load.

Free time

'Free time? What's that?' I hear you say. 'I never get a minute to myself!' It absolutely feels like that for many mums. Sit down with a cuppa and you're lucky to get a minute to unwind before someone needs something from you. Right now.

Researchers talk about discretionary time. That's the time when you're not doing your paid or unpaid work – remember, looking after kids and doing stuff for the household is *work*. Studies find that having less than 2 hours a day of discretionary time leads to unhappiness. However, before you get too caught up in fantasies of moving to that desert island, know that having *more* than 5 hours of discretionary time a day also makes people unhappy. There is a sweet spot in the middle of this for most people where they feel purposeful but not harassed.

This element of happiness is particularly important for working mothers, who chronically feel time-poor. A 2020 study by researchers from both London Business School and Harvard Business School estimated that time poverty was as influential as money poverty when it comes to our overall well-being.

Religion and spirituality

There is a well-established correlation between belonging to a religious group and increased happiness levels, and it doesn't matter which religion. This is related not only to the spiritual comfort religion can provide but also to a gained sense of community and cohesion with like-minded individuals.

Spiritual practices not related to an organised religion also correlate with well-being, things such as yoga, meditation or simply spending time in nature. Fractals – the repeating patterns we find in nature – are known to have a physiological calming effect on the body.

Happy habits

The great news from the field of happiness science is that by altering our behaviours and implementing positive habits in our lives we can actively make ourselves happier. Based on extensive research, leading academics and advisors within the well-being field recommend that we incorporate the following ten behaviours into our daily lives to improve happiness levels. In her book *10 Keys to Happier Living*, Vanessa King uses the acronym **GREAT DREAM** to summarise them[27]:

- **G**iving – do kind things for others.
- **R**elating – connect with people.
- **E**xercising – take care of your body.
- **A**wareness – live life mindfully.
- **T**rying out – keep learning new things.

---

[27] The Action for Happiness charity website actionforhappiness.org has many useful resources including access to well-being support groups and online coaching. These ten tips are taken from there and from Vanessa King's book *10 Keys to Happier Living: A Practical Handbook for Happiness*.

- **D**irection – have goals to look forward to.
- **R**esilience – find ways to bounce back.
- **E**motions – look for what's good.
- **A**cceptance – be comfortable with who you are.
- **M**eaning – be part of something bigger.

In the following sections, I'll look at each behaviour in turn, but at this point don't panic thinking you need to add all of these things to your already epic to-do list. You can just pick whatever resonates with you from the list and give it a go.

Even just implementing one or two of these behaviours consistently has been proven to significantly increase happiness. Dr Rangan Chatterjee gives one of the best pieces of advice I have ever received about putting intentional habits into practice. He recommends when you start a new habit don't make it too big; make it easy and then you will persist with it. He says to start with 5-minute habits that you can do every day. He gives the example that he has made a habit of doing 5 minutes of arm strengthening exercises every morning while he waits for his coffee to percolate. My acupuncturist told me she takes time to be mindful every time she goes for a pee! She says that no matter how busy your day is, you can always take a minute extra when you go to the bathroom. She is a firm believer that 60-120 seconds to yourself in the solitude of a locked loo is a marvellous way to realign.[28]

Also, keep in mind that working on a behaviour in just one area of your life can boost your overall happiness. Note

---

[28] The ability to have time in the bathroom on your own may vary. A while ago I called my sister, and my niece answered the phone. I asked to speak to Mummy and she had no hesitation in passing the phone over to my sister who informed me that she was now sitting on the toilet with full audience participation including not only me and my niece, but also the baby on her knee and the dog at her feet.

how a number of these behaviours can be work-related (keep learning new things, have goals to look forward to), a number can be home-related (do kind things for others, connect with people), and several are individual practices (take care of your body, live life mindfully and look for what is good). The theory of the *enrichment model* finds that people who have multiple roles in life tend to be happier. If you have lots of irons in the fire, there is a buffering effect when one area of life is not going well. So, if work sucks you can always go home and hug your family. And when your kids are busy being teenagers – 20 dirty cups in their bedroom and eyes rolled so far in the back of their heads you worry they've gone blind – you can always console yourself with a job well done at work.

Now, let's explore each of these ten key behaviours that can help us feel more positive about getting out of bed in the morning.

Giving – do kind things for others

Dr Dacher Keltner of the University of California, Berkeley explains the evolutionary benefits of altruism in his book, *Born to Be Good*. We are hard-wired to want to co-operate and we feel happy when we give to others. Keltner lays out how the skills of co-operation and altruism were essential to our survival as a species. He explains, in the context of survival of the fittest, that it wasn't just an individualistic, competitive process, but one where group cohesion and co-operation had value in promoting survival and, therefore, the passing down of genes. He argues that societies with individuals who demonstrated empathy and were able to form strong social bonds were more likely to thrive. This evolutionary advantage is then coded for, and we are primed to feel good when we look out for other people.

In fact, being kind to others has been shown to actively elevate levels of dopamine in the brain, sometimes known as the *helper's high* – dopamine is the neurochemical responsible for reward and pleasure. People who do volunteer work have much lower rates of depression than the general population.

For mothers in particular, always giving to others seems to be part of the job description. Remembering emergency snacks, checking in on our neighbour who has fallen, picking up a friend's children from school when they are poorly, packing 'I love you' notes in school lunchboxes, or volunteering for the school PTA. The list is endless, and sometimes we feel like it never ends, but the truth is by giving to others in all these little ways, we're boosting our happiness.

Dr David Hamilton explains in his book, *The Five Side Effects of Kindness*, five fabulous benefits of looking out for others and doing good things:

- We feel happier. Kindness actively releases dopamine.
- We protect our hearts. Kindness stimulates oxytocin.
- We slow ageing. In a study, participants who did a loving kindness meditation for 6 weeks improved the length of their telomeres. These are strands of DNA which unravel as we age – they act a bit like the plastic cap on the end of a shoelace to keep DNA together – and can be used to determine our biological age.
- We improve relationships. We feel bonded to others through acts of kindness and reciprocity.
- We spread happiness. Kind acts have been shown to spread in a ripple effect to three degrees of separation – to friends of friends of friends.

Doing random acts of kindness for others really does improve our own happiness. However, it is also relevant to point out that caregiver fatigue is real for mothers. So many mothers are burned out; I feel pretty confident saying that when it comes to giving to others, we've probably already reached our quota by 9 am on a school day! So be kind to *yourself* too and take this tip in the context of *your* life. Don't feel you have to be endlessly giving if you're already overloaded.[29]

Relating – connect with people

People with good relationships are not only happier, but they are also healthier and may even live longer. Good relationships help protect our immune system, our hearts and our brains from ill-health. For survival, humans have been evolutionarily wired to connect and bond with others. One of the longest and most comprehensive happiness studies, the *Harvard Grant Study*, followed more than 200 men and their families from Boston, USA over more than 75 years. They chose people from opposite ends of the socioeconomic spectrum. A significant finding from the study was that it was strong relationships, rather than money, which made the greatest difference to overall happiness.

So, make time for your friends, grab that coffee and fill your relationship cup. Book a date night with your partner. A wise friend said to me a long time ago that if you could

---

[29] Interestingly, when it comes to performing random acts of kindness, it has been shown that we can get an even bigger high from loading our kindness acts as a weekly activity rather than something to be done every day. In one experiment, participants were told to perform acts of kindness every day for 5 days each week and another group were told to perform five acts of kindness per week but on the same day. They did this for 6 weeks. The group who performed their acts all on one day increased their happiness levels whereas the group who stretched their kindness out over 5 days found no difference. Researchers thought this finding was because doing them all in one day gave participants a bigger one-off buzz and was less draining than thinking about it every day. Rather a useful tip for mums!

manage to count on one hand the number of people you could call in the middle of the night knowing they would respond, it was as lucky in life as you could get.

In relation to happiness behaviours, researchers find that the connections you make with people don't always have to be deep and meaningful to make a difference. Simply having a random chat with a stranger at the bus stop or the person serving you in the supermarket is proven to give a happiness boost not only to you but to the person you connected with. For an immediate buzz, make a point of starting a conversation with a stranger, or look for something you can give someone a sincere compliment about. This happiness-boosting technique has even been shown to work for introverts!

Exercising – take care of your body

Hippocrates, known as the Father of Medicine, claimed all people in a bad mood should go for a walk, and if it does not improve, walk again. Quite simply, exercise doesn't just improve our physical health, it makes us happier and it's an effective tool for treating depression.

Historically, medicine often treated the body and mind as separate entities, but contemporary research in neuroscience emphasises the intricate connection between the two and has reversed our assumption that emotion starts in the brain and feeds to the body. We know now that if we alter how we feel in our body, our brain will respond. There is a complex interplay with significant information going in the direction of body to brain: for instance, the physical act of smiling can trick our brains into feeling happier.

It is common for mums to report feeling *touched-out* and overstimulated in today's frenetic climate. But by learning more about our bodies and finding ways to stimulate our vagus nerve, which is responsible for regulating a number of bodily functions such as heart rate, digestion, immunity and emotional responses, we can physically train our bodies to help us emotionally regulate. Stimulating this nerve can be as simple as learning how to breathe in a diaphragmatic way, humming, singing, cold water therapy, massage or yoga.

The World Health Organisation recommends a minimum of 150 minutes of moderate-intensity aerobic physical activity per week plus a strengthening activity twice a week. Of course, good luck to the mothers for finding time! Women with children not only exercise less but we also tend to eat less healthily than women without children. Exercise and eating well should be something we do to make ourselves feel good, but for many mothers, it is just another thing to feel guilty and body-shamed about.

The WHO targets are not do or die, however. A 2024 study published in the Journal of the American College of Cardiology found that while regular physical exercise does extend our lifespan, women need only do half as much as men for the same beneficial effect. A 2023 report by Public Health England found that even walking for 10 minutes a day can increase physical fitness and improve the chances of a longer life by 15%. Thumbs up, then, for the school run! Well, school walk usually, unless it's One of Those Days and you're super late.

In Michelle Obama's biography, author Liza Mundy explains how and why Michelle decided to prioritise exercise as something she was going to do for herself:

> 'Michelle had a revelation: She had to stop being angry and expecting him (Barack) to change, and focus instead on how she could gain control and extract happiness out of her life… "This was an epiphany," she said. "I am sitting here with a new baby, angry, tired and out of shape. The baby is up

for that 4 o'clock feeding. And my husband is lying there, sleeping." She figured out that if she left (and went to the gym), he would have to cope. "I would get home from the gym and the girls would be up and fed. That was something I could do for me." She told an interviewer for the *Chicago Tribune* that she realised she could not live her life being resentful: it would wreck her and it would poison their relationship. "I cannot be crazy, because then I'm a crazy mother and I'm an angry wife." In that interview, she allowed herself the luxury of adding, "What I notice about men, all men, is that their order is me, my family, God is in there somewhere, but me is first. And for women, me is fourth, and that's not healthy.'"

Michelle is absolutely right. For far too many women, *me* comes at the end of a long list of the needs of other people. This doesn't serve anyone. So take that time to look after yourself by eating well and exercising – and if you know something's not quite right, make a doctor's appointment. Even if you have to stagger into the GP practice with a sticky toddler on one hip and a squalling baby on the other, do it. *You* matter. And your health matters.

Awareness – live life mindfully

Mindfulness is a state of active, open attention to the present moment. It involves observing our thoughts and feelings without judgement and having a heightened awareness of the present. The ancient Chinese philosopher Lao Tzu said that those suffering from anxiety spend too much time worrying about the future, those with depression spend too much time hung up on the past, and it is only those who live in the present moment who are able to be happy.

Mindfulness is so effective, the NHS in England now prescribe 8-week mindfulness courses for a variety of conditions.[30] Studies have shown that people with a regular mindfulness practice are likely to be happy, optimistic, self-confident and satisfied with their lives, and less likely to be depressed, angry, anxious, hostile, self-conscious, impulsive or neurotic.

Professor Ellen Langer of Harvard University – author of several books including *The Mindful Body* and sometimes known as the mother of positive psychology – has made a lifelong study of the power of the mind-body connection. In her research, she found time and time again that the way we think about things actively impacts our physical health and happiness. To develop positive thinking, we need to start with being mindful. She says if you are new to the practice of mindfulness, a simple technique to get started is just to notice three things about someone or something that you have not noticed before. She also recommends having more fun! If you are having fun, you are by definition enjoying the moment and therefore being mindful. Bring on the tickling of tiny toes!

With our busy lives and busy brains, mindfulness can often feel like just another thing to do. However, a mindfulness practice is more a way of being than an activity to tick off your list. Playwright William Saroyan puts it this way:

> 'Try to learn to breathe deeply, really to taste food when you eat, and when you sleep really to sleep. Try as much as possible to be wholly alive with all your

---

[30] Although, note that mindfulness is not a panacea. Those with significant mental health concerns such as bipolar disorder or schizophrenia are advised to consult their doctor before implementing this technique as it does not work for everyone, and some may need additional support. nhs.uk/mental-health/self-help/tips-and-support/mindfulness/

might, and when you laugh, laugh like hell. And when you get angry, get good and angry. Try to be alive. You will be dead soon enough.'

Trying out – keep learning new things

A pretty self-explanatory happiness habit! This is about trying something that you haven't done before – sign up for a wine-tasting course, book an art class, learn a new language, go salsa dancing or simply just take a different route home. Interestingly, studies find that when couples try new activities together, the act of seeing their partner in a new and novel situation increases intimacy and relationship satisfaction.

Humans have a psychological need for mastery. The stimulation of trying something new and the accomplishment we feel when we have achieved it gives a great boost to our self-confidence and well-being. By doing and achieving new things we accumulate evidence that we are capable, and this gives us a more open and curious attitude to life.

For this technique to work best for boosting happiness, the key is to find something that relates to your personal interests and skill set and to stretch yourself a little with it – around 10% out of your comfort zone. We often conflate happiness with success, and received wisdom around success training is that you must do the thing you are most scared to do. This is a brilliant way to conquer fear and achieve success, but for happiness, it is more about finding things that speak to our hearts and getting good at doing them. Rather than adding stress, we are looking for *eustress*[31], the type of stress that comes from positive challenges and exciting experiences that float *your* boat.

Direction – have goals to look forward to

According to personal development coach Brian Tracy, only 3% of the population write down their goals. Yet those who do are not only substantially more likely to achieve them but are also happier. Goals give us purpose and provide us with a sense of direction – remember, happiness is a combination of pleasure and purpose.

For happiness, the goals we set should be something that aligns with our values and interests, not something we think we *should* be doing. Goals can be related to our hobbies or our home life, but for many people, goals come from work. And if we aren't interested in goals relating to work, it may also be time to ask whether the work we are doing is the right work for us.

The Action for Happiness charity recommends starting goal setting with something as simple as writing down a goal that you want to achieve. Make this time-bound so, for instance, once a week for the next 3 weeks. In order to make sure you can achieve it, also write down the steps you will take and predict any obstacles which may get in your way as well as what you will do to overcome them.

This might seem rather simple. Working mums are already pretty experienced with to-do lists! It seems to come with the territory. That glorious, satisfied feeling of a fully ticked-off list – do you ever write the extra stuff down just to be able to put the tick next to it? What we aren't quite as adept at, is to-dos which are focussed on something *we* want to do! We need to make sure that things we want to do are

---

[31] Eustress is a type of stress that is positive, healthy or fulfilling. It is known as the *good stress* and is the opposite of distress.

on that list. Creating a vision board is another hugely effective way of goal setting that is more long-term. Ask yourself: What does my ideal life look like and what do I want to achieve by the time I die?

You can create a vision board for your life by sticking images that you crop from the internet or magazines onto a pinboard. These goals will be very personal to you and can be anything from fitness goals, relationship goals and financial goals, to travel and adventure goals. The idea is to keep the vision board where you can see it daily, so it gives you a sense of direction and purpose. Of course, as any businesswoman or mother will know, the key to a good goal-setting strategy is for it to also be adaptable. So, if circumstances change or new ideas come along, we can add them to the mix.

Resilience – find ways to bounce back

'Find ways to bounce back and be resilient' may seem a little waffly. How do we actually do that?

First of all, you can consider your mindset. Psychologist Carol Dweck has explored the difference it makes to have a growth mindset rather than a fixed mindset:

- With a *growth mindset*, you have the attitude that setbacks are temporary and an opportunity to learn.
- With a *fixed mindset*, you think things are immutable and you can't influence them. For instance, you may think that you are either good at sports or you aren't.

No prizes for guessing that people with growth mindsets are more resilient. Growth mindsets aren't just wishful thinking either: we know that even intelligence can be malleable – neuroplasticity helps our brains make new connections all the time, and high-performance learning, where we anticipate that *all* students can master any subject though some may just take longer, is now a goal in many schools.

Another way to develop resilience is to embrace change. This means changing your attitude towards stressful events and seeing them in a different light. Author Spencer Johnson in *Who Moved My Cheese?* tells the tale of four characters who live in a maze: two humans, Hem and Haw, and two mice, Scurry and Sniff. Everyone is happy because they have found a big source of their favourite food, cheese. But then, one day, the cheese is gone. Scurry and Sniff quickly accept the loss of the cheese and go off into the maze in search of other sources. Hem and Haw, on the other hand, feel they are the victims of some kind of fraud or theft; they are devastated because they have built their lives around the big cheese, moving their house to be near it. Yet their clinging on only makes things worse because it ensures that they go hungry. Meanwhile, Scurry and Sniff have long moved on and found new cheese.

The moral of the story is that the more you can start to see change as an opportunity rather than a threat, the happier you become. One of my mum's favourite sayings is 'This too shall pass.' The one thing that we can guarantee in life is that nothing stays the same, and the more accepting we are of this fact, the easier our life becomes.

The Dalai Lama says that we must remember that *not* getting what we want is sometimes a wonderful stroke of luck. Happy people tend to trust that things happen for a reason and will work out for the best. I remember a guy I dated for a while telling me that he had just always known he was lucky. He said that whatever happened to him, he always managed to land on his feet, and he inherently believed that things always worked out for him regardless. The great thing was, they always did; he had his fair share of traumas, but he was naturally upbeat, and fate seemed to smile on him because of his attitude. I now tell my children to trust that everything will work out okay. If you believe in your heart that regardless of what happens to you, it happens for a reason or that something good can be made from it, your life will ultimately be happier.

Author Frances Rodman says: 'Just think about how happy you would be if you lost everything you have right now – and then, got it back again.' This concept originates from the Stoic philosophers who practised it as a technique they called *negative visualisation*. The idea is to spend time thinking about how your life would be if you had lost the things you value. By contrast, you will start to appreciate what you have even more.

Emotions – look for what is good

Research shows that intentionally practising gratitude not only improves overall life satisfaction but also has positive effects on mood in the moment. So how do you go about practising gratitude? A good way is to write down the things you are grateful for in a daily, or at least weekly, journal – choose, say, a Sunday night and reflect on the week. Be specific about the things you are grateful for – for instance, rather than just being grateful for your family, you might be grateful that your toddler learned how to wipe her bum, or that your teenager laughed at your joke. Even if you feel you haven't much to be grateful for at the moment, start with the small things: I am grateful the sun is shining; I am grateful for the flowers in the park; I am grateful for soft fluffy slippers after a day of high heels or the ahh feeling of removing my bra at the end of a long day!

Over dinner, I ask my children to share the best bits of their day, the worst bits and also the funny bits. Being grateful for what you have isn't about ignoring what is bad and brushing problems under the carpet. Instead, it is about reframing the bad in the context of the good.

If there is a particular person you are grateful for, why not tell them? You could simply send a text to someone you love – do it now! In one study, participants had to think of someone who had made an important difference in their lives. They wrote them a detailed letter saying what they did for them and how it affected their life, and they visited the person and read the letter out to them. Results showed that from just this one intervention, participants felt happier, and they still felt happier a month after the visit.

Who would you write to?

Acceptance – be comfortable with who you are

In 2012, Bronnie Ware wrote a best-selling book called *The Top Five Regrets of the Dying* about her experiences as a live-in carer for those with end-stage illnesses. She found people's top regret at the end of their lives was not having lived a life that was true to themselves.

For some, this whole concept of being authentic can sound a little new age-y. However, all being authentic is really about is accepting yourself and understanding the difference between self-acceptance and self-esteem. Self-acceptance is crucial for well-being. The ability to understand ourselves fully – know thyself, says Greek philosophy. Being compassionate to ourselves, despite our imperfections, is far more important than the self-esteem which we often covet more. Self-esteem is related to ego, value and worth, but chasing self-esteem can actually be quite damaging. By contrast, self-acceptance is being able to be OK with ourselves *exactly as we are*.

One way to develop more self-acceptance is to work on how you speak to yourself. Pay attention to the critical voice in your head. Professor Steve Peters – the sports psychologist who coached the UK's Olympic-winning cycling team – calls this voice our inner chimp. Do you find that the voice in your head speaks kindly to you? Or does it berate you when the slightest thing goes wrong? 'Oh my God, I can't believe you said that. You're SO stupid.'

The truth is, we often speak to ourselves in a way we wouldn't dream of speaking to anyone else. Try this exercise, used by therapists with their clients:

1. When you notice your critical voice is speaking, write down what it says or record it as a voice note.
2. Read the words back and ask yourself: Would you say this to your best friend or your child?
3. Rewrite the words with compassion, speaking to yourself as you would your child: 'It's alright, these things happen. You are great. Just try again next time.'

Dr Peter Attia, a researcher on health, well-being and longevity, tried this for 4 months on the advice of his therapist, and he found he developed more compassion for himself in his late 40s than he had ever had at any point in his life. He credited this technique for saving his marriage. When you're full of self-criticism and loathing, it is hard to be present for other people. Give it a try!

Meaning – be part of something bigger

Cultivating meaning in life is related to having purpose. In his 2020 film *A Life On Our Planet*, David Attenborough, at the grand age of 93, presents what he calls his *witness statement* to the changes humans have brought to the natural world over his lifetime. He explains in vivid language how different our perspective of the world became when American astronauts landed on the moon in 1969; the illuminating moment when humanity peered at the grainy images on our television screens, and we saw ourselves for the first time from far away. At that moment, we became aware of how finite our world is: we could literally see the edges of our existence on the Blue Planet in the context of a vast universe.

Few of us will lead a life as rich and diverse as that of David Attenborough, but we all have to cultivate our own meaning during our time here. We can make meaning from our work, our sense of community, our family, our faith, from nature, music or art.

We can even develop meaning from overcoming adversity. Viennese psychiatrist, Viktor Frankl wrote a book in 1946 called *Man's Search for Meaning*. It details the horrors he encountered when he was held prisoner in Auschwitz and Dachau concentration camps during the Second World War. He suffered every possible deprivation and endured extreme hunger, cold and brutality. His wife, father, mother and brother died in the camps. Alone and with every possibility of imminent death, he came to understand that even in the most dire and horrific circumstances, a person still has their last freedom. This is the freedom to choose how we respond to our circumstances and how meaning can be created out of even the darkest despair. He noted how those who had given up hope suffered mental anguish far more than he, and he emerged from the camp as an optimist.

Optimism can be cultivated and grown despite any predisposition to Resting Bitch Face or the unfortunate lack of a longer 5-HTT gene! We can train our brains to focus on the good things and make efforts to be connected to something bigger. Try the following exercise:

Imagine you are at the end of your life and looking back over it. What were the most important and meaningful aspects of what you have accomplished? Think about it. Write an advice letter to your today-self about what matters most in life.

Pressure to be happy – no thank you!

Having read plenty now about how to feel happier, I wonder how you're feeling. Inspired, motivated? Or perhaps… exhausted?

The perverse irony is that all this talk about happiness sometimes creates an expectation of happiness that makes us unhappy. The pressure to be happy with the inference that other emotions aren't acceptable can end up being counter-productive.

My children's school has revamped their image recently and developed a new motto: *Be More*. School assemblies and social media posts are accompanied by hashtags such as #bemorecurious, #bemoresporty, #bemoreresilient, et cetera. The effect of this is simply to weary my daughter into asking why she can't just *be*? Why does she have to be *more*?

Relating this to happiness, author Caitlin Moran has talked openly about her daughter's eating disorder and how Caitlin felt she was doing the right thing as a parent by telling her daughter that she didn't have to be successful, she just wanted her to be happy. After significant amounts of therapy and soul searching, she found that it was partly a *pressure* to be happy – #bemorehappy – that was causing her daughter's misery.

Social media is horribly responsible for much of the angst of today's teenagers. Silicon Valley chief executives know this and don't let their own children near it. For the rest of the population, however, they persist in developing algorithms that lure us in and keep us doom-scrolling and addicted. Try leaving your phone in a locked drawer for several hours and count how often you have a compulsion to go and look at it. Kids today see only an unfiltered view of everyone's best bits and they think it is real, with no context of people's worst bits which never get posted. Both the pressure to be happy and the power of social comparison are hugely detrimental to happiness levels.

For working mothers, being happy can become just another bloomin' thing on your ever-increasing list of things to do. I haven't got *time* to be happy! I distinctly remember a birthday when my children were little: I was so busy and harassed that I was actively irritated about having to thank people for sending birthday wishes. Not good, hey? I didn't have time to get my hair done or pee on my own, never mind celebrate a birthday and try to be *happy*.

Being pleasant and agreeable can feel like a requirement of womanhood, not only for ourselves but to suit the rest of society. Being Miss Congeniality comes as part of the role of social glue-stick that I previously discussed. When I was 18 I got a bar job, and I remember one incident where I was told by a male customer around 30 years my senior to 'Smile, love' and that I would look better if I was wearing red lipstick. My response at that time, I am now ashamed to say, was to helpfully demur with a big grin and an agreeable flash of my pearly whites.[32] As opposed to returning the favour and giving him my unsolicited opinion regarding his moustache and general demeanour.

---

[32] A 2019 survey of 520 women conducted by the American dental company Byte, found that nearly 98% of women had been told at some point in their lives to smile by complete strangers. 56% said they were told to smile by men in public and 15% said this happened regularly, around twice a week. We know that social status affects how often people smile. In many cultures it is a sign of submission and agreeableness. Those in higher positions in the hierarchy do not feel the need to smile as much as those who have less power.

Along with countless other women since the dawn of time, I have found being pleasant, happy and accommodating to be my job as a woman: both for the comfort of others and to keep the peace. There is an additional safety element to this which I will come to in Chapter 5. Oiling social wheels is partly about making everyone around us happy, and partly about making ourselves attractive. And, like so many women before me, I am now coming to the conclusion in middle-age: bollocks to that pressure to be happy and congenial. Wearing a determined Resting Bitch Face when we feel like it is the way to go!

Four significant things women need for happiness

Much of the happiness data above relates to both men and women. But there are four particular areas which are impactful for women's happiness and can look different for each gender. The first is relationships. Not that men don't also participate in relationships! But it is often women who spend more time cultivating relationships in the community and performing acts of caregiving. The second is money. Women simply don't have access to as much of it as men do and this is a problem. The third is time. Working mothers have less leisure time than working fathers. And the final is gender equality. As outlined in Chapter 1, women's inequality directly leads to a reduction in our happiness and quality of life.

Good relationships

Connecting with others is one of the behavioural tools already discussed which we can use to improve our happiness levels. It is clear and categoric in the research that good, healthy relationships are one of the most important indicators of well-being. This is within romantic relationships, friendships, relationships with our children and with our work colleagues. Motivational speaker Jim Rohn says we are the average of the five people we spend the most time with; therefore, it is important to choose those people carefully. People rub off on us! Psychologist Adam Grant finds in his research that one bad apple definitely does spoil the bunch. It is critical for our happiness that we distance ourselves from toxic relationships.

Researchers find that humans are evolutionarily wired for connection – even the introverts like me. Psychologist John Bowlby's influential work on attachment theory explains how crucial to our well-being the attachments that we form with our caregivers as infants are. His work was extrapolated by clinical psychologist Sue Johnson to explain adult pair-bonding relationships. Dr Johnson explains that as humans we are programmed to scan the horizon and look for our tribe, people who will accompany us through life and who we can reliably trust and depend upon – and also have fun with!

Relationships affect our happiness so much that they also impact our health. Interestingly, one large study of 9000 people, the *Alameda County Study*, found that it was women's friendships with *other women* which determined their longevity, whereas men's longevity was affected by whether they were married or not. This is thought to be related to the fact that women often develop same-sex friendships in a different way than men do. In times of stress, women are more often found to *tend and befriend* – when faced with a threat, we tend to our children and befriend those around for support and comfort – whereas men are more likely to *fight or flight*. In my experience, women communicate by having supportive chats – we put kisses at the end of our text messages. Whereas men have entertaining bants – 'How's it going, dickhead?' – and are more likely to not bother responding to texts! Females are socialised from a young age to share problems, and this behaviour can strengthen relationships and have a protective effect on women's happiness levels. Bring on meeting friends for coffee and cake.

This is not to say that women never feel isolated, though. Sometimes we're drinking that coffee and eating that cake alone. *Matrescence*, or the physical and psychological process of becoming a mother, is bamboozling in itself and can have drastic effects on relationships not only with partners but with friends as well. Work and motherhood can also divide women, rather than bring us together. Parenting styles can clash and competition between parents can create upset and disharmony in relationships. A friend calls this the 'yummy-mummy pecking order'. Then there's a push-and-pull dynamic about who is going back to work, when and for how long. Which camp do you belong to? I remember all too well the feeling of being left out of the mums and tots swimming group my antenatal friends had joined with their babies. I couldn't go as I had to be in the office.

Beyond relationships with partners, family and friends, the connections we form at work also make a big difference to our happiness. Bad relationships at work, especially with line managers, can take a big toll on us and poor line management is one of the main reasons why people leave employment. On the flip side, for many women good working relationships with like-minded colleagues often provide a much-needed and welcome diversion from Dora the Explorer and toddlers who don't yet talk!

So, as most women already know, the people we gather around us are significant and can provide both great levels of comfort and great levels of distress. At funerals, it is rare to speak about the deceased's jobs or accomplishments. Instead, our lives our spelled out by what we meant to each other as friends, parents, siblings and partners. This is an important area of our life to focus on, and for many women, of course, this is the reason we instinctively prioritise cultivating good relationships with people we care about.

Money

Money is a significant contributing factor in the having-it-all issue for women. There is no escaping the fact that a job inside the home does not give us money, whereas one outside the home does.

It has been argued that primary caregivers should be given financial compensation in the form of a monthly stipend from the government for doing this job. Wouldn't that be wonderful! One 2019 estimate from Salary.com put the median annual salary of replacing a housewife at £142,188. This took into account the myriad roles a stay-at-home parent performs, such as psychologist, sports coach, dietitian, event planner, photographer, cleaner, logistics manager, teacher and nurse. Yet too often, we find that society has little appreciation for the role of stay-at-home parents, approximately 90% of whom are mothers. Somewhere along the way an assumption sprang up that domestic labour is either free or cheap.

So, how much does having both sufficient money and financial independence matter for mothers' happiness? The answer, of course, is quite a lot. We don't need to be rolling in money, but it does matter when women don't have money. It *does* matter that women are substantially more likely to live in poverty than men. It *does* matter to women's health, happiness and well-being when the vast majority of the world's wealth, and therefore power, is in the hands of men. A 2020 study by Boston Consulting Group found that two-thirds of the world's wealth is controlled by men, and according to the World Economic Forum, women own less than 20% of land worldwide.

This matters for women at a global and societal level but it also matters to us as individuals. Women who have their own money have more power in their relationships, more latitude for decision making and more ability to influence their own and their children's lives. In the UK, 1 in 5 women experience financial abuse. Lack of money is a primary reason for women continuing to stay in coercive or abusive relationships.[33]

It all comes back to the research which finds that money makes you happy to the extent it gives you *choices*. Repeatedly and persistently, choice and autonomy are flagged in research as a key component for happiness.

Money has been said to be the final frontier for gender equality for women. It can be a touchy subject and one that women sometimes steer away from. A study from Fidelity Investments found that 80% of women refrained from discussing finances with their close family and friends. To explain this, a third of women agreed with the statements, 'It is uncomfortable.' or 'I was raised not to talk about finances.'

In the same way that society conditions men to think their worth stems from their money, women are conditioned to not be money-motivated. We are supposed to want to do things from the goodness of our hearts, not because there is money involved; women mustn't come across as money-grabbing

---

[33] Financial abuse can range from a partner not allowing you to access work or education, to controlling finances and not sharing information, to placing debt in your name. For more information or to be signposted for help, see: refuge.org.uk/i-need-help-now/how-we-can-help-you/economic-abuse/

gold-diggers. In this perverse dynamic, women need to prove they don't want or need money. Although, of course, we need money just as much as men do. Like it or not, it's money that makes the world go around.

It is actually unsurprising that these differences between men and women still exist, as women have a long history of financial inequality. Consequently, we find the following today in the UK:

- The gender pay gap is 15%. To put this into context, it means that women essentially work for free for 54 days of the year before their wages are the same as men's: from 1st of January up until the 23rd of February.[34] Note that British women of Pakistani or Bangladeshi heritage earn around 33% less than White British men and over half of Black women are paid less than their White peers.
- The gender investment gap is 20%. The amount of income this accounts for is the equivalent of Switzerland's gross domestic product.[35]
- The gender pension gap is a whopping 38%. That means that women, who on average live longer than men, are significantly more likely to be poor in old age.

It is ingrained in our societal structure to think that money is men's business. These stereotypes and gender roles around money can be difficult to break. A friend of mine who works in finance told me recently that her husband does all the financial management for their family – even though

---

[34] In America, Black Women's Equal Pay Day is the 27th of July. So, despite the fact that Black women are the most educated demographic in America, they essentially work for half of the year before their wages are the same as men's. This is every kind of wrong.

[35] Some studies have shown that women investors outperform men. According to Fidelity Investment's 2021 Women and Investing study, women outperformed their male counterparts by 40 basis points (0.4%). Women were said to be more cautious with their decisions and to think longer term rather than making regular trades.

financial management is literally her job – as it is just a gender thing in their house, so she lets him get on with it. We still have a way to go when it comes to levelling up these disparities and getting on an even playing field.

Women *do* need money. As 20th century novelist and feminist Virginia Woolf writes in her famous essay 'A woman must have money and a room of her own if she is to write fiction.' The good news is that compared to Virginia's time, significantly more women today can do paid work to get some money *and* a room of their own.

Time

However, in order to write that book that Virginia mentions, women also need time. Feminist writer Simone de Beauvoir positions in her book *The Second Sex* that the energy women spend on *othering* is the reason for women writers' comparative lack of success to men in the same field. She claims that women arrive out of breath at the same point where men create their masterpieces. Othering is the idea that men come as the standard model and women are other, or secondary, to men. Society is still not used to women belonging in the world of work, so we perform time-consuming mental labour to justify our existence there. Beauvoir's book was published in 1949 but this kind of mental labour is still highly relevant: researchers today talk about women's identity work, our imposter syndrome and the mental labour women perform to justify our seat at the table.

Further, when it comes to time spent on mental labour at home, mothers typically take on much more of this than fathers. Researchers examine the consequences of the cognitive load of motherhood and confirm the increased stress this places on mothers. Studies find that contrary to popular belief, women are not better multitaskers than men: we just do more of it due to social conditioning. It's like having 100 tabs open on your laptop all at the same time. The whirring of your brain as you anticipate, organise, negotiate, arrange, caretake, schedule and *remember*. Not just for ourselves but for the rest of the family. Women make 70%–80% of purchasing decisions for their families. And this mental workload doesn't just extend to remembering whether the cottage cheese in the fridge is out of date. It is also the emotional workload of a human thermometer – temperature checking the well-being of the family at regular intervals. Was that look your teenager gave you just a standard roll of the eyes or is there something else afoot? Does your 5-year-old's persistent tummy ache mean they are anxious or constipated?

When it comes to time-use studies comparing total workload for women and men, they typically examine the number of hours of paid work and unpaid work. Research consistently finds that women in every country of the world spend more time per day than men on total work. This is typically between half an hour to an hour a day in the Global North, and at least double this in the Global South. Of course, these studies don't count emotional labour and the cognitive load. They also don't count the labour involved with living in a female body. Things like periods, breastfeeding, pregnancy, menopause, physical safety and ill health. So, even without accounting for mental and emotional labour, it is clear that women's total physical daily workload is unfairly distributed. This costs us time and has significant consequences for gender equality.

As explained earlier in this chapter, studies show that time is just as important as money to well-being. To put it simply, working mothers are more likely than fathers to struggle with both money inequality *and* time inequality.

Typically, it is mothers who make the decision to reduce their paid work hours or increase their domestic load at home in order to emotionally compensate for working full-time. We are between the rock and the hard place of losing either money or time. A friend of mine gave up work during the COVID-19 pandemic and has never gone back. Other friends have given up their jobs because of their children's ill health, their parent's ill health or health problems of their own. There is no flexibility in our workload for extra demands. And many mothers find that nonsense schedules and permanently prioritising the needs of others have broken them by the time they reach mid-life, if not before.

Gender equality

Quite simply, we need this to be better for our children. I outlined in Chapter 1 how women are basically fed up and this is backed by science. Research has found women's happiness to be declining both absolutely and in relation to men since the 1970s, and many academics in the well-being field believe this issue to be due to gender inequality. Women's level of overwork in two different spheres is creating frustration and unhappiness. Time poverty and constrained choice are issues for women. Our expectations of what we can achieve have been raised but our reality has not.

So, what do we do?

The issue is clearly one of inequality. Significant research shows that both women *and men* who live in more gender-equal countries are happier. The 2024 World Happiness Report found Finland to be the happiest nation. Scandinavian countries regularly vie for the top spot in the well-being stakes. Denmark often ranks first – it was second in 2024 – and even has its own unique word, *hygge*, which denotes an atmosphere of warmth and camaraderie, enjoying good things with good people. Other countries which regularly appear in the happiness top ten are Norway, Sweden, Switzerland, Netherlands, and Iceland. Tables which rank gender equality also put these countries high on their list, which is no coincidence. The UK's 2024 happiness ranking was 20th, Canada was 15th and the USA was 23rd. Unsurprisingly, Afghanistan, with their atrocious record on women's rights, ranked last for happiness out of 146 countries.

I will say it again: happiness is highly correlated with gender equality. As Laura Bates says in her book of the same title, we need to fix the system, not the women. We need to support each other and recognise not only our own struggle but those of others who additionally deal with issues of racism, sexual orientation and disability.

For happiness, women need equality. The Global Gender Gap report of 2020 put gender equality at 100 years away. In post-pandemic 2023, the UN Secretary-General António Guterres said that at current rates of change, gender equality is more likely to be 300 years away. Data released by UN Women estimated that the 3 years of the pandemic put back gender equality by 25 years as a result of women quitting paid work – we couldn't keep up with our workload when we were co-opted to be full-time teachers too.

This chapter has explored the latest research on happiness in the positive psychology field and has hopefully provided you with some things to consider regarding habits to improve your own happiness. I will revisit the thorny issue of gender inequality in further detail in Chapter 6 to discuss what we need from society to eliminate this gap. Chapter 6 will also outline 11 additional tips specific to the happiness of working mothers. First, a summary of happiness, and then Chapters 4 and 5 will explore women's work: the work we get paid for, the work we *don't* get paid for, and the work of living in a female body.

Happiness: in a nutshell

- Happiness is defined as a combination of pleasure and purpose. Purpose includes things that contribute to a meaningful life, such as self-growth, the realisation of one's full potential and living a life true to your values.
- A reasonable proportion of our happiness is dictated by genetics (we are naturally predisposed to being a bit more Tigger or Eeyore); a lesser proportion comes from our life circumstances but a sizeable chunk is down to personal behaviours which we can modify.
- Having money impacts happiness, but the amounts don't matter as much as you may think. Living below the poverty line or having your cost of living exceed your income can make you unhappy. But being a millionaire won't make you happy.
- Money gives us happiness because it enables choice. It matters for women's happiness that we have control of money in the same way as men do. Women who work to earn their own money have more autonomy and decision-making power for themselves and their children.
- Good relationships are one of the most important indicators of happiness. Good marriages are strongly correlated with happiness, although this effect is less-so for women who can be very happy on their own. Married men tend to be happier than married women. Single men are the most unhappy category.
- Children make you happy from a purpose perspective – and once you start sleeping again!

- When it comes to age, happiness is u-shaped – greatest in childhood and old age and dipping in middle-age.
- Being beautiful, intelligent and educated can be a double-edged sword. These things make you happy primarily in terms of the opportunities they afford for providing greater income, but they aren't nearly as significant to happiness as things like having good relationships or a fulfilling job.
- Living rurally can lead to happiness through having a sense of community, but a sunny climate doesn't seem to make much difference to happiness levels.
- Work makes people happy and being unemployed is one of the greatest indicators of unhappiness. This effect holds for both men and women.
- Less than 2 hours a day of free time makes us unhappy but so does more than 5. Time poverty is thought to make us as unhappy as material poverty.
- Spirituality helps happiness through any religious practice – or even simply an appreciation of the natural world.
- Happiness levels are not fixed. You can change them by actively practising certain behaviours such as: doing kind things for others, connecting with people, taking care of your body, practising mindfulness, learning new things, setting goals, developing resilience, practising gratitude, being authentic and creating meaning.
- The bottom line for women's happiness is that we need equality. Both men and women are happier when they live in more equal societies. The Global Gender Gap report of 2020 puts equality at 100 years away. Post-pandemic, the UN Secretary-General said it was more like 300 years away. This simply isn't good enough for us or our children.

Chapter 4

Women's Work: Paid and Unpaid

Over(under)whelmed

For sure I'm not the only working mother who feels damned if I do and damned if I don't. My social media feed is full of these sentiments. A shout out here to the Facebook algorithms for (disturbingly!) understanding me better than I understand myself. My sister tells me the new phrase bandied about on the school run is #mommyburnout. This phrase goes hand in hand with #whymummydrinks. We try and make light of the pressures heaped on us but so many mothers truly are at breaking point.

Podcaster Glennon Doyle discusses at length how women have to be all the things to all the people. Researcher Brené Brown finds that shame and guilt are gendered, with women experiencing it as: '… a web of layered, conflicting and competing social and community expectations.' Author Mallory O'Meara observes that worldwide and throughout history women have been allocated responsibilities but not the power or resources to fulfil them. *This* is why we are guilty and conflicted. We are overwhelmed by responsibility and yet underwhelmed by power.

When speaking to women for my research, not only did I find that women regularly felt guilty, but many described complicated and conflicting feelings about their work. In my experience, working mothers often fall into two categories: those who feel resentful that work is getting in the way of their parenting, and those who feel resentful that the domestic load is getting in the way of their work and sense of self. Sometimes these feelings happen on the same day! None of this is straightforward. Many women can simultaneously feel a confusing mixture of pride, love, frustration and ambivalence about their roles. Researchers find that at any point in time, there are similar numbers of mothers wanting to work *more* paid hours as there are mothers wanting to work *fewer* paid hours. Tension exists between not having enough money and not having enough time.

This chapter will further explore some of the reasons for this conflict and why it is that working mothers feel so guilty. I will explain the counter-intuitive finding that paid work does make us happy, despite the challenges we face. I explain why caregiving also makes us happy and outline how it isn't always the parenting load but rather the domestic load – in my case the laundry – which tips us over the edge. I outline why part-time work for many women can help overall well-being but how this still ends up holding us back. I summarise the research which shows which types of jobs are likely to make us more – and less – happy. I conclude the chapter with a plea to follow your heart and do what's right for *you*. I ask you also to consider a portfolio career, one which is made up of a lifetime of different interests.

Judged, belittled and underappreciated

It is highly likely that working mothers feel guilty because we *are* actively judged. Much more so than fathers. Researchers find that society reveres the role of mother and acknowledges its importance while simultaneously belittling the day-to-day tasks involved in carrying out the role. 'Well done, you, for being a mother, but really, finger painting and soft-play parties? That's not work, is it?' I argue that if it were men who were primarily responsible for this role, society would undoubtedly acknowledge both the value and the difficulty of it. Quite simply, the role of father in today's society still does not carry the same weight as the role of mother.

The brilliant comedian Tina Fey noted that when she was promoting the movie *Date Night* with Steve Carell, she was grilled several times by reporters on how she balanced her life in terms of career and motherhood. Her co-star, Steve, although a father of two, was never asked that question. As Tina wrote in her book, *Bossypants*:

> 'What is the rudest question you can ask a woman? "How old are you?" "What do you weigh?" "When you and your twin sister are alone with Mr Hefner, do you have to pretend to be lesbians?" No, the worst question is "How do you juggle it all?"… People constantly ask me, with an accusatory look in their eyes. "You're fucking it all up, aren't you?" their eyes say.'

A few years ago, when my eldest daughter started high school, one of my friends told me that unless one parent is at home full-time being a 'proper parent', children are bound to be messed up. She didn't say this with malice; it was simply her honest assessment of just how hard being a good parent is. However, the impact of her words was breathtaking. The mixture of guilt and shame practically brought me out in a rash!

Of course all mothers want to be good mothers, and the idea that we aren't if we go out to work is bunkum. However, things that keep me up at night – and you can happily read shame, guilt and fear of judgement into all of this on my behalf – include:

- Which members of the family are wearing raggedy, grey underwear that needs replacing (bad mum).
- When I've run late for a meeting (again) because I was trying to squeeze too many things into my schedule and ended up letting someone down (bad boss).
- When I've been tired and grumpy from seemingly 'all the things' but I am not even sure what they are (bad person).

This is not to say that mums who don't go out to work don't struggle too. A good friend of mine who is a stay-at-home mum was in tears recently. She explained that as she sat in her beautiful home, with her loving husband and lovely children, she felt underappreciated, overwhelmed and unheard. I related wholly to her frustration with the never-ending cycle of domesticity: I remember it all too well from my maternity leaves. Picking up discarded socks and towels, and the voicelessness that comes from the family's and society's lack of appreciation. 'Nobody listens to me. I might as well be talking to myself.' Or to the wall, as Shirley Valentine did.

The problem with the enormously important role of caregiving is that not only is it undervalued, but once you start doing it you start to notice how you are treated like a second-class citizen – and therefore start to lose your confidence and feel like one. You become 'just a mum' or your new identity becomes 'X's mum' rather than an actual person in your own right. A beautiful friend with four children and endless patience was asked by her husband recently, 'Why don't you have any ambition?' Another friend's teenage daughter now defers to dad to answer the important questions. Dad gets respect – *he* has a job so *he* will know the answer.

Any mother who has stayed at home with children, whether full-time, part-time or on maternity leave, will understand the double-edged sword of the role. Caring for children is joyful, but it's ridiculously hard work! Not only is it incredibly taxing in terms of the ability to multitask, problem-solve, organise and provide care, but at the same time, it's financially unrewarded and underappreciated. We wipe the little noses, and sweep up the cereal tsunamis, and sing the lullabies, and go to the park and toddler groups and swimming lessons and dance classes and Cubs and Brownies and school sports days and harvest festivals and… so much. We do so much. And this is before considering the 11% of parents who care for children with disabilities and even greater numbers who care for children with health issues, learning difficulties and behavioural challenges. Primary responsibility for all this care still falls on mothers. Mothers of disabled children experience more health problems of their own, including depression, insomnia and migraines.

We all need to have each other's backs with this. Caregiving is crucial and if society belittles the job of mothering, how will women ever get the respect for this job that is their due? We need to champion the role of parent and caregiver at every opportunity. And it is not just mums who can do it. Dads can too. Because how on earth can you know how hard a job is and have an appreciation for it unless you do it yourself? More than one dad I know has only stepped up to the parenting plate in the aftermath of divorce when faced with the realities of co-parenting. And more than one mum I know wishes desperately that the co-parenting penny had dropped for their husband long before the divorce.[36]

Work, choice and happiness

For the vast majority of women, work is not a choice, it is a financial necessity. Approximately 30% of women in the UK and around 40% in the US are the breadwinners for their families; 15% of families are single parents and 85% of single parents are women. One of my single-mum friends tells me how frustrated she is that '… after everything is done, there is just nothing left for me.' She works her ass off earning the dough and making the sandwiches. Another friend who is married but whose husband works away several weeks at a time says she '… feels like a married, single mum.' A third laments being financially pressured back into work so soon after giving birth – long before she was physically or mentally ready. While stay-at-home mums suffer from society's lack of appreciation, working mums suffer from the double load. So, what's the answer?

Research repeatedly shows that choice is essential for happiness. Yet, the bottom line? Mothers often make decisions about work from positions of limited choice, and when this happens, we are invariably less happy. For instance:

- Mothers who want to go back to work but can't afford childcare.

---

[36] A 2023 Mamma Mia podcast discussed the phenomenon that it is now primarily women (70%) who initiate divorce. They outlined the trend reported on social media of women watching Greta Gerwig's *Barbie* movie and then breaking up with partners who *just didn't get it*. The podcasters drew the conclusion that now that many women have more choices because they are less financially beholden to men, they leave when they get fed up with doing it all: the work-work, the house-work and the emotional-work. They finally just break and think: 'I'm sick of this crap!!'

- Mothers who don't want to leave their children but can't afford not to go back to work.
- Mothers who end up taking jobs below their level of skills and expertise because it was all they could find to fit in with school hours. This is known as The Paula Principle; more on this later.
- Mothers who wish their partner would take a more equal role in domestic work and caregiving, enabling them to do paid work, but whose partners are not prepared to do this or have a completely inflexible job.
- Mothers who take time out to parent but then find the gaps in their CV are too large when they want to return to work, so they become stuck.
- Single mothers who are either criticised for being on welfare benefits or criticised for leaving their children while they go out to work. While single dads often have our sympathy – *How does he do it? Let's bring him a casserole.*

We can argue that nothing in life is perfect and today's women do have many more choices than they did previously. This is true. However, researchers term the work choices for mothers today *constrained choices*. There is currently not enough support from governments in terms of maternity leave, paternity leave, or high-quality childcare. Nor is there yet enough involvement from dads. It is still primarily mums rather than dads who juggle work arrangements around childcare – the ratio of mums to dads at pick up time in my children's school playground was at least 3 to 1. This invariably leads to frustration and unhappiness for many working mothers who are stuck in positions over which they feel they have little control.

Autonomy is not just about having a choice about what work to do and when to do it, it is also about money. When women can earn their own money on the same terms as men, we can have more control over the decisions in our lives, which leads to greater happiness. This is worth repeating: researchers find that money buys happiness simply through the mechanism of giving us more *choice*.

To work or not to work, that is the question

Taking into account the guilt, judgement, constrained choice and conflicted feelings women have about work and mothering, what does the research say? In general, are women happier working or staying home with kids? Well, research consistently finds that women are happier if they have a paid job.

Studies find that mothers in paid employment report less depression, sadness, worry and anger. Being a working mum is no walk in the park – poorly child + work deadline = frazzled mother – but the working bit of the equation is important for our happiness. Work is good for us. For me, it was this part of the research which finally made me able to let go of my guilt around going out to work.

The juggle

If you are reading this and thinking, *Well, I am still not sure that work makes me happy, mainly because it is so bloody stressful*, you can join me and Bridget Jones as neither of us initially bought into this. Bridget was my alter ego throughout my thirties and one of her diary entries in Helen Fielding's book reads: 'It is proved by surveys that happiness does not come from love, wealth, or power but the pursuit of attainable goals.' Bridget writes this while still preoccupied with both Daniel Cleaver and Mark Darcy but is trying to convince herself that she should distract herself by getting a new job. She was right to do this! As we saw in

Chapter 3, goal setting is a key tool we can use to improve our happiness.

However, I still remember regularly feeling engulfed and overwhelmed when I went back to work while my children were little. I remember one particular phone call I had to make from home – timed for when the baby would be asleep and with my 3-year-old propped in front of the television. The call was made from the bathroom while I stood in the shower cubicle, my mobile phone pressed against my ear with the door closed to muffle out the sound of *Dora the Explorer*. It had been prearranged with an important potential client who was apparently unable to speak at any other time or to any other person. Looking back on how the conversation went – me and my best posh phone voice huddled in the shower, 'Yes, yes, you will see from our company performance in the last 12 months that…' and my 3-year-old knocking on the door and demanding biscuits – something definitely needed to give! I hung up the phone mid-sentence, pretended to the client that we had been mysteriously disconnected, and gave my daughter three biscuits *and* the iPad.

Work *is* stressful, and juggling work and family with inadequate help is beyond stressful. But I have good news! Exhausting as the juggle can be, it's more likely to leave you happier – albeit somewhere deep down beyond the 'WHY is the hamster loose?' rant.

Studies show that the very act of *doing* this juggling – with a variety of interests between work and home – makes a significant difference to women's happiness. This is the enrichment model. Women who participate in multiple roles both inside and outside of the home have better overall levels of mental well-being and greater life satisfaction. The idea is that if one area of life is not going well, like Bridget being unlucky in love, this can be buffered by another area of life which is going well. So despite the challenges of the juggle-jungle, having multiple aspects to our identity – being a mum *and* a hairdresser/teacher/executive/nurse et cetera – is good for our well-being.

Compare this to men: although losing a job can cause depression in both men and women, studies find that men can struggle even more when this happens. It is still not as common for men to divide their identities between work and home in the same way as women do. But we women often wear several hats, and that's good for us.

The guilt, again

Another word here about the guilt. Because parenting can be tough. As the Jeff Green joke goes: 'If you want to know what it is like to be a parent, get up every hour in the middle of the night and burn £100.' We are brought up to believe that mothering will come to us naturally, but there is so much to learn. I can count on less than one hand the women of my acquaintance who took to mothering like a duck to water. Most of us spend our time flailing about in the reeds and paddling in circles. I distinctly remember comparing my own pitiful new-mother skills to those of a friend from antenatal classes. Post-birth, while I was busy eyeing up my stitches and wondering how it would be possible to leave the house to find nappies or if I should just leave my daughter wrapped in a towel for the time being, she was out with the pram buying her baby a Christmas card. Bearing in mind our babies couldn't control their bowels, never mind read, buying baby Christmas cards seemed like an unnecessary job to me!

Struggling with the practicalities of parenting doesn't mean for a second we don't love our children. Of course we do. This includes mothers with post-natal depression.

Approximately 17% of mothers experience this and the struggle is wretched. Happily, the concept of *maternal ambivalence* is now spoken about on Mumsnet and other internet forums in less hushed tones than was previously deemed decent. Those perfectly natural mixed emotions of love, joy and fulfilment, alongside frustration, doubt and even resentment. Mothers are conditioned to think these feelings are wrong, but they are real and acceptable.

Doing another job that plays to our particular skill sets alongside parenting is good for us and improves our happiness and well-being. Of course, we'd quite like time to draw breath and maybe let our stitches heal before we're levered back on the bike!

The housework, again

Studies find that women prefer paid jobs to housework. No surprise there. I know I'd much prefer to sit in a team meeting sipping a nice coffee than be hoovering. Or mopping. Or dusting. Or pulling hairs out of a drain… good grief, anything but that!

Here's a key finding from research studies: women's happiness directly increases with increased paid working hours and decreases with increased hours of housework. In particular, having responsibility for a large share of housework negatively affects women's happiness, especially for women who work more than 30 hours a week. A 2019 study found that fewer than 7% of couples split the domestic load equally.[37] Therefore, many women find themselves working part-time in order to cope with domestic responsibilities or running themselves absolutely ragged

---

[37] A free quiz you can take which assesses the total workload in your own home can be found at: quiz.equalitystartsathome.org

trying to do a full-time job, be a good mum *and* stop the laundry mountain teetering over into an avalanche.

A friend of mine tells a story of how frustrated she was the week she came home with her first baby. All she wanted to do was sit on the sofa and cuddle her new daughter. Not one of the stream of visitors who arrived offering help did anything practical like vacuum or load the dishwasher. Instead, they offered to cuddle the baby *for her*, while she ran around making *them* cups of tea and tidying up. She felt viscerally that she did not want them holding her new baby; what she wanted instead was help with the housework! It tends to be the domestic load rather than the mothering load or the paid workload that really naffs mothers off.

Happy mum equals happy family

Freud proclaimed that happiness is to love and to work. As discussed in Chapter 3, good relationships and secure attachments to others, especially family members, are crucial to happiness. But in addition, work that contributes to the wider world and is personally interesting to us is important for a sense of meaning and purpose. Freud is right on this one: as humans, we do need a balance of both love and work in our lives.[38]

I sincerely hope that working mothers find this information comforting. Work outside the home is good for our well-being and by doing the best thing for ourselves, we are also doing the best thing for our families. You've heard

---

[38] Of course, Freud also had some fairly sexist views. Many are familiar with his startling theory of penis envy. This was a developmental stage he identified in young girls, apparently characterised by their sexual attraction to their fathers and rejection of their mothers who they punish for not giving them a penis. Another little gem of his comes from a paper he wrote in 1925 claiming: '… women oppose change, receive passively and add nothing of their own.' Surely that kind of nonsense wouldn't get published if academic review boards weren't predominantly male? (And they still are.)

the saying, happy wife, happy life? Well, it also applies to being a mum. Mums are sometimes called the heartbeat of the home and when mum is happy, the rest of the family is too. Research consistently finds that self-nourishment is not selfishness but rather a prerequisite for effective caregiving. We cannot pour from empty cups.

Work challenges

I'm not going to pretend that it is easy and that mothers and women in general don't face extra challenges, because we do. It is well-known that girls now outperform boys academically at school. This is a significant issue for boys and is, of course, cultural rather than based on intelligence: it's not cool to be clever. Women also succeed equally well in the workplace – *up until the point that they become mothers*. The workplace pay gap between women and men is primarily one of motherhood rather than gender. It is specifically mothers (rather than women) who earn less than fathers, spend more time in unpaid work and find it harder to reach the top of the career ladder. I explore working-mother-specific challenges, along with those faced by all women, below.

'Unsuitable candidates'

There is a hugely irritating phenomenon called the *motherhood penalty* which finds that being a mother makes a woman 44% less employable than their childless counterparts, whereas being a father makes a man 19% more employable than his childless counterparts. When men have children, it adds to their credibility – 'Aw, he must be a good guy, other people love him and depend on him.' Meanwhile, motherhood has completely the opposite effect. People assume that mothers won't prioritise work and, of course, that is bad for business.

When running my recruitment business, I witnessed this first-hand. Women in their forties were fine, they were past it fertility-wise, but women in their thirties who hadn't yet had children and were applying for full-time roles could easily find themselves usurped. And women with children, well, would they be hired over other candidates? I remember one female candidate who was ideal for a position we had with a client. Feedback from the interview was glowing apart from one slight problem; the client was not happy that we hadn't told him she had three children. Although the candidate insisted it was not a problem, the employer didn't think she would be able to manage the travel required with the role because of her responsibilities at home. She was therefore rejected in favour of 'a more suitable applicant.' I had no doubt that a man of the same age with three children and the same skill set would have been offered that job.

Money, money, money

So, getting a job in the first place is harder if you are a mother, even with all the right skills, experience and a willingness to put in the hours. And that's before we've even considered trying to find a job which might be vaguely compatible with caring for a family. Because the domestic load is still not shared equally between genders, women with dependent children are seven times more likely than men to work part-time. Women, therefore, earn less. In the UK, the gender pay gap is 15% across the board, and part-time work is a substantial reason for this pay gap – when we compare men and women who work full-time, the pay gap is much less at 8%. Note that differences in pay in *feminised* industries[39] as well as issues of direct discrimination also contribute to the pay gap.

The confidence code

As Bette Davis said, 'When a man gives his opinion, he's a man. When a woman gives her opinion, she's a bitch.' Studies suggest that women's inability to climb the career ladder to the same degree as men is due to a lack of confidence. This phenomenon seems to be another case of damned if you do and damned if you don't. Research confirms that successful women are less likeable than successful men, and assertive behaviour in women is frowned upon much more than assertive behaviour in men. Women walk a precarious tightrope of being both competent and likeable. We are told it is our fault we don't earn as much because we don't put ourselves forward for pay rises or promotions. However, it's all too obvious to us that we're known as the bossy cow if we ask for a pay rise whereas a man doing the same is a cheeky chap.

A viral story posted online by writer and copyeditor Martin Schneider in 2017 described his experience of swapping his email signature with his female colleague, Nicole, for 2 weeks. When clients he had no previous issues with perceived Martin to be female, they became rude and dismissive and just didn't bother getting back to him. On the other hand, Nicole signing as Martin had a much easier time. Martin concluded: 'Folks. It f***ing sucked.'

---

[39] Feminised industries are those in which a significant majority of the workforce are women. For instance: nursing, social care, retail, clerical and caregiving. Societal expectations and historical gender norms have influenced the perception of certain occupations as *women's work*. This has contributed to the devaluation of this labour and consequently lower pay compared to similar roles in male-dominated industries.

Here's another example from a study at the University of Columbia. They asked students to appraise matching CVs for a man and a woman: Heidi and Howard. Although students were provided with exactly the same CV, and both candidates were rated as competent and worthy of respect, Heidi was considered '… selfish and not the type of person you would want to hire or work for.'

This is the very reason we make ourselves small, don't offer opinions and don't ask for pay rises. Women aren't stupid: we know we have to come at things from a softer angle – or use a different name! – to get the same response. It feels like women have been trying to make our voices, our opinions and our waistlines smaller forever.

Me too

Hollywood's Me Too movement, a term coined by activist Tarana Burke in 2006, catapulted awareness of sexual harassment into the mainstream in 2017 when a famous Hollywood producer was accused of rape, sexual misconduct and abusing his position of power on the casting couch when offering women jobs.

In the UK, a 2021 survey by UN Women found that 70% of women experience sexual harassment. The Fawcett Society finds that 40% of women have experienced harassment at work and that prevalence increases for women who are marginalised in relation to ethnicity, disability or LGBTQ+ status. Newspaper headlines abound with reports of widespread institutionalised sexism, particularly in male-dominated industries such as policing, finance and politics. This phenomenon is pervasive and persistent and these statistics, much like those for the more serious crimes of sexual assault and rape, only represent those who report incidents. The UN Women survey found that a shocking

95% of UK women don't report sexual harassment. There's a culture of not rocking the boat and even laughing it off when in reality, it's anything but funny.

A substantial amount of sexual harassment is subtle, which can make it hard to address because people think incidents are too small to complain about. But tiny papercuts add up to a serious bleed out (pardon the bleeding analogy but, for women, it seems appropriate). In isolation, incidents like this can be dismissed as minor: get over yourself. But they form part of an ecosystem that erodes our confidence over time like the drip, drip, drip of an open vein.

When I was a pharmacy manager in my early twenties, the regional manager sometimes popped into my branch unannounced. He was a big, burly man in his fifties, with a moustache not unlike Hercule Poirot. He would roam the sales floor and pounce on the nearest underling, firing a variety of obscure questions to keep you on your toes. One particular day, I happened to answer a question correctly and he was so delighted with my response that he enveloped me in an enormous bear hug and squeezed so tightly that he lifted me entirely off the floor. What do you do with that gesture? I couldn't decide how I felt anyway; was I pleased I got the question right, or was I mortified to be lifted in that way? Of course, it was both. This kind of thing just wouldn't happen in reverse or to a male employee.

A few years later as an employer, I saw a similar conflict on the face of my 23-year-old employee after she finished a phone call with one of our big-billing clients, a 40-odd-year-old male. He had chatted her up and asked her about her plans for the weekend, he laughed and told her he '… could picture her out on Saturday night, lying in the gutter with her legs in the air.' I was livid and wanted to give him a piece of my mind. However, this man's business accounted for 50% of my company turnover at the time. I'm ashamed to say I took the coward's way out and apologised to my staff member saying that I would take the man's calls in the future. He went on to give us a lot more business. Money talks and so does fear; it's common for women not to speak up.

The glass ceiling and other cautionary tales

Women can be put off by how bloody hard it all is. It not only feels harder to reach the top but if you do, other people don't like you for it. A woman who is successful in the workplace is not admired in the same way as a man who is successful in the workplace. Even if you do manage to make it, you've got to deal with:

- Judgement from other women and not fitting in.
- Online abuse – there is an actual term for this: cyber misogyny. Women are targeted far more than men for this type of abuse. Keyboard warriors seem to be particularly keen to put women *back in their place*.
- Managing the emasculation of your husband. Flipping charming! [40] We can't seem to get out of the housework either way.

It is no wonder that many women conclude it's too much. As historian Helen McCarthy says, given all the challenges that women have faced breaking into the world of work, it is astounding to think how far we have come rather than how far we have to go. It's genuinely awe-inspiring to me that women have managed to push back against this crappy system at all.

---

[40] A dating advice column I read when I was in my twenties advised that 'alpha women' with high powered careers should make sure to switch to 'beta Suzy Homemaker' mode when they got home in order to remain attractive to their man.

Caregiving challenges

As we saw in Chapter 3, research shows that giving to others and forming social connections brings happiness. Mothers specialise in this area. A beautiful friend of mine, an amazing mother as well as a full-time worker and a part-time student, gave me feedback about the first draft of this book. She said that so far, I had mainly explained all the problems with juggling. She understood them, completely! But she wanted me to '… make sure you include how wonderful mothering is despite the juggle, how much we get from it.' The little faces on Christmas morning, snuggles before bed, watching the milestones (from taking their first steps to having their first kiss), nurturing family traditions, the unconditional love (unlike any other love we experience), inhaling the smell of them, their different little funny quirks and moments of fun. There is nothing in the world like your baby's belly laugh. These things are a joy and a privilege of parenting.

In addition, caregiving and domestic life as part of raising a family can extend to other pleasurable things such as forming bonds with wider sections of the community, creating a pleasing home environment, gardening, cooking, caring for family pets – pets are known to provide not only happiness but health benefits to families – and volunteering. School Parents Associations are run primarily on the goodwill and camaraderie formed between mothers. In fact, women make up two-thirds of the voluntary sector workforce. Caregiving for a family is a job which has many facets and requires a broad range of skill sets; it is a job which provides many parents with a lot of pleasure. When we talk about women working so they don't put all their eggs in one basket, this doesn't negate the fact that volunteering jobs and hobbies also create the kind of happiness we are looking for which brings meaning and purpose. Often with less stress – although, unfortunately, with no money attached.

For many women, it is not that we don't get pleasure and purpose from mothering, but more that it is a job which is chronically undervalued, unpaid and prone to overwork. Picking other people's pants off the bedroom floor tends to be one of the less joyful parts of the role. A friend tells me her husband just steps out of his underwear and leaves them warm on the bedroom floor for her to collect and deposit in the laundry basket. She now has a horror of other people's warm pants – apparently it's *not* an aphrodisiac!

Both caregivers' fatigue and postnatal depression are the unintended consequences of primarily women over-working in a job which is relentless in its demands. Caregiving for family members doesn't come with an off-switch. Even when children are grown and start families of their own, it is often the grandmother who adapts her retirement plans to help care for her grandchildren.

Additionally, caring for elderly parents is a job vitally important to society and is primarily done by women who spend as much as 50% more time doing so than men. A friend explained her predicament as the only female sibling who lived within travelling distance of her elderly parents. Because she worked part-time and from home and her brothers said they couldn't take time off from their jobs, the whole family considered it to be her responsibility to provide this caregiving. The strain this placed on her marriage, on her children and on her work was unbearable. By the time her dad passed after nearly 2 years of illness, my friend described being broken, and she had acquired a health condition of her own. Another friend with two teenage daughters explained the immense cultural pressure she faces in her British Asian community to look after her elderly mother-in-law who needs round-the-clock nursing care. She is barely able to leave the house to do errands, never mind think about getting a paid job of her own. Culturally, it's considered her job rather than her husband's to look after his mother.

By middle age, many working mothers, who now often delay starting a family until into their thirties, become the sandwich generation straddling caregiving responsibilities between elderly parents and still dependent children. The fact that so many women are overworked is a problem with cultural expectations and a lack of support, rather than a problem with the job of caregiving or women themselves. It's no wonder we lose it about picking up pants! We need more support. A thank you would go rather a long way too.

The value of care

Economist Katrine Marçal asks 'Who cooked Adam Smith's dinner?' in her brilliant book by the same name. Adam Smith is widely known as the father of economics and he claimed, 'It is not from the benevolence of the butcher, the brewer, or the baker, that we expect our dinner, but from their regard to their own interest.' The idea is that it is people's selfish desire for profit that makes the world turn – goods are produced when and where there is demand. However, as Marçal points out, Adam Smith never married and lived at home with his mother. Therefore, rather than the free-market economy and the self-interested butcher and baker alone providing Adam Smith's dinner, it was likely also through the benevolence of his mother making it for him that Adam managed to be fed.

The key point Marçal makes is that the value of caring labour is consistently dismissed and unaccounted for when discussing the economy. The only work considered worthwhile is that which is done for money. Caregiving and domestic labour – women's work – has always been presumed to be cheap, if not free. I don't know about you, but this kind of presumption makes me want to start a one-woman protest. You'll find me next outside Parliament with a placard: *Women's Work Has Worth!*

In the UK, the Women's Budget Group has done some excellent work on this subject. They explain there are deep-rooted biases in our system which result in infrastructure spending being accounted for as investment – for roads and buildings which creates jobs for men – and social infrastructure spending being accounted for as expenses – such as healthcare and childcare which creates jobs for women. They argue there is no good rationale for this as investing in caregiving creates twice the number of jobs as the same investment in the construction industry.

In both the UK and the USA, childcare is considered a personal matter that families, mainly women, are expected to figure out on their own as opposed to something that is an essential contribution to the functioning of society. After all, if women stopped having children, things would grind to a halt pretty quickly. The United Nations estimates that worldwide 16.4 billion hours are spent on unpaid care work every day. This is the equivalent of 2 billion people working 8 hours a day without pay. It is primarily women who do this unpaid work.

In terms of valuing care, it also strikes me that when men step up and provide care for their families, it is often more valued and appreciated than when women do it. I think of the encouraging smiles I give to any dad I see out for a walk with a baby strapped to his chest or pushing a pram. I've watched some men do this one-handed, casually, like they know the pram is there but they aren't really associated with it! It is taken for granted that mothers will do the caring – we own the prams the way we own the handbags, and the presumption is we will just get on with it. So we do.

Dads can too

Research tells us that mums are happy working outside the home. Research also tells us that dads doing their fair share makes a world of difference as to whether mums are able to do this. But what about dads' happiness? And what about children? Just because mums are happy going out to work, does that mean the rest of the family suffer? Well, let me also reassure you on that front.

Firstly, children don't suffer when their dads look after them. Dads, of course, are just as capable as mums at providing care for their children. We need to move on from the tired old trope of hapless Homer Simpson and silly Daddy Pig who can't seem to function in the world without being rescued by Marge and Mummy Pig. We know that when dads are more involved in their children's lives, children have better academic outcomes and better mental health. In particular, girls who have close relationships with their dads are found to have greater self-esteem and more confidence. Children need close attachments with warm and reliable caregivers, and it doesn't matter whether this is mum or dad. Of course, it is the quality of the care which is important rather than the biological relationship. For single parents, it is also important to know that it really isn't as binary as only mum or dad. Children form happy and healthy bonds with a variety of caregivers including grandparents, extended family members, nannies, nursery workers and family friends.

Secondly, we know that dads are happy to look after their children. Fathers often want to have close relationships with their kids. Studies find that men are less keen on the housework – aren't we all – but most frame their responsibilities as parents as a significant part of their identity. Children matter to fathers just as much as they matter to mothers.

However, according to Statista, only 7% of fathers stay home full-time with children compared with 28% of mothers. It is more frowned upon for men to ask for flexible work than women. 'Really, mate? Did you grow a vagina overnight?' And socially, daddy daycare infrastructure is just not in place for men in the same way as it is for women. When our children were little, I know my husband would have been delighted if his friends had been reliably available to meet mid-week for coffee and a pram around the park. But they were all at work.

Finally, what about nursery care? If mums don't have the help of dads? Several studies show that high-quality daycare is good for children, especially children from disadvantaged backgrounds. In particular, when mothers work part-time this turns out to be actively beneficial for children. There is some debate over full-time working parents when children are very young, but this is what paid parental leave is for.

If the thought of leaving your little angel(s) at a nursery sets you rocking in a corner with horror and guilt, think of it this way. Childcare, especially that of young children, is a 24/7 job. That's 168 hours a week. No one is meant to do that kind of shift work alone. Where the hell is the Working Time Directive for motherhood?! And even mothers who work full-time outside the home still have plenty of time left over for our second shift. Allowing for 8 hours of sleep a night, and 8 hours of work during the day, we still then have 72 hours a week to love, care and spend time with our families.

What families genuinely need is for mums to have more support and to say no to our side-serving of guilt!

Laundry wars and the domestic load

It is often said that money and sex are the two main things that couples argue about. Well, not in our house. Our marital spats centre fully around the domestic load and our laundry wars have raged for years. I distinctly remember an argument I had with my husband on my 40th birthday in our local Italian restaurant. We had organised a babysitter for the night, I'd gone to the bother of shaving my legs and we were both looking forward to a lovely evening. I can't even tell you how the subject of laundry came up. All I know is that the evening ended far before it was meant to with my husband complaining that I was always trying to turn him into a girl and me insisting furiously that just because I owned the boobs did not mean I liked doing the laundry.

Daily Mail sexpert Tracey Cox claims that the biggest marriage killer is actually *not* arguments over sex or money, but over who does the housework. Not just me then! Studies show that unfairly divided housework leads to a greater risk of divorce.

There is a term floating around social media: The Doesband. This is a husband who does stuff without being asked. Opinion is divided on this as either patronising – of course husbands don't need to be bossed about and told what to do – or right on the money when it describes men like this as an anomaly. Also doing the rounds on the internet are any number of caricatured depictions of mothers' mental load including our emotional load and mum maths: how many days has that leftover chicken been in the fridge and can I get away with reheating it without killing anyone?

I encountered a retired couple last summer while I was walking along the beach – the woman was trying to get a nice picture of her partner against the sunset. I stopped and offered to take a picture of them both. The woman enthused gratefully and commented that her family photo albums look like their children don't have a mother as she is always the person behind the camera. This kind of work that women do for our families is often unrecognised and, in this case, the consequence was to literally make her unseen.

Many modern dads do take a more hands-on approach to childcare but are just still not as on board with domestic responsibilities. Time management studies find that housework is one of the least pleasurable tasks that people perform. A 2023 British Attitudes Survey finds that despite the fact that the vast majority of people (75%) think housework should be split evenly, 66% of women say they still do more and 32% of men admit to not pulling their weight. Studies show that women do more total labour than men on average – this is combined paid and unpaid work. A report by the charity ActionAid finds that in the UK, the extra work that women perform adds up to a total of 2.5 years of our lives.[41]

When it comes to jobs that earn the big bucks, these have chronically long working hours and a culture of being permanently *on* and accessible through technology. More often than not, these big jobs – which garner power, money and influence in the way society is run in politics, law, healthcare, technology, media etc. – end up going to men. Wives are left holding the baby and putting on a wash and cooking dinner and organising everyone else's schedule.

The COVID-19 pandemic sparked a change in expectations of working patterns, leading to more requests for flexible working and working from home. A greater culture of flexible and home work for both sexes is certainly a step in the right direction. It makes life much easier when you can be home to get dinner on the go or nip out and pick up the kids from school. The tricky bit is that it is often

---

[41] In developing countries the disparity is even greater, adding up to 4 years of a woman's life.

women who choose part-time, home-based and flexible working. While studies show that this is great for maintaining women's working hours, otherwise women may quit altogether, the knock-on effect is that it exacerbates inequalities in housework and childcare. Flexible working and home working are good, but unless both sexes do it equally, it doesn't properly solve the problem of women's unequal domestic load.[42]

Does part-time work, work?

If the findings are that paid work is good for women's well-being but that women struggle with the juggle, is part-time work the answer? The research says: not entirely. What would actually work best is flexible hours for *all* parents.

In the UK, 38% of women work part-time compared with 13% of men. This model of 1.5 workers per family with women nearly always being the part-time earner, is common in several other countries such as the Netherlands, Germany, Greece and Italy. In America, 22% of women work part-time compared with 11% of men.

Undoubtedly, there are benefits to part-time work; research finds that it leads to less work-family conflict and this in turn improves happiness. Studies show that many women's preference is part-time work. It's easier to show up for the nativity play, to fit in a doctor's appointment or to invite friends over for a play date. You might find that you even have time for the odd yoga class and that bit of self-care you so rightly deserve.

---

[42] A book I'd highly recommend for your bedside table is called: *Porn for Women*. One page shows a man cleaning a kitchen while insisting, 'I like to get to these things before I have to be asked.' Another man gets out of bed in the middle of the night wondering, 'Is that the baby? I'll get her.' From the straw poll I conducted, the majority of women were in agreement that this was better than sex…

In addition, mothers get more societal approval when we work part-time. UK society sanctions a structure where women put our mum duties first and don't try to emasculate the men by out-earning them. According to our new contract, women should contribute somewhat financially to the family, but not too much. Public opinion finds that only 7% of the UK population think that women with children under school age should work full-time.

The difficulty with this expectation, of course, is that it doesn't work terribly well for full-time working mothers who are shamed for not taking care of their families properly and nor does it work for stay-at-home mums who are shamed for not doing enough. And unfortunately, despite working part-time for substantial parts of my own career, I'm not convinced that part-time work for mothers is the panacea we like to think.

The problems with part-time work

Let's look at the tricky realities of being a mother who works part-time. Society thinks this is the ideal balance for mothers, and researchers find part-time work does relieve women's work-family conflict. But, as with most things in life, it comes with trade-offs. Part-time working means that mothers:

- Earn less money.
- Regularly take jobs below our level of skill or expertise just because they are flexible.
- Often end up doing all the domestic work anyway.

I'll take these in turn below.

Firstly, part-time work pays less – it's that simple. We might gain time, but we lose money. It contributes to the gender pay gap, the gender investment gap and the gender pension gap. It means that women are more likely to live in poverty than men.

Part-time jobs are heavily polarised in low-paying occupations and mothers, on average, experience a 60% drop in earnings in the ten years after their first child is born. Women never recover from this pay penalty. It isn't just that part-time hours mean part-time pay, although it is this too, but also that the kind of part-time work you can get which fits around school hours is paid a lot less on an hourly basis.

This is a big issue. Part-time work is a significant reason why women struggle to acquire the same money or power as men. This matters, even if women are married and their husbands have promised to take care of them. Within a marriage, we know that women who have their own money have more bargaining power and autonomy over their own lives and those of their children. In addition, around 40% of marriages end in divorce, and the idea of spousal maintenance is becoming a thing of the past. If you are fit to work and have children of school age, the state now expects you to work – even if your skills and experience have been compromised through spending less time in the workplace. This penalty happens primarily to women. It is more than maddening, but the law of the jungle still holds here: the person who has less money is more vulnerable and has fewer choices.

Secondly, part-time work stalls women's careers through a lack of networking and promotion opportunities. And that's if you even stay in the career you were building pre-children. Mothers often take jobs below their level of skill and expertise and outside their interests to accommodate flexible working. Author and researcher Tom Schuller calls this The Paula Principle and describes it in direct opposition to The Peter Principle – a work organisation phenomenon described in the 1960s where workers, mainly men, were regularly promoted beyond their level of competence in hierarchical organisations.

We typically find that when a couple become parents, it is the woman who automatically becomes the default carer. This is often due to social norms, and when babies are very little and mums' bodies are still leaky, quite often a sincere preference. However, even slight differences in pay or flexibility at work can cement this role, perpetuating the mother as the primary caregiver indefinitely. When initial decisions are being made about how to manage work and family, by and large it is the mother who adapts her schedule and performs the trade-offs and contortions required to decide how best to accommodate childcare. It is typically the mother's career which is penalised.

Finally, when we work part-time, we often end up doing our jobs and most of the domestic work anyway. Does the following sound familiar? Mr Smith works a 40-hour week in his job and then comes home and puts his feet up. Mrs Smith works 20 hours a week in her job *and* does 40 hours a week cooking, cleaning, shopping, ferrying kids about, helping with homework and so on. Simplistic examples, but you get the idea: mums who work part-time often end up doing more hours than dads overall in order to keep up with the domestic load.

These patterns exist because of long-standing gender roles that we all struggle to break free from. A friend of mine found that when she went back to full-time work after a long period of working part-time, her overall workload seemed to magically become much lighter as her partner became willing to help out domestically. Before that point, he'd assumed that she was working the same hours as him juggling her job and the house and the kids. She had also carried an assumption that it was on her to sort it all out: wasn't running yourself ragged what all mothers do?

In her book *Double Lives: A History of Working Motherhood*, researcher Helen McCarthy describes a household dynamic where one woman's husband refused to help his full-time working wife with housework as he said her doing the housework made up the difference between what he was earning and what she was earning. *Ugh.* I imagine you winced at this in the same way I did. Unfortunately, it's not uncommon for many people to think this – even if they don't say it out loud.

The bottom line is that the domestic load is a contentious issue in many heterosexual households, and it doesn't go away when women work part-time. Interestingly, same-sex couples are found to share the domestic load much more equitably. It can be done, and this bears repeating: research finds that equitable marriages with shared housework and paid work lead to greater overall life satisfaction for both partners, lower rates of divorce and better sex and intimacy in relationships. Everyone's a winner!

What works for *you*?

As we have seen, working mothers face challenges both at work and at home. Life doesn't come with easy options or one-size-fits-all solutions. Ultimately, only you know what is right for you. However, it can be helpful to use research to inform our decisions. And what the research tells us, is that paid work for women is a good idea – it makes mothers happy. It adds to the purpose element of well-being and, depending on your job, the pleasure element. It also gives us an income and therefore more autonomy.

In relation to hours of work, we know that being overstretched is not good for anyone. A 2019 study from University College London found that women who work more than 55 hours a week have a greater risk of depression than men who work the same hours or women who work 35–40 hours a week. The researchers suggested that this was due to women's increased domestic load and therefore higher total workload. Forget breaking through that glass ceiling; few mothers are interested in chasing a lifestyle which stresses us out that much. Of course, this was the point my friend Fran was trying to make about advising her daughter not to become a doctor in the current climate.

This over-stretched feeling is the primary reason many mothers choose part-time work as it can improve happiness by reducing work-life conflict. However, there is also research which suggests that women's measurements of overall life satisfaction (rather than day-to-day happiness) are greatest when they work *full-time.* The theory here is that full-time work enables women to more easily achieve their life goals. Part-time working is not the catch-all solution that some think it is.

So, what should you do? At the end of the day, only you know your circumstances, and these often change with time. For me, understanding this research simply helped me to understand I wasn't alone in my frustrations, and it helped me to contemplate my own path armed with knowledge. I firmly believe that all things have a time, place and season. If we can't do it now, it doesn't mean we can't do it later. I implore you ignore what everyone else is doing and to pick the path that is right for *you.*

Which jobs make people happiest?

The saying 'Choose a job you love and you will never have to work a day in your life' is often attributed to the ancient

Chinese philosopher Confucius.[43] However, once women become mothers, they can find that their neatly typed career plan is more useful as a liner for the bottom of the budgie cage! So if we're ready to start over and make a new plan, or if we are trying to advise our daughters, what do we know about the types of jobs which lead to happiness?

Quite a lot, it turns out. With the recent explosion in happiness research, we now have solid evidence about what leads people to be happy at work. We now know that people want work which is:

- Purposeful – something that is meaningful and a reason to get out of bed in the morning.
- Autonomous – where there is latitude for decision-making and choice.
- Engaging – work that is interesting and can lead to a sense of flow.[44]
- Authentic – work that speaks to an individual's sense of self and plays to their inherent strengths and skill sets.[45]

This might sound a little woo-woo or snow-flaky to older generations who may argue they were happy enough just to *have* a job and jolly well got on with it – no need for all this preciousness! However, Generation Z is definitely on board with this concept. They have high expectations of what work

---

[43] Note that Confucius was also quite the sexist: an enlightened thinker for his time, but not that enlightened! He thought that women should focus solely on domestic responsibilities and did not see education or intellectual pursuits as necessary for women in the same way as for men. He believed: 'A woman lacks a sense of virtue if she cannot serve her husband.'

[44] Flow is a mental state which leads to complete immersion and absorption in a task and is associated with happiness. Hungarian-American researcher, Mihaly Csikszentmihalyi introduced the concept in his 1990 book: *Flow: The Psychology of Optimal Experience*.

[45] The Japanese have a term *ikigai*, which is finding work at the intersection of: 1) something you love (your passion), 2) something you are good at (your profession), 3) something the world needs (your mission) and 4), something you can be paid for (your vocation).

will deliver to them and are more likely to leave a job if their terms and conditions aren't met.

I see two sides to this. We can argue that Gen Z is correct in looking for more happiness in their work and are demanding a lifestyle where they *work to live* not *live to work*. We can also argue that this philosophy may lead to less happiness as expectations are unmet. Of course, any work has periods where it can be frustrating, dull, or require delayed gratification.

The types of jobs where people tend to report higher levels of happiness include:

- Entrepreneurs and the self-employed, due to autonomy and latitude for decision-making.
- Creative professionals, due to artistic and authentic engagement in their work.
- Healthcare and education professionals, attributed to the sense of purpose in helping others.
- Charity workers, who find engagement in something personally meaningful.
- Outdoor and environmental jobs, as they involve spending time in nature.

On the other side, these are the kinds of jobs that make us less happy on average:

- Jobs with low autonomy and high stress levels, such as middle management positions.
- Repetitive jobs, like factory work.
- Low-paying jobs, with women disproportionately represented in this category.
- Call centre jobs, which may involve dealing with rude or difficult people.
- Jobs with poor work-life balance, characterised by extended or inflexible working hours.

Looking back on my own career, I think the word happiness is a misnomer when used to describe what work brings many women. For me, work often made me stressed and sometimes made me bored and frustrated. However, and this is key, on balance it gave me a sense of pride and satisfaction.

In one of my first jobs after qualifying as a pharmacist, I worked for a large retail business and ended up managing a department of 25 staff. I found middle management difficult. It felt like a chronic piggy-in-the-middle situation, with bosses dictating terms in which I had limited input, and then me trying to get staff to buy into things I didn't necessarily agree with. Added to this were relentless hours in a 24/7 retail environment that didn't allow me sufficient downtime as I could be called in at any time to cover sickness or other issues. I ended up quitting that job to work for myself and have more control over my work-life balance. I then owned three different businesses over 20 years, two of which overlapped. The balance between stress and satisfaction when you are in charge is the subject of another book, but I can definitely vouch for the fact that having more control adds to your well-being.

Researchers consistently find that autonomy is the main reason self-employed individuals are found to have greater levels of happiness than those who are conventionally employed. It also helps enormously if we choose something that aligns with our interests. It doesn't matter whether we work in a supermarket, a hospital, as CEO of a bank, in childcare or as a postwoman; if a job is not aligned with our interests and skill sets it's unlikely to make us happy. By the way, I would make the worst postie – I hate the early mornings! But I know my local postman loves the fresh air and exercise and the fact his day is done by 2 pm. There are any number of character tests on the internet which can help you explore your unique strengths and interests. One excellent resource to help you figure out your personal strengths is viacharacter.org.

Building a portfolio career

In 2021 the business networking site LinkedIn added the ability to list stay-at-home parent as a job title. Finally! Parenting requires a multitude of transferable skills, and it is about time that it's recognised in the business world as a legitimate job rather than some kind of suspect career break. It's not like you've swanned off around the world to find yourself; it's rather more like the most intensive crash course of your life, where your ability to quickly upskill literally keeps a vulnerable human alive.

On average, life expectancy across the entire world has doubled in the last 200 years: we are living longer, more productive and more purposeful lives. With people regularly living to 100, gone are the days of one job for life. It is high time we started approaching our careers in a different way. Ideally from the perspective of acquiring a portfolio of different skills over a long lifetime. One of which is parenting.

I would like to emphasise again here that according to the enrichment model, having a variety of skills and interests is good for our well-being, and we know that work which is engaging, purposeful, authentic and autonomous is good for our happiness. While not all the jobs we do will always tick all the boxes – life doesn't work like that – we can strive to look for different aspects of these qualities in the different types of work done over our lifetimes.

Maya Angelou, author of *I Know Why the Caged Bird Sings*, first became famous for her work in her forties – as did renowned fashion designer Vera Wang and chef Julia

Child. Businesswoman Pattie Sellers says to think about your career as a jungle gym and not a ladder. It doesn't have to be an upward trajectory; you don't have to do everything at once and it is good to try different things. It is increasingly common for women to reinvent themselves when their children have grown – they have time to focus on different aspects of their lives. Of course, you don't have to be famous or award-winning. For happiness, choose work that is both purposeful and interesting to *you*.

Both my mum and dad had a wide range of diverse interests, epitomising the idea of having a portfolio career. The way they supported each other's work throughout their lives was a great inspiration to me. We lost my dad in 2022, aged 75, and although we felt like we lost him far too soon and far too suddenly, we took comfort in the fact that he led a life true to his interests and full of variety. And despite being busy with work, both my parents managed to convey to us children that we were their priority; we knew there was a listening ear and comforting hug available whenever we needed it.

My parents started out as teachers, and both were the first in their families to go to university. My mum taught English and later specialised in teaching children with learning difficulties. My dad was a music and geography teacher and played guitar, piano and clarinet. He also loved driving and as a young man not only drove rally cars, but taxis, ambulances and hearses to earn extra money on the weekends. He and my mum got the travel bug and decided to move to Canada as an adventure when they got married in 1970. They stayed there for 24 years, during which time they both earned master's degrees. My mum's master's was in early years education and my dad's was in educational psychology. My dad then worked as an educational psychologist for many years before becoming a school headmaster. My mum climbed the career ladder too and ended up with a swish job as assistant superintendent of the local school board, including overseeing my dad's school.

When my parents were in their late 40s, they decided to move back to England. My mum started a business renting holiday cottages in Wales and the Cotswolds, and my dad went back to school again instead of continuing his teaching career. This time, using his A-Level in biology from when he was 18, he did a university correspondence course to learn how to be a chiropodist! He then set up a business visiting nursing homes and fixing old people's feet. On the side, he learned how to tune pianos and how to play the organ. He and my mum ran the holiday cottage business together and also renovated several houses. My mum's aesthetic flair made the houses they worked on warm and welcoming, and her persuasion skills were legendary; she could upsell you to a 3-day holiday break from a 2-night weekend stay in the blink of an eye. Meanwhile, my dad became a grandmaster at DIY – you name it, and he could fix it.

My mum is a plate-spinner extraordinaire, with a myriad of social interests outside of work. She sings in the church choir, volunteers in two charity shops each week and for many years cleaned the church on a Wednesday morning. When she visits me and my two sisters, she brings a bag of tricks filled with puzzles and games to entertain her seven grandchildren. She has taught them magic tricks as well as how to read, knit and sew. She is a wonderful cook and party host, having made thousands of cookies, cakes and meals for us all. Both my parents always stayed active in their work, with my mum particularly interested in the detail and organisation of financial plans and investments, and my dad never fully putting down tools and retiring. Just 10 days before he died, he organised the move from one of the holiday cottages my parents sold. At his funeral, I read my dad's favourite poem, Max Ehrmann's *Desiderata*, which includes the following advice:

> 'Enjoy your achievements as well as your plans.
>
> Keep interested in your own career, however humble;
>
> it is a real possession in the changing fortunes of time.'

It doesn't matter what our work is, but it does matter that we keep on trying to find work that is purposeful and interesting to us. We are all only here once.

Women's paid and unpaid work: in a nutshell

- Society now mandates women to work outside the home; however, it only wants us to work part-time. Women who work full-time are shamed for being bad mothers, and those who stay at home are shamed for being lazy.
- Mothers are between a rock and a hard place in terms of our choices about work. It's a systemic issue and not our fault. We must stop feeling guilty and allow ourselves to drop a few balls and allow others to pick them up.
- The enrichment model tells us it is good for our well-being to put our eggs in a variety of baskets. Having more than one aspect to our identity can buffer our happiness levels. Working outside the home is found to improve the happiness of mothers.
- Working mothers have higher stress levels than both women without children and men with children. Mothers often work part-time to manage the stress from work-family conflict.

- However, part-time work is not necessarily the answer as it leads to us earning less money and having less satisfaction with our work, and it doesn't always fix the gap in the domestic load.
- It is tough out there. Women still face gender discrimination at work when it comes to pay, leadership, sexual harassment and breaking through the glass ceiling. Caregiving is a tough job too: chronically underappreciated and consistently underpaid.
- The types of jobs that make people happy are those which create a sense of autonomy, authenticity, engagement and purpose.
- Jobs that make people less happy are those which give us limited choice, are repetitive, have low pay and give us a poor work-life balance.
- Lives are complex and life is longer than ever before. We don't have to do everything at once and we should give ourselves a break. We can treat our career like a jungle gym rather than a ladder and ideally think about having a portfolio career made up of a lifetime of different interests.

Chapter 5

Women's Work: Our Female Bodies

Women's third job

As my friend empathised with her daughter recently, living in a female body is a full-time job. That evening, her 16-year-old not only had to prepare for an upcoming test at school but was also dealing with crippling period pain and changing bloodied bedsheets. She was under additional pressure to get up an hour early the next morning to wash and dry her long hair, apply make-up (all the other girls do), shave her legs (God forbid anyone saw leg hair) and pack a healthy lunch (watch the waistline).

Balancing work and kids is one thing, but I contend that females also have a third job related to dealing with our sexed bodies. In this chapter, I'll explore the themes of biology, beauty, safety and sexuality. In addition to the outside work of careers and the domestic and caregiving work of families, female bodies literally create *labour*. More flipping things to do!

First, we work to manage our biology: periods, pregnancy, birthing, breastfeeding, contraception, the biological clock, fertility treatments, miscarriage, menopause and abortion.

Second, we feel the pressure to do a lot of beautifying things that men don't do nearly so much: make-up, hair dye, nails, eyelashes, skincare regimens, outfits, high heels, handbags and dieting fads just to get started. My friend tells me she's completely hairless from the eyebrows down, but it's taken significant time and money to get that way. *Girl math* for my teenage daughters isn't just algebra, it involves things like calculating outfits around period cycles and how much sleep they will get if they stay up to wash and dry their long hair before bed.

Third, women's work to keep safe isn't just about planning our route home, going to the toilet in pairs and paying extra for taxis. It's also the work of worthiness in a world where we are seen as less than, and the simpering smiles and smoothing of the waters to ward off offence or physical threat.

Finally, you wouldn't think that having sex is work. It's fun! Or is it always for women? For many women, sex is still a bargaining currency in a variety of large and small ways. Model, actor and activist Cara Delevingne explores the orgasm gap in her 2022 BBC series *Planet Sex* and why women should be pretty ticked off that men are far more likely to experience pleasure and orgasm from sex than women. Sex is too often seen as something women 'give' to men and where women's pleasure is either not prioritised, or worse, shamed.

Sometimes it can feel like we've rocked up to the starting line in the race of life with one hand tied behind our backs. However, before we explore these four themes in detail, I want to examine what female biology means in terms of our place in the world. If we are so beholden to the meat suits we inhabit, is inequality inevitable? Should we just surrender already?

I say, not quite yet.

Nature versus nurture

In a poignant scene at the end of the movie *Forrest Gump*, Forrest ponders whether life is a matter of fate or chance, and in the end, he concludes he thinks it is a bit of both: 'I don't know if we each have a destiny, or if we're all just floatin' around accidental-like on a breeze, but I, I think maybe it's both. Maybe both is happenin' at the same time.'

Having researched the subject of gender differences for many years, I have come to the same conclusion as Forrest: the answer to the nature versus nurture debate is that a little bit of both are happening at the same time. Both nature and nurture feed into women's problem with equality. There is no doubt in my mind that our biology matters, but this has been used as a poor excuse over millennia to limit women's opportunities and consequently, happiness. Let's unravel it a bit.

It's trickier than you think

Gender wars seem to be the hot potato topic doing daily rounds in tabloid newspapers. Whether you are woke or not, everyone's hopping mad and you're about as likely to set sail to Mars on a banana as you are to have a nuanced conversation about gender on the internet.

In the academic world, those who are gender-affirming assert that gender exists on a continuum, and we primarily perform our gender based on social constructs. Those who are gender-critical, argue that biological sex differences are impactful, and in circumstances such as shelters for domestic violence or in women's sports they should be given precedence over gender identity. These debates are contentious as they dig deep into the psyche of personal identity.[46]

It is important to clarify the wording. Discussions around *sex* – males and females – explain biological differences: our chromosomes and reproductive organs. Those around *gender* – men and women – are more about cultural and sociological differences, and these, of course, are more fluid.

It is clear that there are biological differences between males and females. However, far too many sex differences get lumped into the category of being 'natural' for women, when there is far more nurture and social conditioning involved – like women's propensity to do the bloody laundry! Happily, we now have substantial scientific evidence which refutes a number of myths around the types of things we used to think were inherently female.

For instance, Victorian scientists used to carve up people's brains looking for evidence that brain structure was related to personality and intelligence – this study was called phrenology and has since been debunked. Male scientists got quite far with this type of propaganda, and for many years used the fact that female brains were smaller than male brains to argue that females had less intelligence. Today, we know what utter codswallop this is: females are *not* less intelligent than males – and if brain size were the key issue then surely we'd have blue whales and elephants telling the men what to do? Funnily enough, men didn't sign up to *that* theory.

---

[46] Approximately 1.7% of the population are intersex and approximately 0.5% are transgender. These definitions over-simplify an incredibly complex subject which is beyond the scope of this work. I have cited references at the end relating to both gender-critical and gender-affirming views for those who wish to read further.

The peculiar thing about getting research published in this field is that researchers find there is limited interest in work concerning similarities between the sexes. *'Breaking news: males and females are both equally as good at tying their shoelaces!'* No one cares, do they? What we really want to know is something juicy like, 'What is it about females that makes them cry more than males? Are our tear ducts shaped like ovals and just spout differently?' And, in case you are wondering, no, they aren't, and no, they don't.

The boring answer to the vast majority of research on sex differences is that scientists have not found many extreme examples other than those which are accounted for by our reproductive organs. The research simply doesn't show that males are inherently more clever which is why they get better jobs, or that females are more emotionally intelligent which is why we should stay home with children.

When we study differences between males and females, we typically find that there is far greater variance between *individuals* in the gender group – the difference in height between the tallest male in the world (105 inches) and the shortest male in the world (21 inches) – than the *average differences* between two genders – females on average are about 4.5 inches shorter than males. With such variety in the world, it just doesn't work to lump all of humanity into two categories and extrapolate behaviour, and therefore life outcomes, into two distinct groups.

So, for instance, when we look at studies which find that males are slightly better on average at spatial tasks than females and females are slightly better on average than males at verbal tasks, this in no way means that females aren't capable drivers, or that males aren't able to give speeches. In fact, females drive more safely on average, and our insurance premiums reflect this. And many male politicians I can think of seem to have overcome their verbal disadvantage pretty well!

Further, while stereotypes that we have previously put down to biology might still be observably true – women cry more than men and men carry more senior leadership positions than women – we now know the reasons for them are far more influenced by nurture than has previously been portrayed.

We know that neuroplasticity[47] affects our inherent wiring causing our nerve pathways and brain circuitry to change depending on the experiences we have. Between males and females, it is substantially this kind of social influence over time which accounts for many gender differences including emotional intelligence, maths, risk-taking, leadership and anger. I'll take these in turn below.

Emotional intelligence is for boys

Emotional intelligence is defined as the ability to identify and manage both your own emotions and the emotions of others. There are no differences found here between the sexes, with females and males having equal overall capability.

However, gender differences are found in different *types* of emotional intelligence, one of which is empathy. Several studies show that on average, women demonstrate slightly more empathy than men. Researchers find that this is substantially the result of social conditioning as women are more often encouraged and rewarded for this trait. It is less likely to be a purely biological phenomenon as we know

---

[47] Interestingly, the more we learn about the brain and neuroscience, the more we know that change is possible. Historically, it was believed that after childhood the brain was fixed. We now know that when we learn new things through repeated behaviour, we actively make new connections between nerve cells which in turn impact the expression of certain genes.

there are no DNA differences between males and females in genes relating to empathy.[48]

What I *can* tell you from my experience of empathy and mothering is that when my babies were little, I reacted to their cries like I was on fire.[49] Whereas my husband... not so much. Similarly, my friend used to tell me that when her husband got up to attend to their babies in the middle of the night, he'd hear them cry, take his time to go to the loo, put on his dressing gown, *tie up the belt*... and wander down the hallway. Of course, her reaction in the wee hours, like mine, was more akin to the emergency services being called.

Science now tells us these behaviours can be learned and unlearned. And if we think that our partners are primed to hear burglars and we are primed to hear the baby, this is primarily down to social conditioning and who thinks they are responsible for which jobs.

Maths is for girls

When I was at school, this idea that girls were better at English and boys at maths just seemed to float in the atmosphere. The American toy company Mattel caused a furore in the 1990s when they launched a talking Barbie which said, among other things, 'Math class is tough!' The idea that women don't perform well in STEM subjects is a big deal as these careers are often where the money is.

---

[48] Some genes predispose people to struggle with how to express empathy – for instance, those on the autism spectrum. Autism spectrum disorder has traditionally been more diagnosed in men than women. But it is now thought that some of this difference is due to social conditioning: girls mask their autism more frequently and are therefore under-diagnosed.

[49] In relation to breastfeeding mothers, however, both lowered oestrogen levels and the sleep deprivation associated with breastfeeding can biologically cause increased anxiety and lead to mothers' hypervigilance. For sure, this was me!

Interestingly, the gender gap in maths performance from 50 years ago has now disappeared. This gap was largely a result of stereotype threat: women negatively perceived themselves to not be very good at maths and therefore lived up to that stereotype. In multiple studies, women are shown to perform better on maths tests when there are no men in the room, and this finding has been extrapolated to ethnicity as well. When Asian American women are reminded of their ethnicity, they perform better on a maths test but when they are reminded of their gender, they perform worse. Girls *can* do maths. Don't let anyone tell you differently.

Risk-taking is subjective

Females do not inherently take fewer risks than males when all things are considered equal. However, *perceived* risk can vary for males and females and therefore lead to different outcomes. For instance, females are less likely to have a one-night stand than males, but this is because both the pregnancy and safety consequences of a one-night stand are higher for them. When risks are equal, females and males do not demonstrate different levels of risk-taking. This finding of men being more likely to take risks has also been demonstrated to be a White male, hierarchical situation. More than other groups, ethnic minorities in particular, this group have been found to sincerely perceive society to be a safer place and therefore they are more willing to take risks.

As researcher Cordelia Fine points out, it would be helpful if other researchers started asking questions about risks that resonate with women, like 'How likely is it that you would bake an impressive but difficult souffle for an important dinner party, risk misogynistic backlash by writing a feminist opinion piece, or train for a lucrative career in which there is a high probability of sex-based discrimination and harassment?' Instead, researchers often ask questions about things like skydiving, and how many women – mums, especially – are going to reply in the affirmative? We're already too busy. Interestingly, pregnancy and childbirth are approximately 20 times more likely to result in death than skydiving. Risk really is relative to our perception of it.

Leadership is for everyone

We now know that on a corporate board, diversity of both gender and ethnicity substantially improves company performance and leads to better decision-making and less groupthink. Through this metric alone you could argue that women are just as good at leadership as men.

Studies find that when it comes to leadership, men and women tend to have different styles: women are more collaborative, and men are more directive. Some people argue that women's leadership style is better. However, many others say they just can't picture any woman as a leader. A 2020 United Nations study found that 25% of people in the UK think men make better leaders – globally the figure was 40%.

Women are all too aware of this pushback. A woman I interviewed for my research, the CEO and owner of a business with more than 300 employees, said she felt like she was permanently stepping on eggshells when it came to giving instruction to the men on her board. She instinctively knew she would get better buy-in from them if she lightened her approach rather than being direct. Research backs this up. When women and men behave in the same assertive way, women are punished, and men are rewarded. Women know this. And it's exactly the reason why many of us either don't go for leadership positions in the first place, or when we get them we feel we have to lightly tiptoe. This phenomenon is deeply influenced by social conditioning.

Women *want* to be leaders just as much as men. The 2023 McKinsey *Women in the Workplace* report found women to be equally as ambitious as men to climb the career ladder to the top. Saatchi & Saatchi's Kevin Roberts should put that in his pipe and smoke it!

Females get angry too

Another area that is more nuanced than it first appears in terms of nature versus nurture is the regularly explored fact that the overwhelming majority of violent crimes are committed by men. Testosterone *does* play a role in violence, but simply having a body that contains testosterone doesn't trigger violence. The equation is not nearly as basic as male = testosterone = violence. It is much more complicated. Biologically speaking, testosterone *is* a factor, but a personality trait low in impulse control is also hugely influential in this equation. It feels like the right time here to say, #notallmen are violent. Nurture plays an enormous role in violence, and studies prove time and time again how societal factors such as poverty, education, family environment and gendered cultural norms affect violence. And just because violence exists doesn't mean we should tolerate it or that it can't be managed or controlled.

Contrary to popular belief, females experience anger at similar rates to males, but we don't demonstrate violence to nearly the same degree. Social conditioning dictates that it is more acceptable for men to express anger and for women to express sadness. We see this in our everyday lives: women cry more than men. Women are more likely to direct their anger inwards[50] towards self-destructive behaviours like self-harm and eating disorders – which are hugely more prevalent in women.

In terms of physical aggression, females are more likely to back down from males simply because it is often the most sensible strategy due to physical size and power disparity. We are likely to be losers in that fight, so we have developed typical behaviours to cajole and placate and make efforts to please instead. More than one woman I know takes a kind of horse whisperer role in their relationships when difficult issues arise, predicting moods and behaviours and heading them off at the pass.

In many areas of life there is a push and pull between nurture and nature, and it can be complicated to unravel not only what the myths are – intelligence levels – but also the dynamics and interplay between the two – anger. However, some sex differences between females and males are just down to pure nature. We will look at these next.

Biology matters

When my daughter was eight, much to her disgruntlement, she was told by her male physical education teacher that the boys could run faster than the girls. He was completely wrong about this in primary school children. However, we know that after puberty there absolutely *are* differences in speed, bone density, muscle mass and height between males and females, and these lead to different consequences for

---

[50] Dr Gabor Maté's research on stress and physical health suggests that the repression of healthy anger and behaviour such as people-pleasing disturbs the immune system. He indicates a link between the fact that 80% of those with autoimmune disease are women, and women struggling to express their anger and therefore internalising it.

both sexes.[51] Despite sensationalised headlines along the lines of *Revealed: men and women do think and act differently!* we know the vast majority of consequential differences between males and females are simply down to our sex bits. Females have the babies and the boobs, and males have the testes and the sperm.

Having explored a few of the nuances around gender differences which are primarily nurture, let's now look at differences affecting females' lives which are absolutely in the nature category. First, I will start with the story of a woman whose work influenced the life of nearly every one of us.

Choice and contraception

Born in 1879, Margaret Sanger was a nurse living in New York who brought contraception to the masses in an era when females' lives were dictated by pregnancy. Margaret witnessed her mother die at age 49 after 18 pregnancies over 22 years, with 11 live births. The very idea that one woman had so many pregnancies and births has me crossing my legs as I write this. However, this situation was not uncommon at the time. Through her experience with her own mother and through her work with other families, Margaret became convinced that the only way to liberate women from the constraints of unwanted pregnancies and dangerous self-abortions was through sex education.

In America at that time, discussing sex openly was seen as shockingly perverted, and spreading information about how to prevent pregnancy was therefore outlawed by federal anti-obscenity laws. Defiantly, Margaret started distributing

---

[51] There is typically about a 10% difference in endurance sport performance (e.g., marathons) between males and females but this difference reduces to about 4% in ultra-endurance sports and females generally outperform males in extreme-distance swimming.

leaflets and information in 1914, and 2 years later opened a clinic in Brooklyn supplying contraceptives such as condoms and diaphragms. It was closed down by police within 9 days, and Margaret was arrested and sentenced to 30 days in a workhouse. The judge who sentenced her said – wait for it – no woman had '… the right to copulate with a feeling of security that there will be no resulting conception.' In other words, do make sure to procreate, but please don't enjoy sex.[52]

However, only two short years later in 1918, the birth control movement in America won a victory when a Court of Appeals judge issued a ruling which allowed doctors to start prescribing contraception. The publicity Margaret created paved the way for donations to her movement and spearheaded the development of oral birth control pills in the 1960s, which nearly all of us have used in some form or another today.[53] The ability to control our reproduction has transformed the lives of females all over the world.

---

[52] Women are still prohibited from sexual pleasure in cultures around the world today. Either brutally explicitly through practices such as female genital mutilation, or through the well-known orgasm gap which finds that 95% of men but only 65% of women usually-always have orgasms with their spouse.

[53] When the contraceptive pill was first developed, the seven-day break to create a withdrawal bleed was put in place, in part, due to the so-called Pope rule. One of the inventors, John Rock, thought the Pope would be more willing to accept the use of the pill if females still had a bleed. Also, the original pill had much higher doses of hormones than the pills today and this created side effects in some females, so a break from the high-dose hormones in order to bleed was thought to be helpful. Contraceptive pills today are not only substantially lower doses, but we now know that it is not only safe, but better to not have any seven-day pill break as there is less risk of pregnancy (or side effects if people are taking it for conditions like endometriosis or painful periods). This means if we take the pill we don't need to have periods. The idea that we need to bleed to cleanse is not true. In fact, regular bleeding can cause substantial health problems – more than a third of females under the age of 50 are iron deficient.

It's a female thing

Author and feminist Caitlin Moran says a good litmus test to see if a subject is a woman's issue is to look at whether men are worrying about it. This part is irrefutable: male and female lives differ because our bodies are different. Females deal with the physical aspects of periods, pregnancy, birthing, breastfeeding, contraception, the biological clock, fertility treatment, miscarriage[54], abortion[55] and menopause. Yet somehow, talking about *female problems* is deemed a bit unsavoury. So while males obliviously carry about their day at work, the females sitting next to them are often bravely getting on with business whilst sweating cobblers from hot flashes or contorted from period pain.

When my mum first told me about periods, I thought it had to be a joke. This happens every single month? Who made that up? Not only can periods be painful, but they are irritatingly expensive. The charity Bloody Good Period estimates it costs on average £4,800 for a lifetime of period management. New car, anyone? In 2021 the UK government finally abolished 'tampon tax' after some messy demonstrations through the streets of London by females wearing white, blood-stained trousers. Previously, sanitary wear had been subject to VAT as it was considered a luxury item.

Periods also affect females' equal participation in sports.[56] A 2021 survey by Adidas found 1 in 4 girls dropped

---

[54] About 25% of pregnancies end in miscarriage resulting in significant physical and/or emotional pain.

[55] About 25% of pregnancies end in abortion. Worldwide, around 45% of these abortions are unsafe.

[56] There are also many social factors which have precluded women from playing sports. The Football Association banned women's football in 1921 saying it wasn't suitable for female bodies, and only reinstated the women's game in 1971. In England, the Women's Super League went fully professional in the 2018-2019 season.

out of sports in adolescence due to fear of period leakage. This is madness – physical activity is so important for our health and well-being. A friend's daughter who was a competitive swimmer quit when she got her period. She simply didn't want to deal with bleeding on top of everything else. In 2023, Wimbledon conceded that females could wear dark-coloured shorts under their tennis white skirts to help anxiety around period leaking. As one campaigner on this issue said: About Bloody Time.

And if 'normal' vaginal bleeding for 1 week a month isn't enough, 1 in 10 females suffer from endometriosis, which currently takes an average of 8 years to get diagnosed. Endometriosis causes horrifically heavy and painful periods and can lead to problems with fertility.

Of course, periods are all about fertility, and here again we have to put in plenty of work. Females, rather than males, tend to make most of the decisions around contraception primarily because of the reality of the consequences of unintended pregnancies. When I was a teenager, going on the pill was a pretty standard decision regardless of the side effects. Not only for contraception but also for acne and painful periods. More recently, a friend told me about the agony she endured getting her contraceptive coil fitted. The nurse couldn't find the thread from the previous coil, so an awful lot of rummaging was required. Her story reminded me of things my Uncle John said about his cattle needing help from the vet to give birth: describing how the vet's arm would disappear up to the elbow like he was searching for a lost set of keys. My friend had already had to take the morning off work for the appointment, but the whole thing was so painful she then spent the afternoon in bed dosed on painkillers and clutching a hot water bottle.

The fertile window for females is much less than for males and therefore the tick-tock of the biological clock means many females in their twenties are already thinking about the best route to pick through the minefield of work-family balance. We are acutely aware that having a baby over the age of 35 puts us at increased risk of a complicated, geriatric pregnancy. There is nothing quite like a mother's guilt – starting in our early thirties – about an inability to conceive in a timely way.

However, it is worth noting that although fertility has traditionally been seen as a female problem, declining sperm quality in ageing males is a significant factor in couples' fertility. Between 9–15% of couples will have fertility problems and these problems are experienced equally – about 30% of infertility is related to females and 30% related to males (the rest is a combination of both). Fertility and ageing affect both sexes; the difference, however, is that infertility treatments for females are infinitely more invasive.

And while fertility and contraception should be shared responsibilities, pregnancy, childbirth, breastfeeding and menopause truly are not.[57] It is only females who experience the blooming of pregnancy and the accompanying miracle of childbirth. In my case, 9 months of vomiting that made any scene from *The Exorcist* look tame, followed by a failed epidural and pain not unlike having something amputated. After 16 years of taking the contraceptive pill, 80 weeks of pregnancy and 2 years of breastfeeding, I only got about 5 years off for good behaviour before menopause started. It then became necessary to start slapping on a patch to stop

---

[57] The Huichol tribe in Mexico believe that the pain of childbirth should be shared. The mother ties a string to her husband's testicles and with each contraction she gives the string a tug so that her partner can share her burden. Of course, I am not recommending this, but it did make me wonder what happens afterwards? Does this sincerely make the woman's partner more sympathetic, or does he go home and lie on the sofa with a bag of peas on his groin while his wife still does all the heavy lifting with the baby?

me from soaking my bedclothes in sweat and jibber-jabbering my way through brain fog. All females go through menopause and 75% of us experience symptoms; 10% of us leave our jobs, not only due to symptoms but also to a lack of understanding and support from employers.

Further, it is estimated that about one-third of mothers have ongoing health problems as a result of childbirth. Not only do females get more cancer of their reproductive systems than males, but they deal with any number of gynaecological issues related to owning a womb. A friend of mine has just had to have a hysterectomy necessitating several weeks off work and a crisis of childcare because she couldn't drive the kids to school. Another friend needs a corrective operation on her stomach muscles which separated giving birth to a large baby and has been putting it off for the last 7 years. This is before we get to plumbing issues and problems with incontinence and reconstructive surgery after tearing during birth. It's enough to make us all cross our legs and vow, 'Never again!'

Then there's the fact that female bodies are still being commoditised and viewed as public property for sex and reproduction. The year 2022 brought a roll-back of abortion law in the United States of America meaning that there is no longer a federal constitutional right to an abortion. Some states still allow abortion, but others have made it illegal either from conception or 6 weeks of pregnancy.[58] Some states don't even provide exemptions in cases of rape or incest. Much was made of a picture which went viral of an all-male group of politicians under Donald Trump's tenure debating a woman's healthcare bill. In response, *The*

---

[58] As most women know, a 6-week ban on abortion does not mean you have 6 weeks to get one. It means, if you have a regular 28-day cycle, you have, at best, 2 weeks. Unfortunately, the male governor of Texas responsible for the passing of this law didn't understand this pregnancy math and actually claimed in a 2021 press conference that women had 6 weeks to decide.

Guardian newspaper journalist Martin Belam insightfully tweeted: 'As long as you live, you will never see a photograph of seven women signing legislation that defines and controls what men can do with their reproductive organs…'

Women should always have the right to make decisions about their own bodies – without criticism or judgement. But that's just not always the case. On a 2023 episode of BBC *Women's Hour*, women with large breasts complained about how they are seen to be public property as if people have the right to ogle. A friend's teenage daughter with large breasts complained that at college it was only the larger-breasted girls who were penalised for not complying with the dress code – even when wearing exactly the same tight T-shirts and V-necked tops as girls with smaller breasts. Another friend who had a breast reduction due to serious back pain said her dad told her she was being ridiculous to do that. He pointed out that her stepmother had gone to the trouble of getting implants so he thought she was lucky to have the breasts that she did, and she shouldn't mess with them – despite the physical agony they caused her. This is not good enough. We are more than our meat suits.

Beauty standards and body bashing

I reckon I spend around 300 hours a year on what I would consider basic maintenance. Geek alert: I have gone to the trouble of totting this up. Things such as shaving my legs, blow-drying my hair, applying make-up and painting nails, et cetera. My husband's routine, in contrast, amounts to an awful lot less. He doesn't even go to the barber anymore – he just shaves his head over the bathroom sink.

The idea that women are valued for their beauty and men for their bank balance is still pretty pervasive. Not an ideal situation for anyone. The Kardashian crew and the media in general don't help. Women are expected to navigate high heels, handbags, make-up, thongs and waxing. We end up spending far more time and money than men on manicures, haircuts and clothes. Business attire is more complex than a suit, and jeans and a T-shirt simply won't do for that night out. Women feel judged, and therefore valued, by our appearance. We worry more about our weight.

You can argue that spending time on beauty is women's choice and that we don't need to wear make-up or do any of these other things. But many of us feel chained to social conventions. I will admit to feeling positively naked without my non-existent eyebrows painted in. I made the mistake one day of dropping my children at school without my make-up mask on. My daughter's teacher pulled me aside and asked, worriedly, and in hushed tones, whether I was feeling OK.

Why is it that so many women dislike the wonderful life-giving entities that are their bodies? An amazing friend of mine with three grown-up daughters and an enviable amount of sexual body confidence demonstrated for me recently the best body-beautiful attitude I have ever come across. We were on a girls' trip, and I caught her coming out of the bathroom: she turned around and showed me her body and told me how proud she was of it and that her scars and rolls meant she had lived life and birthed babies, and she was comfortable and happy in her skin. In that same moment, she both inspired me and made me sad that there aren't more women who look at their bodies this way.

Over the years, I haven't treated my body with tenderness and care, but rather more like an uncooperative part of me that hasn't quite got with the programme. For as long as I can remember, I've felt like I've been doing some kind of battle with it. I berate it for making me puke my guts up during 9 months of pregnancy, for giving me an almighty and unexpected period flood whilst wearing white jeans in the middle of the supermarket, for making me leak breastmilk through my blouse on the way to my first business meeting after going back to work and for making me crying and crazy in menopause. I have never spoken nicely to my body or told my body that I appreciate it – the way my friend does hers. I hope her daughters learn from her as I am trying to.

All I can tell you about my acquiescence to this merry-go-round of beauty is that I know I could ignore society's expectations, but complying with these standards feels like some kind of compulsion:

- I feel compelled by a friend's husband who hasn't seen me in years and says, 'Are you okay? You look tired.'
- I feel compelled by another friend who tells me that eyebrows are everything, and I should consider microblading as it will change the whole shape of my face – this was before it occurred to me that my face shape needed adjustment!
- I feel compelled by every other mum on the school run who is sporting make-up and lacquered nails and who doesn't have 2 months of root growth.
- I feel compelled by a variety of friends and family who love me just as I am but who are approving when I lose weight.

Taylor Swift tells us that 'Happiness and confidence are the prettiest things you can wear.' Of course this is true, but the battle with beauty can be deep-rooted for many women. It flies in the face of Every. Single. Thing. we encounter growing up which tells us that beauty for women is necessary. For thousands of years, women were the legal property of men and wholly reliant on them financially. In many cases, our ability to attract and secure a mate was necessary for survival. This runs deep. In my experience, modern-day women have a variety of reactions to the legacy of this societal pressure. Some, like me, acquiesce while resenting the fact that we do, some rail against it entirely[59] and some embrace it as an aspect of femininity and how they enjoy expressing themselves. None of these reactions are wrong but, of course, they all create work.

To top it all off, it is not just the emotional labour of managing society's beauty expectations which cost us dearly. It's also actual time and actual money. A study of women in 93 countries found that worldwide women spend an average of 2 hours and 40 minutes more a week on beauty than men. Already, mothers do more combined work and caregiving than men; add on this beauty premium and our remaining leisure time takes a substantial nosedive. Does styling your hair count as leisure? According to Forbes, women make up around 80–90% of spending in the beauty industry which is globally worth around $500 billion. It is a purely commercial proposition to make women unhappy with how we look.

To keep us purchasing, beauty standards change all the time as well. And not just decisions between bell-bottomed or skinny jeans. Actual body types. A friend saved up for a breast implant in her twenties in the days of the tabloid newspapers having page three girls. Several years later she is not happy with her breasts again and is going for a reduction as the style now is athletic and toned, not big and busty. And don't even get me started on pubic hair. Thanks to porn, beauty now means being waxed or lasered within an

---

[59] I have a marvellous friend who was shamed by another mother in the school playground for her grey roots. This woman literally said with disdain, 'You've let yourself go.' My friend decided then and there that she wasn't going to be told what to do anymore. She made a decision to stop dying her hair and let the grey grow out entirely. Go girl!

inch of our lives to look like some pre-pubescent child. Just another job to do. And it hurts, dammit!

Safety and the water we swim in

I'd like men to imagine living in a world full of basketball players, where around half the population is significantly taller, faster and stronger than you. Capable of strangling you with their bare hands if they choose. Women are sometimes not even conscious that this is the water we swim in. It ends up being *just the way it is*, and we don't even question the fact we've developed gills while others are breathing on land. It becomes a way of life to never leave our drinks unattended, to text each other on the way home, to go to the bathroom in pairs and to not leave the house alone after dark.

A 2021 survey by the UK's Office for National Statistics found that 1 in 2 women feel unsafe walking alone after dark on a quiet street close to their house compared with 1 in 7 men. My husband recently empathised with me about this, and I can't tell you how much it means when the men in your life get this. He said he imagines it to be like how he feels walking around a dodgy part of a big city late at night. It's a chronic state of altered alertness. He doesn't feel this when he walks through our local park during the day or gets on a crowded train into the city; he doesn't startle when he hears a loud noise behind him, but I do. I was alone when I came across a naked guy walking through the woods this summer by the beach in Portugal. It was funny in a way, but it also put me on alert in a way that a naked woman in the woods would simply not do for a man. I imagine most men stumbling across a naked woman walking through the woods would be delighted by the view!

The issue of safety pervades women's psyche as we make our way in the world. With every step I take, for example, I carry these experiences from my life:

- Every time I've been honked at and catcalled. I can remember the first time it happened when I was 15; I even know what I was wearing – a white skirt and navy-blue jumper. I reacted with the uncomfortable mix of flattery and mortification many women will be familiar with.
- The three times I've been followed through the woods in the last 4 years whilst out walking on my own. On one occasion, when I had my headphones in, I stopped to stretch my back in the middle of a deserted path. As I turned, I realised there was a man less than a meter behind me; no one else was around and he had been directly stalking me that close for I don't know how long. When I startled he went into the bushes at the side of the path and beckoned me to join him. Of course, I ran.
- The five women I have known over my lifetime who have been raped. Only one reported it to the police.

There is work in this hypervigilance. I do all the normal things many women do: I carry a rape alarm; I glance behind me regularly when walking during the day; I keep my headphones low so I can hear noises around me; I avoid walking anywhere on my own after dark; if for some reason I end up having to make a late-night journey by myself I carry my keys tightly gripped between my knuckles as a makeshift weapon; I think carefully about what I am wearing and whether I can run in it and I spend time, energy and money planning the safest way to travel if I am going alone.

Sadly, we have good reason to fear for our safety.[60] Some statistics for the UK:

- 70% of women experience sexual harassment in public places and 95% don't report it.
- In the UK, 1 in 5 women and 1 in 20 men will experience sexual assault during their lifetime. Globally, the figure for women is 1 in 3.
- Conviction rates for rape are a disgrace. Of the 55,130 cases of rape reported to the UK police in the 12 months leading up to March 2020, only 1.4% resulted in a conviction. This finding was cited as indicative of a system which has effectively decriminalised rape.[61]
- 5 out of 6 rapes are never reported to the police in the first place.
- Men are 230 times more likely to be raped themselves than to be falsely accused of rape.

Post Me Too, there has been a pervasive dialogue among men – and some mothers I know too – who worry that things have gone too far and that men are now at great risk of having their lives ruined through false allegations. In response to this, I would invite you not only to fact-check the statistics above but also to sense-check the following: feminist activist Nimco Ali says her female friends all know a woman who has been raped but her male friends are never

---

[60] We know, of course, that violence affects men too. It is often quoted that men are more likely to experience violence outside the home and women inside the home. Although 95% of perpetrators of violent crime are men and only 5% are women, both men and women are the victims. In addition, transgender people are twice as likely as cisgender people to be victims of violent crime.

[61] Historian Philippa Gregory explains in her book *Normal Women*, that even in medieval times, the rate of conviction for rape was more like 1 in 5. However, there were also horrific historical practices such as: 1) the fine for rape being paid to the woman's guardian, or 2) the rapist marrying the victim as reparation. In the UK in 1960, conviction rates for rape were more like 1 in 3. Now, only around 1 in 100 prosecutions result in a conviction.

aware of a friend who is a rapist. This was her experience from speaking to her friends and friends of her four brothers. Something doesn't add up, does it? Her point is that transgressions are often not discussed openly – unless you are Wayne Couzens[62] on a WhatsApp group – so good and decent men understandably find it difficult to imagine other men behaving this way. Women are blamed for exaggerating or attention-seeking, so of course they often don't report sexual assaults. London's Metropolitan Police force has 2.5 times more men than women on the force, and institutionalised misogyny is said to be the reason many women don't report to the police – they don't trust them to deliver justice.

The work of worthiness

As well as physical safety, humans have an innate desire for *emotional* safety. L'Oreal tells women that we are worth it! However, research abounds around women's confidence gap and the imposter syndrome. Why is it that so many women feel like we're not worthy?

There is emotional labour in this struggle for worthiness. Both in the continual questioning but also in keeping ourselves small – literally and figuratively. A friend on a diet

---

[62] Wayne Couzens, was a serving Metropolitan Police officer found guilty in 2021 of murdering Sarah Everard who was walking home from a friend's house through London around 9pm. Not that it should have made a difference if she was skipping home in her knickers at 3am. The media seized on this story as Sarah was a beautiful White woman who had done nothing 'wrong.' Assaults on ethnic minority women are rarely as widely reported, and further victim blaming if women are drunk, disorderly or engaging in sex work practically makes us disposable. A public protest was organised and police were heavily criticised at the time not only for their heavy-handed management of the protest (this was during COVID-19) but for inane suggestions to women such as 'Flag down a bus if you feel unsafe.' or 'Ask the police officer for ID.' Women, but not men, were also warned to be vigilant and stay indoors. If perpetrators are primarily male, shouldn't it be men rather than women who are punished with a curfew?

recently told me that her partner just likes her to be tiny. She reckons it makes him feel big. I must tell you that this man's physique could best be described as hippopotamus-like so I'm not sure how much bigger than her he wants to be. My friend is already a little hummingbird. And while she spends effort making her body smaller, I've spent years shrinking my opinions. Requests to male colleagues prefaced with lots of affable smiling and business emails that start with a tentative 'I wonder if you wouldn't mind…'

There is a physical safety element to the work of worthiness for women too. Women are more likely to be people pleasers than men. We more often feel the need to smile and to be pleasant and agreeable. Author and influencer Jen Hatmaker talks about this kind of behaviour as women being the 'clean-up crew' – women being vigilant of other people's emotions and pre-emptively making attempts to calm the waters and smooth things over. There is labour in both this kind of behaviour and also the swallowing-your-own-emotions kind. In the UK, 1 in 4 women experience domestic abuse.[63] Women with long-term illnesses or disabilities are more than twice as likely as the rest of the population to experience domestic abuse. Abuse is not just physical, it can also be emotional, sexual or financial. Someone who controls your friendships or your money, or who criticises you and then tells you it's all in your head and you can't take a joke. Far, far too many of us have been there or know someone who has. As well as people-pleasing behaviour being more prevalent in women, gaslighting is also a gendered phenomenon with those on the

---

[63] Rates of domestic abuse are shockingly high. It is a problem that few of us talk about, and which primarily happens behind closed doors. Men are also the victims of domestic abuse with 1 in 7 men suffering. However, simply due to the strength and size difference between men and women, the consequences of domestic violence are much more often lethal for women. This link is repeated from Chapter 1: nhs.uk/live-well/getting-help-for-domestic-violence/

receiving end of this power play more likely to be women or minorities.

Of course, alongside the work of worthiness goes the work of feminism, justifying to ourselves and to others that we aren't ranty harridans who hate men, but rather that the accumulation of micro-aggressions over time has taken its toll and *enough is enough*. It's also the stark knowledge that in many countries around the world, having a son is preferable to having a daughter. More than 130 million women are estimated to be missing worldwide due to infanticide, ill treatment, or selective abortion. A 2020 United Nations global report finds that 90% of people are biased against women, with 30% of respondents thinking it is acceptable for men to hit their partners and 50% of men saying they have more right to a job than a woman. This feeling that women carry, that we must justify our place in the world and our seat at the table, is real. It's not just in your head.

Girls in crisis

The digital age and social media have been damaging for young women. A BBC report on struggles girls face today speaks not only about sexting and online abuse, but also the anxiety associated with how many likes they get on their social media posts. Girls feel pressure to simultaneously get good grades, be popular and, most importantly, look good. When I was a teenager, if you weren't invited to a party, you'd be none the wiser. Modern-day 24-hour social media culture means that not only do you know you have not been invited to a party on a Friday night, but you can sit at home alone watching your peers post about what an amazing evening they are having without you.

A report from 92 secondary schools in England found that at age 18 girls were twice as likely to have poor mental health than boys. This same report found that at age 11, girls have 30% poorer mental health than boys: the problem gets worse rather than better during the teenage years. This is compounded for children from ethnic minorities. A 2023 Girlguiding survey found that 89% of girls aged 7 to 21 felt generally worried or anxious, and only 59% of girls were happy with the way they looked compared with 72% in 2009. The organisation called on the government to urgently tackle this crisis in girls' mental health by addressing sexual harassment, online abuse and appearance pressure. Boys also struggle with body image issues but not to nearly the same extent as girls do; nearly twice as many girls as boys are unhappy with their looks.

I see this in our young people. I know teenage boys who weigh chicken breasts to monitor their protein intake, who obsessively pump iron in their bedrooms in pursuit of muscle tone and who drown themselves in Dior Sauvage – it was Lynx Africa in my day! But what I mainly gather from mums is that they hear less from their boys who, on the surface, tend to get on with it.[64] Not like their teenage girls who seem to engage in so much *drama*. This makes me cross! Girls are not making their feelings up in a vacuum; they are swimming in a toxic stew of society's double standards and conflicting expectations.

In my experience, teenage girls are still up against the unfeasible requirement to be both sexy and virginal at the

---

[64] Let me be clear. I am *not* saying that teenage boys aren't struggling as well. We know there is a male mental health crisis also stemming from a patriarchal culture which doesn't encourage boys to share their problems or seek help. We buy into the idea that boys are emotionally uncomplicated when, in fact, they are socialised to repress their feelings. Teenage boys struggle more with addictions to drugs, alcohol, gambling and gaming, and boys are now not doing as well academically at school as girls are. All our children need our help.

same time. And the rise of the internet means these expectations are on steroids compared to what we had to contend with 30 years ago. Girls are now coerced into sending nudes to engage in a relationship but are then called out by both girls and boys when they do. They are encouraged to look attractive on their social media posts, but, of course, not too attractive as they will be called out again for catfishing.[65] We then have the gall to accuse girls of unnecessary overthinking when society sets them the extra homework of navigating these conundrums.

There is a crisis of well-being for women young and old, and things are simply not good enough. It is an issue of gender inequality, and we need to make it better not only for ourselves but for our children. Women often don't want to do too much special pleading on behalf of themselves, but when it comes to our children, we need to turn on our mama-bear and make some fuss. This situation must improve for us all.

Sex *is* work

Female bodies mean that we perform extra labour managing our biological functions, society's beauty expectations and the basics of keeping ourselves safe. And for some women, sex *is* literally work. Not just within relationships – not tonight darling, I've got a headache – but to make ends meet financially. During the COVID-19 lockdown, the BBC reported that 80% of workers pushed into the sex industry

---

[65] I'm told that catfishing in teenage speak means that your social media pictures are too good. Apparently, they don't sufficiently represent what you look like IRL (in real life), so you are accused of being disingenuous. Another tightrope walk. This is not something boys contend with to anything like the same degree.

were single mothers.[66] About 90% of sex workers are women and they predominantly perform this work for reasons of financial insecurity.

However, sex work is not just what we picture in terms of women selling sex on the streets. Women sell sex in lots of nuanced ways. A friend held off having sex with her partner until he agreed to buy her a new kitchen! It is still common for women to use sex as a bargaining chip.

Daisy May Cooper's BBC1 drama *Rain Dogs* is a brilliant portrayal of a smart, sassy, writer and single mum who works at a peep show to make ends meet. When she and her daughter are kicked out of their flat because she can't make the rent, she ends up being offered a place to stay by a man who clearly is expecting sex in return for his offer of lodgings. Sex for rent is a whole thing.

And it isn't just sex for rent. In general, society still has a messed-up view of what female bodies are for. Unfortunately, it is rarely centred on the idea of female pleasure. Snippets of conversations I've heard over the years include things like:

- A professional therapist confessing with an eye roll that she just goes along with her husband who thinks it's a wife's duty to provide him with sex – lie back and think of England.[67]
- Women who argue that it is fair play for a man to cheat if his wife isn't 'giving him' sex – like it's his birthright.

---

[66] The prevalence of women working in the sex industry is difficult to calculate but estimations vary between approximately 0.4% to 1.7% of women in the US and UK. (Ranges are different in other countries – e.g., Africa 0.7%–4.3% or Latin America 0.2–7.3%).

[67] The first written reference of this phrase is from Lady Alice Hillingdon, who writes in her diary that: 'When I hear his steps outside my door I lie down on my bed, open my legs and think of England.' For women, sex in the Victorian era was often framed in this way as both a burden and a duty. Not much fun there.

- Exchanges between teenagers of naked pictures for cash, and payment in cigarettes in return for sexual favours.
- Wives offering anal sex to 'keep him sweet' on the run-up to Christmas and birthdays in the hope of better presents.

Where is the line? Is there a line? Or is it perfectly reasonable to swap sex for favours – financial or otherwise? Of course, sex doesn't have to be solely about love or procreation. I agree with that. But what I will caveat here is that these situations don't happen in reverse. Try them out for size. It is rare for women to pay men for sexual favours[68], and equally rare for men to offer their wives specific sex acts in order to get a better Christmas present – mainly because far too many women I know are buying all the Christmas presents anyway!

In addition, what happens to females who emotionally or physically can't have sex? Up to 16% of females have vulval or vaginal conditions which cause sex to be painful. A 2021 YouGov survey found that only one-third of females in the UK say that they never experience pain during sex. Also, what happens to women when we get to an age where society perceives us as 'past it'? Remember, men are silver foxes and we become barren hags. Ugh. What happens to our bargaining chip?

Wouldn't it be wonderful if the messages our daughters received about sex were that they should grow up to enjoy and embrace sexual pleasure without guilt, fear, oppression or any sense of duty and quid pro quo? The sex positivity movement, which has gained much traction among the younger generation, is making fantastic inroads to champion the idea that sex does not equal shame and it never should.

---

[68] Although, see actor Emma Thompson in the movie *Good Luck to You, Leo Grande* for a great portrayal of this role reversed.

Any kind of sex and sexual predilections which are consensual to all partners and all genders are great sex. This is wonderful and I heartily agree.

However, I still contend that sex for money is just not the fair trade that some like to argue it is: it is always the person with the money who has the power. Anything can be bought with money, whereas sex is only one commodity and selling it can come with consequences like pregnancy and sexually transmitted diseases. Is using our bodies as commodities really fair game? After all, it's our body, our choice. Or does it cause us problems?

A new take on the oldest profession

Sex work has been said to be the world's oldest profession: women have always been, and still are, far more likely than men to live in poverty, and sex work is a way out of poverty. There is a long and interesting history of this profession: from Roman times to the 17th century, where the diaries of Samuel Pepys give an insight as to the enormous prevalence of sex workers in London, through to Thatcher's Girls of the 1980s – women affected by high unemployment who travelled from the provinces to King's Cross in London for sex work.

Today, sex work is increasingly more prevalent and accessible through the online environment. And it isn't just women who are pushed into it for financial reasons who participate, but also those who rightly want to use their bodies in whatever way they see fit. The argument goes that sportspeople earn money through their physical attributes, so how much different is selling sex? Particularly if it can be done in a safe and regulated way online. After all, there is a power imbalance between all employees and their bosses.

Why shouldn't women use what they've got and capitalise on the market that is there?

OnlyFans, a subscription-based service sharing adult content via webcam, increased from 7.5 million to 85 million users during the first year of the COVID-19 pandemic lockdown. I went for lunch with a friend of mine recently who said she can't get in to see her usual hairdresser at the weekends anymore. Her hairdresser has decided to reduce her hours in the salon and is now working on OnlyFans on Saturdays instead. She likes the hours and the flexibility but said the only downside so far is that one of her neighbours has started watching her online which makes things awkward in real life.

This landscape for buying and selling sex has changed completely in the last 25 years. Thanks to dating apps like Tinder, 'putting out' on the first date is pretty standard fare – relationship commitments are now typically formed after you have sex, not before. I'm no prude, but it is important to be aware that these are wildly different sexual expectations from my mother's generation of no sex before marriage. Even growing up in the ladette culture of the 80s and 90s there was quite a lot of effort that men were required to put *in* before they could get a girl to put *out*, as comedian Micky Flanagan put it. The current landscape means sex has never been so available and so commoditised. It is easy to see why many women have come to the reasonable conclusion that they might as well be paid for their trouble. The confusing part comes when what everyone is actually looking for – sincere, life-affirming, heartfelt, reciprocated connection – is then chronically transformed in society as women giving sex in exchange for men giving money. This rarely makes anyone happy.

Porn: a sticky situation

At this juncture, you might wonder what exactly sex work has to do with the happiness of working mothers? Well, according to a 2023 Ofcom report, around 30% of UK adults watch porn: 73% of users are men and 27% are women. Around a third of all internet downloads are related to pornography and it is estimated to be a 97-billion-dollar industry. As researcher Dr Fiona Vera-Gray explores in her book *Women on Porn*, pornography is so embedded in today's society that it permeates everyone's lives – and many people have a complicated relationship with it.

We desperately need to bring this topic into the light and talk about it without shame; shame must be removed from the equation for *everyone*. Shaming women about their sexuality is a means of control; shaming men about their sexuality shuts down communication. That's just patriarchy 101.

We need a comprehensive paradigm shift. First, for sex workers who must have the right to work in a safe environment. Second, for teenagers who, of course, are interested in sex but need much better information than that provided by mainstream porn sites. And third, for couples in relationships who are affected by pornography in a variety of ways. Trust, openness and honesty are the cornerstones of positive and healthy relationships which enhance our well-being. Unfortunately, the stigma surrounding pornography often leads to secretive behaviour and makes it a taboo topic.

Interestingly, women often get shamed regardless of their opinion on porn. We are still grappling with the Madonna-whore complex: being slut-shamed if we are open about our sexual pleasure and then being vanilla-shamed if we express concerns about shifting boundaries. Dr Vera-Gray's research reveals that women's relationship with pornography is complex. Unfortunately, typical tropes pit women against each other once again. We are either the sex-positive cool girl who happily encourages her partner to go to strip clubs or the frigid feminist who wants all sex work to be banned. The reality for most women is somewhere in between. The BBC Women's Hour programme commissioned a captivating series on pornography in the early part of 2024, giving voice to this complicated relationship.

The sticky part of mainstream pornography for women – pun intended – is that it overwhelmingly caters to the male gaze. In the main, pornography is produced by men, for men; many scripts feature the narrative that sex is something that is *done* to women *by* men. Penetrative intercourse features heavily, despite the fact that many studies show this is females' least favourite sex act and most females need clitoral stimulation to orgasm. As a result, when heterosexual women watch porn, popular searches are for either lesbian or gay porn. The reasoning is to remove the misogyny and violence which is common.[69] Ethnic minorities also describe struggling with racism in porn. There is more feminist or ethical porn being made now and more female producers. However, it is often behind paywalls, and it is common for women (and men) to say they are not committed enough to pornography to pay for it, so they just pick their way through the mainstream sites whose algorithms quickly offer a lot of violent content. Of course, this is not to say that kinky sex should be off the table – you should absolutely get your rocks off to anything consensual – but it makes the point that over the last 30 years, mainstream pornography has enormously increased the variety of what is viewed. And this, coupled with the

---

[69] Of course, this is not to say this the case for all women. Nancy Friday does a deep dive on the wonderful variety of sexual fantasies women have, and her book, *My Secret Garden*, encourages openness, exploration and the idea of women celebrating their hidden desires and breaking free from societal constraints.

addictive nature of anonymous online streaming, is a recipe for disaster.

Regarding pornography's impact on our children's well-being, the primary issue again is the lack of open and honest communication and education. A significant majority of children are learning their sexual scripts from online porn. Researchers find sex has become more performative, and women especially are increasingly body conscious. As with so many aspects of a healthy relationship, surely the focus should be on what feels good, not what looks good?

A 2023 report by the UK's Children's Commissioner found that 79% of children have seen violent porn by the time they were 18, and 47% of young people thought that girls *expect* sex to involve things like airway restriction or slapping. Researchers believe it is hard to deny pornography's impact on behaviour and relationships in real life. The charity Refuge finds that in the UK, 41% of girls aged 14 to 17 in an intimate relationship experienced some form of sexual violence from their partner. As a mother of two daughters of a similar age, that statistic took my breath away. The Children's Commissioner report concludes that pornography exposure is now so widespread and normalised that children cannot opt out. Their assessment is unequivocal: online pornography today is enormously more harmful than the quaint-by-comparison top-shelf magazines that titillated previous generations.

One peculiar consequence of all this porn is that 18 to 25-year-olds are having less sex than previous generations – and using far more Viagra. If you ask me, it's hardly surprising that young people are put off sex. The veil of shame and secrecy around sex needs to be lifted. And by far the most perverted aspect of it all is that most of us are too shy to talk about it.

The work of being female: in a nutshell

- Mothers don't need to just balance a career and caregiving. Females have a third job managing our sexed bodies. It is more work, yet again, for us to manage our biology, beauty, safety and sexuality.
- The main differences which occur between males and females have to do with our reproductive organs. Many other differences are either nuanced or science has debunked them. For instance, we know that on average, males and females don't have greater or less intelligence or ability in maths.
- There are socially nurtured reasons around many gender differences. For instance, why men and women show different leadership styles. The finding that women leaders are more collaborative and men are more directive is substantially influenced by social hierarchies: men tend to not like it when women tell them what to do but women are typically more compliant the other way around.
- In terms of biology, females, and especially mothers, must deal with a myriad of issues including periods, contraception, the biological clock, pregnancy, birth, breastfeeding, fertility treatments, miscarriage, abortion and menopause.
- Concerning beauty, socially constructed standards mean that some women feel pressured into spending inordinate amounts of time and money doing things like false nails, false eyelashes, skincare routines, Botox, make-up, hair dye and much, much more.
- Regarding safety, females' smaller size means that we work harder at keeping ourselves safe. This ranges from not going out after dark to the emotional labour of keeping the peace and smiling in situations where we

don't necessarily feel happy. In the UK, 1 in 4 women (and 1 in 7 men) deal with domestic abuse.
- Concerning sexuality: 1 in 5 women are sexually assaulted in their lifetimes (and 1 in 20 men). Online pornography has proliferated in the last 30 years. It affects relationships and can be problematic for young people. For instance, 47% of young people surveyed in 2023 by the UK's Children's Commissioner thought that girls *expect* violence such as choking and slapping during sex. We know that girls today are in crisis with teenage girls at 18 twice as likely to have mental health problems as boys. We need less shaming and more talking.

Chapter 6

The Solution

Striving for more

I saw this quote on Instagram recently (attributed to @seewun):

'The older I get, the more I see how women are described as having gone mad, when what they've actually become is knowledgeable and powerful and fucking furious.'

This summarises my mid-life feelings rather well!

Chimamanda Ngozi Adichie, award-winning writer and feminist, says: 'But in addition to being angry, I am also hopeful, because I believe deeply in the ability of human beings to remake themselves for the better.' I agree with Chimamanda too. I have to, otherwise the anger would eat me whole.

In the 100 years since the Suffragettes won the right to vote, women's lives have changed dramatically. In the United Kingdom, women can now legally control our fertility using the contraceptive pill (since 1967), demand equal pay (since 1970), have our own mortgages and credit cards (since 1975), refuse to consent to sex when we are married (1991) and marry each other if we wish (2014). We have come a long way!

But we haven't finished yet.

Should we tell our daughters to become doctors?

My quest to discover whether women could indeed have it all started with my friend Fran declaring that she would never tell her daughter to become a doctor. She said the juggling was making women stressed and unhappy and I didn't disagree. So, what's the answer? What should we tell our daughters today?

Fran was certainly correct in saying the current system doesn't work for women. Despite the fact that women now make up around half of medical students, only 28% of surgeons and 15% of consultants are female. Women are still not reaching the top of the profession and surgery is still said to be a boys' club. In September 2023, an investigation by *The Times* newspaper found that 1 in 3 female NHS surgeons had been sexually assaulted by a colleague. The report laid bare the high drop-out rates among women trainees and how surgical rotations necessitating moving hospitals every year were just incompatible with family life. One story of many detailed in the report was told by a consultant plastic surgeon from Bristol who said a male colleague attempted to hug her while they were discussing a patient. He made some noises and rubbed himself against her. As he backed away, he said he could see down her top and commented, 'You probably felt my erection then.'

Whether it is wise to throw your daughter into this kind of lion's den is definitely a question worth asking. But before you decide the answer is a resounding 'Hell, no!' let's consider how far women have come in the field of medicine alone.

First, we had to surmount all the obstacles to studying medicine. Men have been studying medicine as an academic discipline at universities in Europe since around the 12th century.[70] In 1870, Elizabeth Garrett Anderson was the first woman in the UK to obtain a medical degree. This was no mean feat considering the culture at the time. Back then, English universities did not allow entrance to women, so she had to learn French and get her degree from the University of Paris. As researcher Anne Fausto-Sterling points out, 19th-century scientists routinely claimed that females were less intelligent than males due to their smaller brains. In 1866, the president of the British Medical Association warned of the danger of women studying; he claimed it would lead them to 'great nervousness' and problems with their periods and fertility. In 1874, Sir Henry Maudsley, an influential Victorian psychiatrist, wrote that a woman '... does not easily regain the vital energy that was recklessly spent on learning... if a woman attempts to achieve the educational standards of men... she will lack the energy necessary for childbearing and rearing.'[71]

In 1869, Edinburgh University did admit seven female students to study medicine – Sophia Jex-Blake, Isabel Thorne, Edith Pechey, Matilda Chaplin, Helen Evans, Mary Anderson Marshall and Emily Bovell. They faced significant prejudice, however, and were ultimately

---

[70] A fabulous fact is that the University of al-Qarawiyyin, the world's oldest existing and continually operating university, was founded by a Muslim woman, Fatima al-Fihri, in Fez, Morocco in the year 859.
[71] In 1871, Darwin published his thoughts on gender relations in *The Descent of Man*. Alongside many of his generation, he was also rather sexist and believed women to be naturally coy, modest and passive. I wonder what he would think today of my very immodest barrister friend who drips in diamonds and totters in skyscraper heels to her luxury convertible car after a triumphant day in court?!

prevented from qualifying as doctors. Difficulties they faced included not only hostility and social isolation but being pelted with mud during an anatomy exam, having to pay higher tuition than the male students and having to organise their own tutorials when the male teachers – who were permitted but not required to teach them – refused to do so. At the time, ongoing campaigning from some of these women such as Sophia Jex-Blake, alongside others like Elizabeth Garrett Anderson, resulted in the opening of the London School of Medicine for Women in 1874 – the first school in the UK to allow women not only to study medicine but to become qualified doctors. This school ultimately became what is known today as University College London. Note that 150 years later, Edinburgh University awarded those seven pioneering women posthumous honorary degrees.

By 1911, there was still only a tiny proportion of women doctors in the UK – 495 recorded. Numbers remained low throughout the first half of the 20th century until the second wave of feminism in the 1960s and 1970s which propelled more women into the field. However, discrimination was still rife. Even in the 1990s, I remember my grandmother refusing to attend appointments with the 'lady doctor' at her GP surgery. She much preferred the male doctor, as he knew what he was talking about.

Despite my grandmother's resistance, we know that for quality healthcare, women need women doctors. Dating from ancient times, traditional roles for women in society included those of healers and herbalists. Women were the midwives too, and we knew all about childbirth.[72] Witch

---

[72] Note that it was male medics in the 17th century who came up with the idea for women to lie down in childbirth; it was an easier position for the doctor to view the patient. There is a widely circulated anecdote that it was King Louis XIV of France who instigated this trend as he wanted to view his mistresses giving birth!

trials, however – which reached a peak around 1600 – surely tried to put women in their place. The influence of the Christian church and suspicion around pagan acts meant many women herbalists became too afraid to practise. Although men were also targeted, this fear of the paranormal was directed primarily at women; the miracle of birth was something otherly that men couldn't control. Witch trials resulted in tens of thousands of deaths across Europe using techniques such as immersing a suspected witch in water – if she drowned it proved she wasn't a witch, and if she floated, she was. An horrific damned if you do and damned if you don't situation to which women in many parts of the world today may still relate.

As author Caroline Criado Perez explains in *Invisible Women*, the historical shortage of women medical professionals has significant real-world consequences for millions of women today. Firstly, it has resulted in inequalities in drug trials. Women are less frequently recruited for drug trials, partly due to concerns regarding pregnancy and the extra expense of recruiting women at different stages of fertility but often simply due to entrenched male bias. Traditionally, men's bodies have been considered the standard, while women, with our 'abnormal' menstrual cycles, were viewed as producing anomalous results. Initiatives such as the National Institutes of Health (NIH) Revitalization Act of 1993 in the USA mandated the inclusion of women and minorities in NIH-funded research. However, due to the legacy of this disparity, a 2020 study by the University of California, Berkeley found that women experience drug side effects nearly twice as often as men. For instance, Zolpidem, a sleeping tablet, remains in women's bodies longer than in men's, leading to increased cognitive impairment and traffic accidents. In response to this issue, the American Food and Drug Association halved the dose of this drug for women in 2013.

Secondly, the paucity of women medical professionals has led to gender bias in the treatment of pain, heart disease and hormonal issues. Ever been to the doctor and felt like you've been told it's all in your head? Well, it's not. Women's pain is often not believed. When we present to Accident and Emergency departments with pain, we wait longer than men and are prescribed less effective drugs. This effect is compounded for ethnic minority women. Women are also more likely than men to be written off with a psychiatric problem and given anti-anxiety medication. Heart disease is the leading cause of death among females – responsible for 35% of deaths worldwide – and yet we still think of it as a male disease. In 2021, the British Heart Foundation found that at every stage – diagnosis, treatment and aftercare – women receive poorer care than men due to gender bias.

Thirdly, there is a problem of inadequate funding and research regarding female health. Systemic issues persist, such as the disproportionately high mortality rate of women of colour during childbirth. In the UK, Black women are four times more likely than White women to die in pregnancy or childbirth. Furthermore, conditions like urinary incontinence, affecting 1 in 3 women, and faecal incontinence, affecting 1 in 10 women, are often overlooked or considered taboo topics. We joke with each other about peeing our pants and think this is simply par for the course. It beggars belief that five times more money has been spent on research around erectile dysfunction (affecting 19% of men) versus pre-menstrual syndrome (affecting 90% of women).

So, with all of this considered, should you encourage your daughter to become a doctor?

I think the answer has to be *yes*, despite the struggles. Unfortunately, we are never going to improve things for women without our participation. Women's happiness depends on us having greater gender equality, not on us dropping out of the workforce. I have never heard anyone say that fathers can't be doctors because it's hard work and incompatible with family life. It is perfectly possible for things to change. Although, we just might have to shake things up a bit and ruffle some feathers. Be *demanding*, even. Junior doctors used to regularly work 100-hour weeks, and now, thanks to the European Working Time Directive, we limit this workload to 48 hours per week and mandate time to sleep. While this is an improvement, there is still a substantial way to go to improve working conditions in today's NHS.

The suffragists asked politely for years for the vote and didn't get very far. It was the attention that the more militant suffragettes brought to the cause which moved the needle on women's voting rights. Suffragettes were so fed up they were prepared to break some stuff: they chained themselves to railings, smashed up shop windows and even committed arson. When they were arrested for these crimes and put in prison, they went on hunger strike and were violently force-fed – horrific. These women *demanded* their rights in a controversial way and were difficult to ignore.

Now, I am not saying that we should break shop windows or go on a collective hunger strike – we are doing enough dieting already of our own accord. But I do think the time for asking nicely has ended. What we need to break are social norms and archaic rules. *We must demand more.*

Things can only get better!

The backwards motion of a wave as the tide creeps out is sometimes used to describe the push and pull of progress. Susan Faludi's 1991 bestseller *Backlash: The Undeclared War Against Women* rails against the blaming the victim mentality displayed in 1980s media which said that feminism itself was to blame for women's struggle to have it all. Feminists were labelled as extreme, man-hating or anti-family, and their concerns were dismissed as trivial or unnecessary.

A 2024 international survey commissioned by the King's Global Institute for Women's Leadership through IPSOS found that 47% of the UK population think that things have now gone far enough when it comes to gender equality – 59% of men and 39% of women. Interestingly, this figure increased from 29% in 2019. It can be hard to know what to make of this. It may well be another backlash – the authors of the study suggest it represents a growing polarisation of views. Personally, and with my optimist-hat on, I would like to think it means we are making strides but that substantial numbers of women, more so than men, understand we still have a long way to go.

A similar IPSOS survey in 2022 conducted on 20,000 participants found that 19% of men in the UK think that gender inequality doesn't exist, compared with 37% of men in Saudi Arabia, 30% of men in Australia, 22% in the United States, and 7% in Japan. Russian men seem to have the most fragile egos around this subject – notwithstanding Putin's infamous bare-chested posing on horseback – with 58% feeling like traditional masculinity is under threat and 56% thinking that feminism does more harm than good.

Again, if we take a positive spin on these figures, although 19% of UK men think gender inequality is a fiction, this therefore means that the vast majority of men, 81%, *do* get it. As it stands in the UK today:

- 47% of doctors are women (although, only 15% are consultants).
- 39% of board positions at the top FTSE 100 companies are women (although, only 8% of CEOs).
- 40% of journalists are women (although, only 24% of top editors).
- 40% of MPs are women as of the 2024 election (although, only 4% of our history's Prime Ministers).

Harriet Harman, one of the UK's longest-serving female MPs, comments in her biography that the Parliament she entered in 1982 was made up of 97% male MPs and reported on by a press lobby made of up 95% male journalists. We have certainly made waves since then. In all kinds of ways, women are breaking barriers that my grandmother, born in 1918, would never have dreamed of.

Change is afoot

Culturally, things are shifting. A review of 12 OECD countries found an improving situation in terms of the gender pay gap, and the millennial generation marked the middle of this change. Not only are women now seen to belong in the workplace, but increasing numbers of educated millennial men are looking for more equal partnerships at home, with both men and women wanting careers and time spent with their children. Studies show the millennial generation to be less constrained by gender stereotypes than previous generations – they are much more likely to see gender on a spectrum rather than two distinct boxes. Both women and men are increasingly looking for a kaleidoscope career model encompassing three things: authenticity at work, a stimulating work environment, and crucially, a balance between their work and home lives.

The BBC claims that Generation Z are the workers who want it all. Gen Z is known for not being scared to make a complaint or leave a job they don't like. They are demanding bigger pay cheques, jobs that provide purpose and meaning, more time off and the ability to work flexibly or remotely. Good for them. Although, older generations sometimes think that younger generations don't know what hard work means!

A glimmer of a silver lining from the grim COVID-19 pandemic of 2020 has been a widespread shift in the perception of flexible working. The 1980s always-on culture has mellowed somewhat so that some companies are starting to recognise the restorative powers of down-time and we aren't all running around being busy bastards for the sake of it – as ex-U.S. Secretary of State, Colin Powell advises us against doing. Claudia Goldin, the first woman ever to win a solo Nobel Prize in economics in 2023 for her work on the gender pay gap, claims a significant reason for this pay gap is the issue of *greedy work*. These are industries which reward a culture of facetime: such as entertainment, sport, finance, accounting and law. To achieve equality, this needs to change.

Generally speaking, average working hours in the UK have been decreasing over the last 70 years. In the last 150 years – since the industrial revolution – hours for the average UK worker have reduced by 40%. We now work fewer hours per day and take more holidays than we ever used to. Having said that, the total number of working hours has increased at a *family* level, as more women are in paid employment. Policy needs to shift to recognise this change.

The four-day workweek is now being trialled in several places with evidence suggesting that it leads to less stress, increased productivity and reduced commute time. In May

2021, Spain's government announced a multi-million-euro investment in supporting a three-year pilot project to test the feasibility of a four-day workweek. Results found that workers were healthier, happier and more productive. In 2022, further trials were arranged by the organisation 4 Day Week Global with companies in Ireland, the USA, Australia and New Zealand taking part and finding similar positive results.

The critical mass required to change a culture is said to be about a third: we need at least one-third of positions to be held by women for things to shift so we are no longer the token minority at work. When women hold senior roles in business and politics, women's perspectives are much more likely to be taken into account. Facebook's former Chief Operating Officer Sheryl Sandberg recounts implementing pregnancy car parking spaces at work but only after realising she couldn't manage the long walk to her building when she was pregnant herself. It is true that women are more visible in senior careers than ever before, but in order to fully effect change, we still need more.

Societal solutions

Women, we have work to do! If we want happiness and well-being, the answer to this quest lies in greater equality for all. Happiness stems from equality – this has been proven time and again. It is not only women but also men who benefit from living in more equal societies. It is not only our daughters we help by demanding change, but our sons too. Societal solutions come from cultural change in our day-to-day interactions with others, but they also come from politics and lawmaking.

The BBC's mockumentary *Cunk on Britain* has Philomena Cunk, played by Diane Morgan, musing whether women 100 years ago would have wanted the vote quite so much if they had realised it was just marking an 'X' on some paper using a pencil tied to a shoelace in a primary school classroom. For many, politics seems pointless. But it remains a significant lever to make change, even if it does sometimes feel like we're a fly trying to shift a boulder.

In the movie *Suffragette*, a historical drama released in 2015 starring Carey Mulligan, there is an exchange between male members of Parliament when debating votes for women which goes like this:

> British MP #1: 'Women do not have the calmness of temperament or the balance of mind to exercise judgement in political affairs.'
>
> British MP #2: 'If we allow women to vote, it will mean the loss of social structure. Women are well-represented by their fathers, brothers, husbands.'
>
> British MP #3: 'Once the vote was given, it would be impossible to stop at this. Women would then demand the right to become MPs, cabinet ministers, judges.'

Oof! It can be hard to take that this is recent history. Around the time my grandmother was born, this perspective was categorically the prevailing view. Women were expected to focus on home and family and exhibit feminine virtues such as piety, purity and domesticity. It was primarily men who participated in the workforce and engaged in public life. I remember watching this scene in the movie with visceral irritation, thinking, *Mansplaining much?*[73] Of

---

[73] Historian Philippa Gregory explains in her book *Normal Women* that it wasn't only men but also some women who were against the idea of votes for women; both wealthy women who gained from their proximity to wealthy men and didn't want this balance disturbed, and working-class women who couldn't see what practical difference a vote would make to their lives.

course, I knew that women couldn't vote 100 years ago but this movie brought vividly to life how so many men in positions of power were adamant in their opinion: the best thing for society was to subordinate women otherwise we would be wanting to do all kinds of things.

My children were younger then, aged 7 and 9, and I remember I ushered them out of the room while I was watching it. What would they think? That there must be some good reason for women to be inferior otherwise why on earth would society be like that? I desperately didn't want my naïve children to absorb the idea – in such graphic technicolour detail – that women were inferior to men. It might give them the idea that *they* were. Today, I am still highly irritated by the idea that many people in society think women aren't equally as capable as men, but I am more inclined to talk about it rather than cover it up. Because we can't fix what we can't fully see.

The following sections summarise four significant areas where improved government policies can make a difference to the happiness of working mothers today: childcare, paid parental leave, flexible working and online regulation.

Childcare

In the 1970s, the decade I was born, the first UK Women's Liberation Movement Conference took place in Oxford and set out the following four demands for women:

1. Equal pay.
2. Equal education and job opportunities.
3. Free contraception and abortion on demand.
4. Free 24-hour nurseries.

More than 50 years later, a case can arguably be made for progress concerning these first three demands, but childcare in the UK is still too often seen as a private rather than public problem. Somehow, it's a personal issue that families, and by this we really mean *women*, are meant to sort out on their own – and not the responsibility of government or society.

I find it baffling that the UK, the sixth largest economy in the world, which takes great pride in its National Health Service, does not prioritise a universal childcare scheme for its most vital resource: the next generation. The standard model of care today for children is a mixture of harried maternal care and woefully inadequate daycare, with simply not enough involvement from fathers or the state. We know it takes a village to raise a child and that involvement from warm and reliable caregivers is critical for good outcomes for children. Yet the way society is structured today means that far too often mothers alone carry the practical, physical and emotional responsibility of child-rearing. Help from extended family used to be commonplace in the work of raising children but now, more and more, people move away from their families. We *expect* women to work outside the home and yet we receive limited support to actually do this – we should just suck it up and sleep less, I guess. And juggle. Endlessly juggle with the invisible octopus arms we've magically grown.

Sarah Blaffer Hrdy's crucial research on alloparenting finds that human evolution benefitted from children growing up in societies where they relied on several caregivers in the community: we developed different skills and formed bonds with a variety of people. We didn't rely solely on the extreme efforts and finite resources of one woman. Marcus, the lead child character in the movie *About a Boy*, is the only child of a mother suffering from depression and comes to an epiphany at the end of the movie:

> 'Suddenly I realised – two people isn't enough. You need backup. If you're only two people, and

someone drops off the edge, then you're on your own. Two isn't a large enough number.'

We know that mothers are happiest when they have a paid job, regardless of the hours. We know that fathers' care is important for children's outcomes. We also know that outcomes for disadvantaged children are better when they attend nursery. These are facts. Every £1 spent investing in early years education saves £13 in later interventions.

Yet, the childcare system in England is currently in tatters. The OECD found in 2021 that the UK had the third highest cost of childcare in the world. Research by the Institute of Fiscal Studies and the Sutton Trust found that at ages three and four, poorer children are, in essence, locked out of early education because their parents can't afford it. In 2023, the Guardian newspaper analysed 18,000 childcare providers and reported that more than a third of nurseries run by not-for-profit organisations have closed, affecting the most disadvantaged children in England. In the same year, the BBC reported that 1 in 4 mothers are giving up their jobs due to lack of childcare. Charities such as the Fawcett Society and Pregnant Then Screwed campaigned relentlessly throughout the pandemic, asking the government to invest in the care of our children in the same way they invest in the care of our roads and buildings. The UK's childcare system currently relies on the goodwill, sweat and tears of exhausted mothers and underpaid childcare workers who do it for the love of their job – but really should be doing it for a decent living wage.

The quality, availability and affordability of childcare provision is key to all of this. The World Economic Forum finds providing quality and cost-effective childcare is not only good for women and families but is good for economies too. If other countries such as Germany, Sweden, and

Iceland can provide comprehensive, good-quality childcare, surely we can do so in the UK?

The province of Quebec in Canada is sometimes used as a benchmark example of universal childcare. Quebec introduced a childcare system in 1997 that gained international recognition as it resulted in a record 85% of Quebecois women aged 26–44 in the labour force with no net cost to the taxpayer due to the increased tax revenues of more women in work. This is crucial data. Childcare is an investment, not a cost. In 2019, PricewaterhouseCoopers found that for every dollar invested in childcare in Australia, 2 dollars were added back to the economy. The whole thing is a no-brainer. Childcare provision not only equals economic growth but, happy mums = happy families = happy societies.

Parental leave

Now, just because we want help with childcare, that doesn't mean we are ready to pop out the baby, pat our hair and scoot back to work the next day. We also need a chance to catch our breath. Not only are there a variety of physical symptoms which mothers need to recover from – tearing, trauma, stitches, mastitis… I won't go on as it makes me wince and cross my legs, but 1 in 5 women struggle with mental health either during pregnancy or for up to a year after birth. In 2023, it was widely reported that women's lives are being put at risk due to substandard postnatal care as 65% of maternity services in England were rated as 'inadequate or requiring improved safety.'

One of the working mums I interviewed for my thesis said she can pinpoint the event that created most of the gender dynamics in her marriage. It all started the night she had her first baby; her husband was kicked out of the hospital to go home and rest, and she became the default carer. I relate to this all too well – bedbound with a baby on my boob and hooked up to a catheter that first night after giving birth, I felt not only emotionally abandoned but like I was being milked from both ends. I needed help from the person who loved our baby as much as me, and he was at home in bed snoring. By contrast, my sister had her first baby a year later in Canada and there, the hospital had a separate bed in the same room for dad who was able to get up and attend baby during the night while mum slept and recovered from labour. How civilised does that sound?

Throughout different cultures and history, women lying in after childbirth – a period of bedrest varying between 2 weeks to 2 months where they were attended to – was commonplace. When giving birth in the UK in the 1940s, my grandmother had 2 weeks lying in at a nursing facility. Now, British mothers are regularly expected to mop up our bits, manage the loo without ripping our stitches and be on our way 4 to 6 *hours* after delivery. New mothers in the UK have the shortest hospital stays of any other high-income country.

There are very few countries that do this well. I might be making Canada sound like some kind of utopia but as my friends there will testify, it isn't always. Healthcare is two-tiered (those who can pay and those who can't) and provision is variable between provinces. Few countries comprehensively provide the support that mums desperately need, but some are doing substantially better than others. It is a matter of public and political will to get this right. Interestingly, nearly all nations in the OECD are doing better than the United States which is the only wealthy country in the world to not provide any programme of national paid parental leave.

A direct link has been made between government policies supporting paternal leave and greater gender equality. Substantial government-funded maternity leave is essential in supporting women's physical recovery from childbirth, but so is paid paternity leave for fathers to establish roles and responsibilities in the early days of children's lives. These early bonds children form with both primary caregivers are essential for their well-being, and the dynamics that are established have long-lasting implications for women's roles at home and at work.

In 2020, Finland's female-led government implemented equal shared parental leave for men and women at 7 months each. In the UK, the Women's Equality Party has fully costed a proposal for an equal system of shared parental leave for up to 9 months at 90% of pay. It would guarantee each parent 3 months away from work with an additional 3 months which could be split however the couple decided. Wouldn't *that* be nice?

Flexible working

A 2019 report by UNICEF found that the UK ranks as one of the worst nations in the OECD for family-friendly policies. After being fired from her job when she was 4 months pregnant, with bills to pay and limited hope of getting another job, Joeli Brearley was inspired to start campaigning not only for better protections for working mothers during pregnancy but for greater support around affordable childcare, paid parental leave and flexible working. The charity she started is called Pregnant Then Screwed. Since 2015, she has done a phenomenal job of increasing awareness around these issues. In 2021, more than 100,000 parents signed a petition asking the government to look at an independent review into childcare, and on Halloween 2022 more than 12,000 parents took to the streets in a fancy dress March of the Mummies to demand reform. Unfortunately, in a post-pandemic era where money is tight, we are still facing an uphill battle to convince the government that this investment in women and children is not only necessary but will pay dividends. A survey by Pregnant Then Screwed in March 2024 found that despite the government providing some increased funding for 2, 3 and 4-year-olds, it was not enough, as 1 in 5 parents were still considering leaving their job or reducing their hours as they could not afford childcare.

The COVID-19 pandemic has been a double-edged sword for many women as it has meant that they left the workforce in greater numbers but also that many employers have opened their eyes to the possibility of flexible working. However, dads are discriminated against more than mums when they ask for flexible working and this needs to change. We know that both mothers and fathers reap well-being benefits from flexible working. The difficulty when it is primarily women who ask for flexible working is that we will continue to see women losing out at work and men losing out at home.

Home-working also comes with its own challenges. One is the time bleed. Another is physical space to do the work. Kitchen table, anyone? While the kids are marauding and asking, 'When's dinner ready?' Many working mums I interviewed talked about this catch-22. One shared a story about her husband who worked in an office while she worked from home. She said it would never occur to him in a month of Sundays to take a day off work if the children were ill. When her little boy had chicken pox and was 'literally sucker-attached' to her, she said her husband was sympathetic and asked, 'How are you going to manage?' but still left for work. Another mum who worked from home asked her husband if he would consider dropping a day at work to help her catch up and he just laughed. If flexible and home-working arrangements are not shared equally between partners, there is a danger of entrenching gender stereotypes.

Online regulation

In May 2024, Meta announced its new advisory council for Artificial Intelligence (AI) consisting of all White males. As a female friend who works in the technology sector remarked, 'There isn't a face-palm button big enough.' Women make up about 27% of the tech workforce and we are sorely under-represented at senior level. The impact of AI in the next 10 years will be profound and multifaceted, affecting everything from daily life to global economic structures. The future is unknown, but what is certain is that a greater diversity of representation is essential if we are to make it a success. It is a well-known glitch that AI learns about existing gender and racial disparities depending on the data it is fed, and can promulgate them further. Imagine what the future would look like if Meta's AI board were made up only of mothers?

Of course, whenever new technology comes along, there is much hand-wringing over the impacts: from Gutenberg's printing press in the 1500s to televisions in the 1950s. But are we just getting our knickers in a knot? In the 1980s, my parents told me I would go square-eyed if I watched too much television. Fast forward and my eyes are still spherical but I'm ashamed to say everyone in my family is now firmly addicted to their phone. A 2019 American study found that people check their phones every 10 minutes and that we are so reluctant to prise them from our sweaty grip that that 75% of us bring them to the bathroom. High phone use is associated with greater risk of stress and depression. It affects sleep, exacerbates social comparison and can increase feelings of loneliness. Social media and violent pornography are especially pernicious for women's happiness. Technology is *designed* to be addictive and millions of us are now ensnared.

This is not to say that all technology is bad; it just needs to be regulated. I'm an information enthusiast and love that so much more is at my fingertips now than when I was a child and had to look things up in the Encyclopaedia Britannica (yes, I am that old). The Me Too movement of 2017 used social media with brilliant effect. It captured the public's attention and made a significant contribution to fourth-wave feminism. However, there's a dark, unregulated underbelly to both the internet and AI that government legislation simply hasn't kept pace with. The current terrain is akin to the Wild West. TikTok algorithms inundate us with a variety of disturbing content ranging from the marketing of anti-ageing skin creams to tweens to frighteningly accessible images of self-harm and suicide.

One prominent campaigner on the issue of online regulation is Ian Russell, whose daughter Molly died after being influenced by self-harm content on social media. The heartbreaking inquest into Molly's death found that social media platforms were using algorithms which repeatedly fed Molly bleak and disturbing images, some of which were provided without Molly requesting them. The content romanticised self-harm and discouraged discussion about problems with people who could help.

After years of campaigning in the UK, an online safety bill was finally passed in October 2023. This bill tasks technology companies with protecting both children and adults from online harms including removing illegal content (including messages promoting self-harm), using age-checking measures and providing clearer ways to report problems online. It's a start, but campaigners agree it's not nearly enough and much more needs to be done. Campaigners want to see stricter enforcement, greater algorithm transparency, improved content moderation, education initiatives and support for victims. It is the minimum we should ask from these enormously powerful global companies who rake in billions and pay little tax.

As well as supporting legislation to promote online safety, things we can do at home and in our communities include:

- Have a policy among your friends not to give your children phones until they go to high school. Some campaigners are pushing for children to not have access to smartphones until they are 16 (analogue phones only until then). Question school policies that allow phones in class.
- No phones in bedrooms. At least charge them outside the bedroom overnight. Take week-long digital detox holidays. Put timers on your social media apps. Talk about sex at the dinner table instead and take shame off the agenda.
- Be aware that your phone and Alexa-type devices are listening to you all the time. I didn't used to mind this – if I wanted to buy something, like a party dress or a new hairbrush, I would just talk about it and wait for an advert to pop up on my social media account. Handy! Except that we know being listened to is actually creepy and we wouldn't put up with it in any other sphere of our lives. Yet we plug Alexa in and treat her like one of the family. At the bare minimum, we need to be aware of the data big tech are collecting about us. For instance, the legal ramifications of period tracking apps are a growing concern for women in the USA in an era where abortion rights are being rolled back.

- Actively curate your social media feed so it feeds you joy and not anxiety. Consider how much exposure you have to alternative viewpoints or whether you are living in an echo chamber. We must talk, talk, talk but also listen, listen, listen.

Polarisation is on the rise globally and is particularly affecting the younger generations. There is a significant gap in the number of young women who describe themselves as liberal versus young men who describe themselves as conservative. Media fragmentation plays a crucial role in this; from politically biased news channels to social media consumption where there is an increasing split between male and female online spaces. This affects our happiness and the connection we experience in relationships. Economic disparities additionally contribute to polarisation. As wealth and income gaps widen, so too do the experiences and worldviews of different socioeconomic groups. This can lead to resentment and a sense of injustice. Education and socio-economic status has a role to play here with young, uneducated men feeling a loss of status and power in the world.

There are undoubtedly nefarious actors who use polarisation for political gain. However, my own observation is that there has recently been a small but growing cultural movement in how people are obtaining their information. An observable post-pandemic trend (as well as daily walks and a new family Cockapoo) is a significant increase in podcast consumption. In particular, long-form podcasts which have the opportunity to give considered thought to more than one angle of a debate. Two popular ones are: *The Rest is Politics* and *A Muslim and a Jew Go There*. I believe that many of us *want* to listen to reasoned conversation rather than rant-ridden sound bites. It's the relief of eating an apple after 3 days of eating

McDonalds. We *want* connection rather than division. There is hope in this.

Make some waves

Let's get political! Change happens through politics and campaigning. If you doubt your ability to make an impact, remember what Bodyshop founder Anita Roddick said about mosquitos: 'If you ever think you are too small to make a difference, try going to sleep with a mosquito in the room.'

At the Vancouver Peace Conference in 2009, the Dalai Lama claimed that the world would be saved by Western women. In 2019, former US President Barack Obama said that he was '… confident that for 2 years if every nation on earth was run by women, you would see a significant improvement across the board on just about everything… living standards and outcomes.' Obama said that in his experience, most of the world's problems came from old people, mostly men, holding onto positions of power.

Worldwide, women only hold 26% of seats in government. A 2022 meta-analysis report by Kings College London found that women who hold political positions of power tend to prioritise issues that benefit the vulnerable in society, work harder than men, on average, to represent their constituencies, counteract corruption and are less likely to go to war or commit human rights abuses.

So, think seriously about standing as a Member of Parliament. See 50:50 Parliament or the campaign MotheRED which supports mothers to stand for Parliament. But if you're exhausted and haven't slept straight through since you can remember – due to breastfeeding, stress, menopause, et cetera – then support other politicians or campaigners. At a minimum, we can vote, even if it is only a crappy piece of paper in a primary school classroom. We can also vote with our social media likes for campaigns like Anna Whitehouse's Flex Appeal (aka Mother Pukka) or Smartphone Free Childhood. Vote in favour of those who support the issues affecting working mothers' well-being: childcare reform, paid parental leave, flexible working and online regulation.

Individual solutions

When I was pregnant, I wanted to have boys rather than girls – don't tell them! I was worried about the responsibility that would fall on me as a female role model when I had no idea myself what the right life answers were. People also kept telling me – unhelpfully – that boys were easy-going, and girls were high-maintenance. With the wisdom of experience, I would now firmly diagnose high-maintenance situations as induced by society rather than invented by girls. I guess I thought when boys were born that the sky was the limit – their trajectory was upward to success. For girls, the path seemed to be more about navigating choices and making trade-offs. This felt like a minefield I was ill-equipped to deal with and although I didn't have the words for it at the time, I simply sensed that mothering girls was complicated. *How would I know what to tell them?*

Having subsequently conducted both extensive academic research and intensive soul-searching on this subject, I have summarised some suggestions below. Whilst we can support government policies and media campaigns, we cannot personally fix society overnight. Sometimes we need to just do an Elsa from Frozen and *Let it Go*! When we can't control the *outside*, we must work with what we can affect and control the *inside*. So, what can we do as individuals, today, to help ourselves?

Well, in addition to the well-being behaviours outlined in Chapter 3 under the acronym GREAT DREAM, I have made my own suggestions here specifically for working mothers. My mnemonic is **EMPOWER LIFE**.

- **E**XPECT LESS – from yourself.
- **M**ORE – ask for more from others.
- **P**ORTFOLIO careers – consider having one.
- **O**PTIMISE your time.
- **W**ORK culture – challenge greedy jobs.
- **E**QUALITY – call sexism out!
- **R**EJECT the guilt.

- **L**IMITS – boundary setting.
- **I**NTEGRATE – with your tribe.
- **F**OCUS – on *you*.
- **E**MPOWER – other women.

I'll take each in turn.

Expect less – from yourself

As Voltaire tells us, 'Perfect is the enemy of good.' I outlined Mo Gawdat's work in Chapter 1 which explains just how important expectations are to happiness. When we set ourselves up with the belief that we can *be* and *do* everything, we are inevitably disappointed. Perfection doesn't exist, and chasing it is a significant reason many of us don't feel content. Women get bamboozled by all the demands – good mother, good worker, good partner, good friend, good neighbour, good homemaker, good-looking – and think we need to achicve in *every* sphere. We don't. We can't. And we need to get better at understanding ourselves and what good looks like for us, and us alone. Put your blinkers *on* and turn Instagram *off*.

Self-compassion is a vital component of well-being, and if we are compassionate towards ourselves, research shows that our children will learn from our behaviour. Parenting guru Dr Becky Kennedy counsels that it's important for our children's development to see their parents prioritising their own care. So take a bubble bath, do some exercise, listen to some music, make time for that art class or simply take a nap. At a minimum, we need to start being proud of having a dusty house or competent children who clean and cook and don't treat their parents like household help. I have a magnet on my fridge that says, 'You can touch the dust, but please don't write in it.' Perfect homemaker definitely needs to be taken off the list!

Ask for MORE – from others

We need more. From the government, from our bosses and from our partners. Actually, I don't mean ask. I mean *demand*. Firmly. Not sweetly. Channel your inner suffragette. More flexibility at work, more help at home. The new sexual contract society has drawn up for us is nearly as rubbish as the old one was and it's time we rewrote the terms and conditions. If shouting is not your style, take inspiration from Meryl Streep who said: 'It is amazing how much you can get if you quietly, authoritatively and clearly demand it.'

Another way to ask for more is just by doing less. Drop some balls. Stop the juggling. It is amazing how dynamics shift when we stop being the pivot around which everyone turns. We think the world will stop and that we are indispensable, but that's just our ego. As a wise boss of mine once said to me in my early 20s, 'We are more replaceable than we think.' He was trying to encourage me to delegate rather than to get rid of me – I think!! He said the sign of a good manager is when you have taught everyone their roles so well that things run smoothly without you.

Gandhi also imparts wisdom here when he talks about us being the change we want to see in the world. Change *does* start with us changing our own behaviour. Gandhi's words:

'As a man changes his own nature, so does the attitude of the world change towards him. This is the divine mystery supreme. A wonderful thing it is and the source of our happiness. We need not wait to see what others do.'

Gandhi mentions men but, of course, this philosophy applies to women too. And to laundry. However, I am not sure it was women and laundry that Gandhi had in mind with this particular quote! For instance, if a working mum always does the laundry, she somehow becomes the default laundry person. But what if she just stopped? What would happen when the other members of the household figured out they were out of underwear?

Portfolio careers - consider having one

Second-wave feminist Betty Friedan contends that 'Women *can* have it all, just not at the same time.' Our campaign for change won't happen overnight. For many women, their current juggle is simply impossible. So treat your career like a jungle gym and not a ladder. Do things in different stages and don't be pressured to lean in more when you can't cope. Women live longer than men! We have more time. A few years out of work when the kids are little or when they become grumpy teenagers? Pah! We'll fit it in later! Life is long and has many phases. There is no right or wrong, only a right or wrong for each one of us in the *now*. We should all consider having a portfolio career made up of a lifetime of different interests. There is absolutely a benefit to doing things in bite-sized chunks rather than all at once.

Optimise your time

Don't get me wrong. I am also sick of women being patronised about time management skills: if only we could juggle better! This is not what I mean as I have complete empathy with all the mums who dream about quitting their job and moving to a desert island. I'm not going to smugly talk you through the classic Eisenhower Matrix which advises you to improve your time management skills by dividing all your tasks into four quadrants according to their urgency and importance. Not only does that not reduce the number of overall tasks on our lists – note the plural *lists*, it's never just one – but it doesn't help with the persistent pester power of the tasks our children deem to be both important *and* urgent: 'Mum, mum, mum, mum, muuuuuuum!'

Instead, I will share a tip from happiness researcher Professor Cassie Holmes who suggests in her book *Happier Hour* that we should at least understand where our time goes so we can prioritise the tasks we like the best, and ideally delegate several of the others! Cassie suggests logging your schedule for a while and noting not only how long you spend on various tasks, but more importantly, how happy these tasks make you.

- Which tasks do you want to do yourself and which do you want to give to other people? Do you prefer feeding the dog or looking after the mail?
- What can you stop doing? For instance, does that third Netflix episode you binge on until midnight make you as happy as the first?

- And most importantly, what can you start doing more of, that you know gives you pleasure? Even if you have to multitask, like taking a hot bath while doing the online grocery order!

One of the dynamics that many women encounter in their relationships is that if one partner earns more than the other, the higher earner may feel more entitled to free time than the person with the lower income. It is common for women who earn less to feel compelled to compensate by taking on more total labour, particularly as society still considers the domestic and emotional labour to be on us. The book *Fair Play* by Eve Rodsky is an illuminating read which addresses this dilemma. Eve asserts that regardless of income earned, each person in a couple is deserving of the same amount of *discretionary time*. She counsels couples to forget about who earns more money and to focus on the idea that they are a team, and both deserve similar rest breaks. She has a card game that goes with her book which is a system for dealing out the domestic load in a more even-handed way. Couples agree on who is fully responsible (including the emotional load) for which household chores. Cards can be swapped and changed – and everything doesn't necessarily have to be even; it just needs to be mutually agreed. It is rather brilliant as she also teases out the mental and emotional labour involved in caregiving and homemaking and attempts to put strategies in place to ensure couples work as a team and can be flexible in changing circumstances. One of you may be earning less currently, but that doesn't mean it will always be that way. The card game gets rave reviews: the idea is to give each partner a sense of agency and to cut back completely on the nagging – which, of course, is the best incentive to play!

Work culture – challenge greedy jobs

Economist and Nobel Prize winner Claudia Goldin says that a significant issue for women's equality at work is greedy jobs which reward an always-on culture: time-hungry jobs in politics, law (billable hours), accounting, finance and the media. Changing these cultures is especially effective from the top down. For instance, a woman I interviewed for my research, the founder of an accountancy practice with 26 staff, said she was enormously proud of the support she gave her female staff; she called herself a *female first* company. She went out of her way to support women with both paid maternity leave and flexible working, and said the company culture paid her back in dividends not only because she was proud of the atmosphere she had created at work but because she had virtually no staff turnover. No burnout! Imagine?!

Since 2014, all UK employees have a right to request flexible working. So make sure you ask. Work-culture change happens when all employees start to demand the same thing. There is power in numbers. Our partners must do this too, so we aren't beholden to their work hours as well as our own. Culture will take time to shift in male-dominated industries, but it is possible. If construction workers start the working day at 7 am then it should be feasible to finish at 3 pm – just in time for the school run!

Equality – call out sexism

To get to equality faster, nip sexism in the bud every time you see it. The big stuff and the little stuff. Because multiple small cuts lead to one big bleedout, and frankly, we're sick of the bleeding. Risk getting called a snowflake who can't take a joke. It is time we stopped feeling uncomfortable on the inside and showed our discomfort on the outside. If no one reacts to what we are saying, we probably aren't saying it loud enough. As 20th-century activist Rosa Luxemburg said: 'The most revolutionary thing one can do is always to proclaim loudly what is happening.' Don't do what I did: stop giving my opinion for years because someone didn't like what I had to say about bacon. Your voice matters, and women are half of the population. Therefore, we need at least half of the money, power and means to make decisions about things that affect our lives. We need to spread the word – share this book!

Practise equality at home. Encourage your daughters to feel comfortable using their voices and your sons to feel comfortable using their hearts. Challenge harmful stereotypes and unrealistic portrayals of sex that proliferate online, particularly in violent or misogynistic pornography. In this digital age, we need to be savvy about polarisation, the information we consume and where it comes from. It is also vital to listen to other people's opinions, as we can only get to equality when everyone is on board. We all need to be understood. As podcaster Elizabeth Day often says, 'Only connect.'

Reject the guilt

Glorifying maternal sacrifice is baked into a mother's job description. Society does this. We aren't making it up. But we do have a choice in how we react to the input.

One thing I found helpful in letting myself off the hook about working mothers' guilt was finding out that women are happier if they have a paid job. Varied interests and activities are good for us. It's that simple. We need to stop feeling bad. If you need permission, I am giving it to you here. Work makes women happy, both day-to-day and because of increased gender equity. Happy mum = happy family.

I also implore you to please just be kind to yourself. Turn off the 'I'm not worthy' voice that invades the psyche of so many of us. Speak to yourself in the same kind and compassionate voice you use to let your children know you love them and that it's all going to be OK. Make this your first priority. You deserve it.

Limits and boundary setting

Alongside self-compassion and rejecting working mothers' guilt, there may also be times when you have to practise getting comfortable sitting with some guilty feelings in order to set healthy boundaries with others. As mothers, it is easy for our edges to become blurred. This has taken me many years to understand, and for me is still a work in progress. The advice here is to embrace the guilty feeling we get from saying no instead of accepting the slow-burning resentment of always saying yes.

The resentment which builds from self-abandonment and failing to assert our needs harms us deeply. It damages not only our relationships with others but significantly our most important relationship: the one we have with ourselves. For happiness, I recommend developing a habit of quick and firm boundary-setting. Rip off the plaster and get used to the discomfort that comes with it. Kindness and politeness absolutely! I'd like to sign all of humanity up to those habits. However, the behaviours so many women are trained in – to prioritise the needs of others, to seek approval, avoid conflict, take on extra work, smile, placate, accommodate and acquiesce – have consequences not only for our position in society but for our mental and physical health. We can only come last in the queue so many times without ending up hungry or starving.

Many women naturally break up with their good-girl persona in mid-life as years of being taken for granted in their households and menopause rage come to a head. There is a reason for the hugely popular Facebook group profanely titled *Gen X Women Are Sick of Your Shit*! However, some women serve all their lives in the good-girl trenches, as for many, self-worth is bound up in it. I am here to tell you that your right to love and worth is *not* conditional on forsaking yourself for the needs of others. We need to retrain our own thinking on this and nurture our daughters away from the trap.

If you are a chronic people-pleaser who strongly identifies with good-girl behaviours, a simple way to start choosing yourself again is to actively acknowledge and give yourself a pat on the back each time you say no. Celebrate being able to tolerate the pangs of guilt from *no*, rather than accepting the poisonous creep of resentment which comes from too many yeses.

Integrate with your tribe

Find your people. They are out there. As author and academic Professor Brené Brown explains in her research, the concept of fitting in is actually the opposite of belonging. She says that fitting in is assessing a group of people and thinking: 'Who do I need to be, what do I need to say, what do I need to wear and how do I need to act?' Spider-Man and Peter Parker have nothing on the gymnastics moves and outfit changes performed by working mothers. By day we don our work suits, by evening smart-casual and by weekend we've slipped into sports gear – or in my case joggers with no bra. We spend even longer on the emotional contortions of decoding acceptable behaviours either in the workplace, down the pub with a bunch of guys or in an antenatal class with a group of expectant mums who you are hoping will be your new best friends.

Brené says that true belonging never asks us to change who we are. Spend time figuring out who you are, and which tribe (or tribes) feel good to you. When we find our people, they lift us up.

Focus – on YOU

We cannot be all things to all people, and we can't be anything to anyone unless we put our own oxygen masks on first. Focusing on yourself is partly about self-care, but it is also about understanding yourself better and living life in an intentional way which aligns with your values and passions.

In her book *Real Self-Care*, Dr Pooja Lakshmin challenges the superficial nature of the traditional self-care market. She encourages women to dig deeper, and carve out their own creative spaces, and she emphasises how essential it is for women's physical and mental well-being to connect with our core inner values and purpose.

A few years ago, a therapist asked me what should have been a relatively simple question: 'What do you enjoy doing?' It astounded me that I couldn't name one activity in my week that I truly enjoyed. It was easy to list the innumerable ways I spent my time, but I couldn't think of anything I actively did to prioritise myself, let alone anything which spoke to my soul. It made me sit up and think about how I had been dragged down a rabbit hole of serving others at the expense of serving myself. Writing this book has been one way of honouring a deeper and more creative part of myself.

What do you enjoy doing? When was the last time you did it?

Empower other women

We are stronger together. Consider working in a career that helps women or encourage your daughters and sons to do so. This could be anything from a charity which supports survivors of domestic abuse and violence, to mentoring women in your workplace to help them succeed. Remember Melinda Gates' advice which was that to move the needle on gender equality, we need more women in technology, finance, media and politics.

You might also advise your daughter to become a doctor or a health researcher and work towards closing the UK's gender health gap – the highest in the G20 and the 12th largest globally. Women spend up to 25% more of our lives sicker than men; let's support efforts to help men live longer and for women to live better.

American diplomat Madeleine Albright once said, 'There is a special place in hell for women who don't support other women.' I used to think that it wasn't harder for women and that I just needed to get on with it and put my big-girl panties on. But life *is* a competition and it turns out that it is genuinely harder for women, especially working mothers. There is a brilliant depiction by Peruvian cartoonist Carlin that does the rounds on social media showing men and women in business suits at the starting line on a running track. The women are in high heels and skirts and have a variety of hurdles in front of them to vault over before they start the race, including a washing line of laundry, an ironing board, an oven et cetera. The men's way is clear.

Therefore, we cannot have women against women – we must support each other to make progress. Chimamanda Ngozi Adichie says that we should all be feminists, and I say we should all be intersectional feminists; aware of promoting gender equality for the sake of all women, particularly when it comes to ethnicity, class, sexuality and ability. Our voices are magnified when we use them to support those with less privilege than ourselves.[74]

We need to learn about other women's stories. Read books and watch movies about women's journeys. Please see the reading recommendations in the back of this book. Don't give up the fight for equality.

The solution: in a nutshell

- Yes, tell your daughter to become a doctor! But insist on substantially better terms and conditions than the woeful ones we currently have.
- Happiness stems from equality. Feminism has taken us a long way in a short space of evolutionary time. However, we still have enormous work to do.
- To improve the well-being of working mothers for the betterment of all of society, in particular the next generation, we need societal change. Governments can help through better policies regarding flexible working, childcare, parental leave provision and online regulation. We can play our part by actively campaigning ourselves or by supporting the campaigns of others.
- When we can't change society overnight, we can look inward to what we can do as individuals to help ourselves feel happier. Consider the GREAT DREAM happiness behaviours in Chapter 3 or choose one or two ideas which speak to you from the EMPOWER LIFE list for working mothers. The ripple effect comes from us all

---

[74] The term intersectional feminism was coined by American researcher Kimberlé Crenshaw during feminism's third wave around the 1990s. Crenshaw used the analogy of a car crashing at an intersection to describe how the intersecting variables of gender and race compound problems of discrimination. Intersectional feminism encourages the recognition of intersecting forms of oppression, it promotes diversity within feminism and builds solidarity and co-operation across movements.

doing one small thing consistently. What action will you take to make yourself happier this week? **E**xpect less from yourself, ask for **M**ore from others, consider a **P**ortfolio career, **O**ptimise your time, challenge greedy **W**ork culture, insist on **E**quality and call sexism out, **R**esist working mothers' guilt, set **L**imits and boundaries, **I**ntegrate with your tribe, **F**ocus on yourself or work to **E**mpower other women.

- We are always stronger together. In the words of mother and Member of Parliament Jo Cox, who was murdered at work in 2016 and cruelly taken far too soon from her two young children, 'We have more in common than that which divides us.' Jo's legacy reminds us that life is short and none of us knows what is around the corner. We must seize the day, stand up for ourselves and for each other to ensure we make the future a happier and more equitable one for all.

Epilogue

In 1912, in response to debates around the divided loyalty that mothers felt around their caregiving duties, the *Freewoman* periodical claimed:

'To whom is her first duty, herself or the coming generation? We hold, that her first, second, and third duty is to herself, and, that duty being fulfilled, she will have done her duty to the coming generation.'

This was a pretty radical thing to say at that time. I hope after reading this book that you don't think it is quite as radical now. It takes a village to raise a child and with the right social structures in place, it is perfectly possible to live in a society where mothers can work for pay, parent well and *have it all* in the same way as fathers do. This must be our collective goal; for the sake of our happiness and that of our children.

Acknowledgements

Thank you to the many friends and family who have tolerated my rather obsessive behaviour over the last number of years whilst I have been on a quest to reel in, gut and finally digest the fish that has been this infuriating topic. It is amazing what a deep dive into the statistics on this subject will do to your sense of injustice and your compulsion to share what you have learned – at length and in-depth – with anyone who is unfortunate enough to be within earshot. Those who know me best got the brunt of this listening exercise not only during the 5 years I was ploughing through my PhD, but also during the year it took me to write this book afterwards.

First, thank you to my supportive and ever-patient husband Adam, who has a wonderful ability to listen with an open ear – even when he doesn't agree with me – for which I am eternally grateful. Thank you also to my mother, Margaret Wrigley, for her love and support, and for instilling in me from a young age the confidence to keep asking questions until I figured out the answer. Finally, thank you to my late father, David Wrigley, who had the same depth of patience as my husband and who showed an abundance of love for his family in the small and large actions he purposefully took to connect with us and care for us. It is men like these who change the world.

Also, a sincere thanks to all the wonderful women and men who gave freely of their time to be interviewed for my PhD and who provided their first-hand experience on the subject of women, work and well-being. The interviewees responded with wonderful insight to my inquisitive and possibly, at times, intrusive questions! And thanks to the friends and colleagues with whom I have had detailed conversations over the years about this subject, most especially my PhD supervisor Dr Carol Ekinsmyth. I would never have completed this project without her support, nor without her offering the initial impetus and opportunity.

A special thanks to those who provided feedback on early copies of this book: Arfana Ali, Louise Belshaw, Tracey Brotherton, Florence Collier, Heather Coppard, Jo Egan, Sarah Ellis, Hayley Fellows, Izabelle Grenon, Gemma Holmes, Tom Holmes, Claire Hunter, Bronwyn Johnson, Sue Kelly, Jane Leach, Frauke Mannaert, Deirdre McHugh, Erika Mountain, Sophie O'Sullivan, Tara Poce, Nikki Pope, Natasha Pye, Claire Thomas and Helena Young. Also to Federica Leonardis for proofreading, Jan Worrall for indexing and Becky Glibbery for the cover design.

Finally, an enormous debt of gratitude to my editor Robyn Rae at Simpatico Editing for rescuing me from a hefty dose of first draft self-doubt and for pushing me with the probing questions needed to make this book its best.

Further reading

Feminism books

Invisible Women: Exposing Data Bias in a World Designed for Men. Caroline Criado Perez

Fix the System Not the Women Laura Bates

Everyday Sexism Laura Bates

Hags: The Demonisation of Middle-Aged Women Victoria Smith

Difficult Women: A History of Feminism in 11 Fights Helen Lewis

Women Are Angry: Why Your Rage is Hiding and How to Let it Out Jennifer Cox

Hysterical: Exploding the Myth of Gendered Emotions, Pragya Agarwal

Fed Up: Navigating and redefining emotional labour for good Gemma Hartley

Emotional Labor: The Invisible Work Shaping Our Lives and How to Claim Our Power Rose Hackman

Living Dolls: The Return of Sexism Natasha Walter

The Paula Principle: why women lose out at work- and what needs to be done about it Tom Schuller

The Feminine Mystique Betty Friedan

The Second Sex Simone de Beauvoir

Gender Trouble: Feminism and the Subversion of Identity Judith Butler

Women, Race & Class Angela Y. Davis

It's Not About the Burqa Mariam Khan

Rants of a Rebel Arab Feminist Farida D

More Than a Woman Caitlin Moran

What About Men Caitlin Moran

The Descent of Man Grayson Perry

Why I'm No Longer Talking to White People About Race Reni Eddo-Lodge

Bad Feminist Roxane Gay

Ain't I A Woman: Black Women and Feminism bell hooks

Wonder Women: Sex, Power and the Quest for Perfection Debora L. Spar

Women and Power: A Manifesto, Mary Beard

Testosterone Rex: Unmaking the Myths of Our Gendered Minds Cordelia Fine

Testosterone: The Story of the Hormone that Dominates and Divides Us Carole Hooven

Backlash: The Undeclared War Against American Women Susan Faludi

I Feel Bad About My Neck And Other Thoughts on Being a Woman Nora Ephron

Revolting Prostitutes: The Fight for Sex Workers' Rights Juno Mac and Molly Smith

Women on Porn: One Hundred Stories, One Vital Conversation, Fiona Vera-Gray

Inferior: How Science Got Women Wrong – and the New Research That's Rewriting the Story Angela Saini

The Power of Women: Why Gender Equality Works for Everyone June Sarpong

Letter to My Daughter Maya Angelou

Normal Women: 900 Years of Making History Philippa Gregory

Happiness books

10 Keys to Happier Living: A Practical Handbook for Happiness Vanessa King

Be Bad, Better: How Not Trying So Hard Will Set You Free Rebecca Seal

Happier Hour: How to Spend Your Time for a Better, More Meaningful Life Cassie Holmes

Beyond Happy: Women, Work and Well-Being Beth Cabrera

The Five Side Effects of Kindness: This Book Will Make You Feel Better, Be Happier & Live Longer David R. Hamilton

Solve for Happy: Engineer Your Path to Joy Mo Gawdat

The Happiness Project: Or, Why I Spent a Year Trying to Sing in the Morning, Clean My Closets, Fight Right, Read Aristotle, and Generally Have More Fun Gretchen Rubin

The How of Happiness: A New Approach to Getting the Life You Want Sonja Lyubomirsky

Authentic Happiness: Using the New Positive Psychology to Realise Your Potential for Lasting Fulfilment Martin E.P. Seligman

Happy Ever After: Escaping the Myths of the Perfect Life, Paul Dolan

The Good Life: Lessons from the World's Longest Scientific Study of Happiness Robert Waldinger and Marc Schulz

Flow: The Psychology of Happiness Mihaly Csikszentmihalyi

Born to Be Good: The Science of a Meaningful Life, Dacher Keltner

The Art of Rest: How to Find Respite in the Modern Age Claudia Hammond

Untamed: Stop Pleasing, Start Living Glennon Doyle

Blue Zones of Happiness: Lessons from the World's Happiest People Dan Buettner

You Are Enough: Embrace your Flaws and Be Happy Being You Cheryl Rickman

The Year of Living Danishly: Uncovering the Secrets of the World's Happiest Country Helen Russell

Motherhood books

The Motherhood Penalty: How to Stop Motherhood Being the Kiss of Death for Your Career Joeli Brearley

Overwhelmed: How to Work, Love and Play When No One Has the Time Brigid Schulte

Heading Home: Motherhood, Work and the Failed Promise of Equality Shani Orgad

Drop the Ball: Expect Less From Yourself, Get More From Him and Flourish in Work and Life Tiffany Dufu

Fair Play: Share the mental load, rebalance your relationship and transform your life Eve Rodsky

Half a Wife: The Working Family's Guide to Getting a Life Back Gaby Hinsliff

The Motherhood Complex: The story of our changing selves Melissa Hogenboom

(M)otherhood: On the choices of being a woman Pragya Agarwal

Raising a Happier Mother: How to Find Balance, Feel Good and See Your Children Flourish as a Result Anna Mathur

Forget 'Having it All': How America Messed Up Motherhood – and How To Fix It. Amy Westervelt.

Motherhood: Feminism's Unfinished Business Eliane Glaser

Double Lives: The History of Working Motherhood Helen McCarthy

Matrescence: On the Metamorphosis of Pregnancy, Childbirth and Motherhood Lucy Jones

I Am Not Your Baby Mother: What it's like to be a black British mother Candice Brathwaite

Dad: Untold Stories of Fatherhood, Love, Mental Health and Masculinity Elliott Rae

The Life of Dad: The Making of a Modern Father Anna Machin

Notes on References

Chapter 1

Child marriage, female genital mutilation and girls' education:

UNICEF. (2024). *Female Genital Mutilation.*
https://data.unicef.org/topic/child-protection/female-genital-mutilation/

UNICEF. (2023). *Is an End to Child Marriage Within Reach?*
https://data.unicef.org/resources/is-an-end-to-child-marriage-within-reach/

UNICEF. (2024). *Girls' Education: Gender Equality in Education Benefits Every Child.* https://www.unicef.org/education/girls-education

Domestic abuse:

National Centre for Domestic Violence. *Domestic Abuse Statistics, UK.*
https://www.ncdv.org.uk/domestic-abuse-statistics-uk/

Women's Aid. *Domestic Abuse is a Gendered Crime.*
https://www.womensaid.org.uk/information-support/what-is-domestic-abuse/domestic-abuse-is-a-gendered-crime/

Refuge. *What is Domestic Abuse? Facts and Statistics.*
https://refuge.org.uk/what-is-domestic-abuse/the-facts/

National Health Service. *Getting Help for Domestic Violence.* NHS Live Well.
www.nhs.uk/live-well/getting-help-for-domestic-violence/

Sexual harassment:

United Nations Women UK. (2021). *Safe Spaces Now.*
https://www.unwomenuk.org/safe-spaces-now/

Gender pay gap:

White, N. (2022, October 26). *Gender Pay Gap in the UK: 2022*. Office for National Statistics.

Demographic data on families:

Vizard, T. (2019, October 24). *Families and the Labour Market, UK: 2019*. Office for National Statistics.

Sharfman, A., Cobb, P. (2023, May 18). *Families and Households in the UK: 2022*. Office for National Statistics.

Percentage of females in the National Health Service workforce:

NHS Digital, Hospital and Community Health Services (HCHS) Workforce Statistics. (2018, September). *Equality and Diversity in NHS Trusts and CCGs in England*. https://www.nhsemployers.org/system/files/2021-06/Gender-in-the-NHS-infographic.pdf

Medical Women's Federation. (2024). *The Voice of Medical Women on Medical Issues Facts and Figures*. https://www.medicalwomensfederation.org.uk/our-work/facts-figures

Fathers' caregiving:

Welsh, J. (2011, September 12). Fatherhood Lowers Testosterone, Keeps Dads at Home. *Scientific American*.

Li, T., Chen, X., Mascaro, J., Haroon, E., & Rilling, J. K. (2017). Intranasal oxytocin, but not vasopressin, augments neural responses to toddlers in human fathers. *Hormones and Behavior*, 93, 193-202.

Davis, M. (2024, January 23). Dad's Involvement Linked to School Success: Study Highlights Impact of Father's Engagement in Children's Lives. *The Science Times*.

Brooks, M. (2014, July 24). In the Brain of the Father: Why Men Can be Just as Good Primary Parents as Women. *The New Statesman*.

Machin, A. (2018). *The Life of Dad: The Making of the Modern Father*. Simon and Schuster.

Herstory:

Harari, Y. N. (2011). *Sapiens: A Brief History of Humankind*. Vintage.

Natalie Portman interview with Professor Yuval Noah Harari. (2021). *International Women's Day*. YouTube. https://www.youtube.com/watch?v=wFisgnYY24o

Pomeroy, S. B. (1975). *Goddesses, Whores, Wives and Slaves: Women in Classical Antiquity*. Schocken Books.

Van De Mieroop, M. (2005). *King Hammurabi of Babylon: A Biography.* Wiley-Blackwell.

Beard, M. (2017). *Women and Power.* Profile Books.

Carlo, M. (2023, May 17). More violence, more equality: What's the current state of LGBTQ+ rights in Europe? *Euronews.*

Gallup. (2023, July 7). *Where do Americans stand on abortion?* Gallup Polling.

Smith, M. (2023, October 12). *Where does the British public stand on abortion in 2023?* YouGov.

Women's new sexual contract:

McRobbie, A. (2007). Top Girls? Young women and the post-feminist sexual contract. *Cultural Studies,* 21(4), 718-737.

British Social Attitudes Survey:

Park, A., Bryson, C., Clery, E., Curtice, J., & Phillips, M. (Eds.) (2013). *British Social Attitudes: The 30th Report.* London: National Centre for Social Research.

Phillips, D., Curtice, J., Phillips, M., & Perry, J. (Eds.) (2018). *British Social Attitudes: The 35th Report.* London: National Centre for Social Research.

Family breadwinners:

Silkin, L. (2021, July 6). *Women in Work: A Brief History of Women in the Workplace.* Future of Work Hub.

Pew Research Center. (2013, May 29). *Breadwinner Moms: Mothers are the sole or primary provider in four in ten households with children; public conflicted about the growing trend.*

Vizard, T. (2019, October 24). *Families and the Labour Market, UK: 2019.* Office for National Statistics.

Cory, G., & Stirling, A. (2015, October 20). *Who's breadwinning in Europe?* Institute for Public Policy Research.

Family and Education. (2011, March 8). The 1970s and 1980s were the 'best time to raise children'. *BBC News.*

Good enough mother:

Winnicott, D. W. (1970). *Playing and Reality.* Tavistock.

Johnston, D., & Swanson, D. (2006). Constructing the 'Good Mother': The Experience of Mothering Ideologies by Work Status. *Sex Roles,* 54 (7-8), 509-519.

Kan, M. Y., Sullivan, O., & Gershuny, J. (2011). Gender Convergence in Domestic Work: Discerning the Effects of Interactional and Institutional Barriers from Large-scale Data. *Sociology,* 45 (2), 234-251.

Alloparenting:

Blaffer Hrdy, S. (2011). *Mothers and Others: The Evolutionary Origins of Mutual Understanding.* Harvard University Press.

Mum guilt:

Bishop, K. (2022, January 25). The Parental Shame That Haunts Working Parents. *BBC News.*

Williams, A. (2014, May 6). *Guilt and the Working Mum.* Working Mums.

Collins, C. (2021). Is Maternal Guilt a Cross-National Experience? *Qualitative Sociology,* 44, 1–29.

Goodwin, G. (2021). *An Exploration of the Eudaimonic Well-being of UK Women Entrepreneurs.* The British Library.

Powell, M. (2019, March 10). Scientists blame working mothers for Britain's childhood obesity epidemic after study of 20,000 families. *Daily Mail.*

Social identity theory:

Tajfel, H. (1982). Social Psychology of Intergroup Relations. *Annual Review of Psychology,* 33 (1), 1-39.

Social comparison theory:

Gerber, J. P., Wheeler, L., & Suls, J. (2018). A social comparison theory meta-analysis 60+ years on. *Psychological Bulletin,* 144 (2), 177–197.

Women's happiness:

Stevenson B., & Wolfers, J. (2009). The Paradox of Declining Female Happiness. *American Economic Journal: Economic Policy,* 1 (2), 190-225.

Plagnol, A.C., & Easterlin, R.A. (2008). Aspirations, Attainments, and Satisfaction: Life Cycle Differences Between American Women and Men. *Journal of Happiness Studies,* 9, 601–619.

Blanchflower, D.G., & Bryson, A. (2024).The female happiness paradox. *Journal of Population Economics,* 37, 16.

DeAngelis, T. (2022). By the numbers: Most women are unhappy with how society treats them. *American Psychological Association,* 53 (2), 88.

Gender equality:

Gawdat, M. (2017). *Solve for Happy: Engineer your path to joy*. Pan Macmillan.

Audette, A.P., Lam, S., O'Connor, H. et al. (2019). Quality of Life: A Cross-National Analysis of the Effect of Gender Equality on Life Satisfaction. *Journal of Happiness Studies*, 20, 2173–2188.

Organization for Economic Co-operation and Development. (2023). *Joining Forces for Gender Equality: What is Holding us Back?* OECD Publishing.

Chapter 2

Society simultaneously fetishises and trivialises motherhood:

Ekinsmyth, C. (2014). Mothers' business, work/life and the politics of mumpreneurship. *Gender, Place and Culture,* 21 (10), 1230-1248.

Obesity and job opportunities:

Van der Zee, R. (2017, August 30). Demoted or dismissed because of your weight? The reality of the size ceiling. *The Guardian.*

Hybrid male/female identities at work:

Lewis, P. (2014). Postfeminism, Femininities and Organization Studies: Exploring a New Agenda. *Organization Studies,* 35 (12), 1845-1866.

Working mothers' stress:

Chandola, T., Booker, C. L., Kumari, M., & Benzeval, M. (2019). Are Flexible Work Arrangements Associated with Lower Levels of Chronic Stress-Related Biomarkers? A Study of 6025 Employees in the UK Household Longitudinal Study. *Sociology*, 53 (4), 779-799.

Bush, M., & Ryder, K. (2020*). Parents at the Best Workplaces: The Largest Ever Study of Working Parents.* Great Place to Work.

McRobbie, A. (2007). Top Girls? Young women and the post-feminist sexual contract. *Cultural Studies,* 21 (4), 718-737.

British Social Attitudes Survey:

Park, A., Bryson, C., Clery, E., Curtice, J., & Phillips, M. (Eds.) (2013). *British Social Attitudes: The 30th Report*. London: National Centre for Social Research.

Phillips, D., Curtice, J., Phillips, M., & Perry, J. (Eds.) (2018). *British Social Attitudes: The 35th Report.* London: National Centre for Social Research.

Gershuny, J., & Kan. M. Y. (2012). Halfway to gender equality in paid and unpaid work? Evidence from the multinational time-use study. In Scott, J. L., Dex, S., & Plagnol, A. C. (Eds.), *Gendered Lives: Gender Inequalities in Production and Reproduction* (pp. 74-94). Edward Elgar Publishing.

Nancy Astor:

UK Parliament. (2024). *Women in the House of Commons.* https://www.parliament.uk/about/living-heritage/transformingsociety/electionsvoting/womenvote/overview/womenincommons/

Dr Dorothy Lavinia Brown:

Hdeib, A., Elder, T., Krivosheya, D., Ojukwu, D. I., Wijesekera, O., Defta, D., Ben-Haim, S., & Benzil, D. L. (2021). History of Women in Neurosurgery (WINS). *Neurosurgical Focus FOC,* 50 (3), E16.

Women and property laws:

UK Parliament. (2024). *Marriage: property and children.* https://www.parliament.uk/about/living-heritage/transformingsociety/private-lives/relationships/overview/propertychildren/

Fertility rate in Japan:

Tsuya, N. (2022, October 27). Why the Japanese don't want to make babies. *Asia Times.*

Working motherhood:

McCarthy, H. (2020). *Double Lives: A History of Working Motherhood.* Bloomsbury.

Gregory, P. (2023). *Normal Women: 900 Years of Women Making History.* William Collins.

Mothers and housework:

Syrda, J. (2023). Gendered Housework: Spousal Relative Income, Parenthood and Traditional Gender Identity Norms. *Work, Employment and Society,* 37 (3), 794-813.

Sex and housework:

Johnson, M. D., Galambos, N. L., & Anderson, J. R. (2016). Skip the dishes? Not so fast! Sex and housework revisited. *Journal of Family Psychology,* 30 (2), 203–213.

Carlson, D. L., Hanson, S., & Fitzroy, A. (2016). The Division of Child Care, Sexual Intimacy, and Relationship Quality in Couples. *Gender & Society*, 30 (3), 442-466.

Frisco, M. L., & Williams, K. (2003). Perceived Housework Equity, Marital Happiness, and Divorce in Dual-Earner Households. *Journal of Family Issues*, 24 (1), 51-73.

Gash, V., & Plagnol, A. (2020). The Partner Pay Gap: Associations between Spouses' Relative Earnings and Life Satisfaction among Couples in the UK. *Work, Employment and Society*, 1-18.

Meers, S., & Strober, J. (2020). *Getting to 50/50: How working parents can have it all.* Piatkus.

Munsch, C. L. (2015). Her Support, His Support: Money, Masculinity, and Marital Infidelity. *American Sociological Review*, 80 (3), 469-495.

Stick, M. (2021, April 5). *Men who identify as feminists are having more — and more varied — sex.* The Conversation. Phys.org.

Stick, M., & Fetner, T. (2021). Feminist Men and Sexual Behavior: Analyses of Men's Sex with Women. *Men and Masculinities*, 24 (5), 780-801.

Fetner, T. (2022). Feminist Identity and Sexual Behavior: The Intimate Is Political. *Archives of Sexual Behavior*, 51, 441–452.

Trends in what people look for in a partner:

Van Lange, P. A., Kruglanski, A. W., & Higgins, E. T. (2012). *Handbook of Theories of Social Psychology*, 2 (1-2). SAGE Publications Ltd.

Saatchi & Saatchi Chairman:

O'Reilly, L. (2016, July 29). Saatchi & Saatchi chairman Kevin Roberts thinks gender diversity in advertising debate is 'over'. *Business Insider*.

Women's domestic labour:

Park, A., Bryson, C., Clery, E., Curtice, J., & Phillips, M. (Eds.) (2013). *British Social Attitudes: The 30th Report.* London: National Centre for Social Research.

Gershuny, J., & Kan. M. Y. (2012). Halfway to gender equality in paid and unpaid work? Evidence from the multinational time-use study. In Scott, J. L., Dex, S., & Plagnol, A. C. (Eds.). *Gendered Lives: Gender Inequalities in Production and Reproduction* (pp.74-94). Edward Elgar Publishing.

Treas, J. (2016, September 28). Todays' parents spend more time with their kids than moms and dads did 50 years ago. *UCI News*.

Men and women's identity and parenting:

Taylor, M. (2022, July 24). *The State of Moms and Dads in America.* National Fatherhood Initiative.

Incomplete gender revolution:

McDonald, P., & Esping-Andersen, G. (2011). The Incomplete Revolution: Adapting to Women's New Roles. *European Journal of Population,* 27, 265–267.

Women's 'second shift':

Hochschild, A., & Maching, A. (1990). *The Second Shift: Working Parents and the Revolution at Home.* Piatkus.

Women's 'third shift':

Wolf, N. (1990). *The Beauty Myth.* Chatto and Windus.

Economics and identity:

Akerlof, G. A., & Kranton R. E. (2000). Economics and Identity. *The Quarterly Journal of Economics,* 115 (3), 715-753.

Cultural differences within the UK:

Dixon-Fyle, S. et al. (2023, June 28). *Race in the UK Workplace: The Intersectional Experience.* McKinsey Institute for Black Economic Mobility.

Tall Poppy Syndrome:

Billan, R. (2023). *The Tallest Poppy: White Paper.* Women of Influence.

Mancl, A. C., & Penington, B. (2011). Tall Poppies in the Workplace: Communication Strategies Used by Envious Others in Response to Successful Women. *Qualitative Research Reports in Communication,* 12 (1), 79–86.

Berti, A. (2018, April 5). *Men account for 90% of all global millionaires.* Verdict.

French Gates, M. (2019, October 5). Melinda Gates: Here's Why I'm Committing $1 Billion to Promote Gender Equality. *Time Magazine.*

Why climate change affects women differently than men:

United Nations Secretariat. (2022, June 1). *Dimensions and examples of the gender-differentiated impacts of climate change, the role of women as agents of change and opportunities for women.* Synthesis report by the secretariat. United Nations Climate Change.

Time use of working mums:

Bianchi, S. M., & Milkie, M. A. (2010). Work and family research in the first decade of the 21st century. *Journal of Marriage and Family,* 72 (3), 705–725.

Intensive parenting:

Henderson, A., Harmon, S., & Newman, H. (2016). The Price Mothers Pay, Even When They Are Not Buying It: Mental Health Consequences of Idealized Motherhood. *Sex Roles,* 74, 512–526.

Rizzo, K. M., Schiffrin, H. H., & Liss, M. (2013). Insight into the parenthood paradox: mental health outcomes of intensive mothering. *Journal of Child and Family Studies,* 22, 614–620.

Humans, chimps and bonobos:

American Museum of Natural History. *DNA: Comparing Humans and Chimps.* https://www.amnh.org/exhibitions/permanent/human-origins/understanding-our-past/dna-comparing-humans-and-chimps

Prüfer, K., Munch, K., Hellmann, I. et al. (2012). The bonobo genome compared with the chimpanzee and human genomes. *Nature,* 486, 527–531.

Itani, J. (1959). Paternal care in the wild Japanese monkey, Macaca fuscata fuscata. *Primates,* 2 (1), 61–93.

Fine, C. (2011). *Delusions of Gender: The Real Science Behind Sex Differences.* Icon Books.

Gender equality and anthropology:

Hansen, C. W., Jensen, P. S., & Skovsgaard, C. V. (2015). Modern Gender Roles and Agricultural History: The Neolithic Inheritance. *Journal for Economic Growth,* 20, 365-404.

Lacy, S., & Ocobock, C. (2024). Woman the hunter: The archaeological evidence. *American Anthropologist*, 126 (1), 19-31.

Hunn, E. (1981). On the relative contribution of men and women to subsistence among hunter-gatherers of the Columbia Plateau: A Comparison with Ethnographic Atlas Summaries. *Journal of Ethnobiology,* I (I): 124-134.

Devlin, H. (2015, May 14). Early men and women were equal, say scientists. *The Guardian.*

Pink trains and blue dolls:

Wong, W. I., & Hines, M. (2015). Effects of Gender Color-Coding on Toddlers' Gender-Typical Toy Play. *Archives of Sexual Behavior,* 44, 1233–1242.

Maternal mortality and World War II:

Kristof, N. D., & WuDunn. S. (2010). *Half the Sky: How to Change the World.* Virago.

Albanesi, S., & Olivetti, C. (2016). Gender roles and medical progress. *Journal of Political Economy,* 124 (3), 650-695.

Happiness and equality:

Pickett, K., & Wilkinson, R. (2010). *The Spirit Level: Why Equality is Better for Everyone.* Allen Lane Publishing.

Feminist theory:

Stanton, E. C. (2007). *Feminist as Thinker: A Reader in Documents and Essays.* (Eds.), DuBois E. C., & Smith, R. C. NYU Press.

Chapter 3

Definitions of happiness:

Dolan, P. (2014). *Happiness by Design: Finding pleasure and purpose in everyday life.* Penguin Books.

Ryan, R. M., & Deci, E. L. (2001). On happiness and human potentials: A review of research on hedonic and eudaimonic well-being. *Annual Review of Psychology,* 52 (1), 141-166.

The importance of happiness:

Aristotle. (2014). *Cambridge texts in the history of philosophy: Aristotle: Nicomachean Ethics.* (Eds.), Crisp, R. Cambridge University Press.

Dalai Lama XIV, & Cutler, H. C. (1998). *The Art of Happiness: a Handbook for Living.* Riverhead Books.

Seligman, M. (2012). *Flourish: A Visionary New Understanding of Happiness and Well-being.* Simon and Schuster.

Layard, R. (2005). *Happiness: Lessons From a New Science.* Penguin Books.

Happiness of parents:

Stanca, L. (2012). Suffer the little children: Measuring the effect of parenthood on well-being worldwide. *Journal of Economic Behaviour and Organization,* 18, 742-750.

Veenhoven, R. (2015). Informed Pursuit of Happiness: What we should know, do know and can get to know. *Journal of Happiness Studies,* 16, 1035-1071.

Happiness stemming from genetics, behaviours or life circumstances:

Bartels, M., Bang Nes, R., Armitage, J., van de Weijer, M. P., de Vries L. P., & Haworth, C. M. A. (2022). *Exploring the Biological Basis for Happiness.* World Happiness Report, Chapter 5.

Lyubomirsky, S. (2008). *The How of Happiness: A Practical Guide to Getting the Life You Want.* Penguin Press: American Psychological Association.

De Neve, J.E., Christakis, N. A., Fowler, J. H., & Frey, B. S. (2012). Genes, Economics, and Happiness. *Journal of Neuroscience, Psychology and Economics,* 5 (4),10.

Happiness and money:

Fischer, R., & Boer, D. (2011). What is more important for national well-being? Money or autonomy? A meta-analysis of well-being, burnout, and anxiety across 63 countries. *Journal of Personality and Social Psychology,* 101 (1), 164-184.

Dunn, E., & Norton, M. (2014*). Happy Money: The Science of Happier Spending.* Simon and Schuster.

Women and poverty:

Rummery, K. (2015). Equalities: The impact of welfare reform and austerity by gender, disability and age. In Bochel, H., & Powell, M. (Eds.) *The Coalition Government and Social Policy: Restructuring the Welfare State* (pp.310-324). The Policy Press.

The Joseph Rowntree Foundation Report. (2024). *UK Poverty 2024: The Essential Guide to Understanding Poverty in the UK.*

Graham, C. (2012). *Happiness around the world: The paradox of happy peasants and miserable millionaires.* Oxford University Press.

Increasing income and happiness:

Kahneman, D., & Deaton, A. (2010). High income improves evaluation of life but not emotional well-being. *Proceedings of the National Academy of Sciences,* 107 (38), 16489–16493.

Muresan, G. M., Ciumas, C., & Achim, M. V. (2020). Can Money Buy Happiness? Evidence for European Countries. *Applied Research in Quality of Life,* 15, 953–970.

Diener, E., Horwitz, J., & Emmons, R. A. (1985). Happiness of the very wealthy. *Social Indicators Research,* 16, 263–274.

Marriage and happiness:

Dolan, P. (2019). *Happy Ever After: Escaping the Myth of the Perfect Life.* Penguin Books.

Cain, S. (2019, May 25). Women are happier without children or a spouse says happiness expert. *The Guardian*.

Divorce and happiness:

Gardner, J., & Oswald, A. J. (2006). Do Divorcing Couples Become Happier by Breaking Up? *Journal of the Royal Statistical Society*, 169 (2), 319–336.

Health and happiness:

Ellingrud, K., Perez, L., Petersen, A., & Sartori, V. (17th January, 2024). *Closing the women's health gap: A $1 trillion opportunity to improve lives and economies.* McKinsey Health Institute.

Barclay, S. (2022). *UK Government Department for Health and Social Care.* Women's Health Strategy for England.

BBC Health. (2022, February 14). Review reveals 'vast' ethnic inequalities in NHS Services. *BBC News*.

Winchester, N. (2021, July 1). *Women's health outcomes: Is there a gender gap?* House of Lords Library. https://lordslibrary.parliament.uk/womens-health-outcomes-is-there-a-gender-gap/

Becchetti, L., & Conzo, G. (2022). The Gender Life Satisfaction/Depression Paradox. *Social Indicators Research*, 160, 35–113.

Mosconi, L., Williams, S., Carlton, C. et al. (2024). Sex-specific associations of serum cortisol with brain biomarkers of Alzheimer's risk. *Scientific Reports*, 14, 5519.

Age and happiness:

Blanchflower, D.G. (2021). Is happiness U-shaped everywhere? Age and subjective well-being in 145 countries. *Journal of Population Economics*, 34, 575–624.

Beauty and happiness:

Diener, E., & Biwas Diener, R. (2008). *Happiness: Unlocking the Mysteries of Psychological Wealth.* Wiley-Blackwell.

Björn Meyer, B., Enström, M. K., Harstveit, M., Bowles D. P., & Beevers, C. G. (2007). Happiness and despair on the catwalk: Need satisfaction, well-being, and personality adjustment among fashion models. *The Journal of Positive Psychology*, 2 (1), 2-17.

Mobius, M. M., & Rosenblat, T. S. (2006). Why beauty matters. *American Economic Review*, 96 (1), 222-235.

Maestripieri, D., Henry, A., & Nickels, N. (2017). Explaining financial and prosocial biases in favor of attractive people. Interdisciplinary perspectives from economics, social psychology and evolutionary psychology. *Behavioral and Brain Sciences*, 40, e19.

Intelligence and happiness:

Ali, A., Ambler, G., Strydom, A., Rai, D., Cooper, C., McManus, S., Hassiotis, A. et al. (2013). The relationship between happiness and intelligent quotient: the contribution of socio-economic and clinical factors. *Psychological Medicine*, 43 (6), 1303–1312.

Judge, T. A., Hurst, C., & Simon, L. S. (2009). Does it pay to be smart, attractive, or confident (or all three)? Relationships among general mental ability, physical attractiveness, core self-evaluations, and income. *Journal of Applied Psychology*, 94 (3), 742–755.

Robson, D. (2015, April 14). The surprising downsides of being clever. *BBC Future*.

Raghunathari, R. (2016). *If You're So Smart, Why Aren't You Happy?* Vermilion.

Happiness and where you live:

Burger, M. J., Morrison, P. S., Hendriks, M., & Hoogerbrugge, M. M. (2020). *Urban-rural happiness differentials across the world*. World Happiness Report, 67-94.

Schkade, D. A., & Kahneman, D. (1998). Does Living in California Make People Happy? A Focusing Illusion in Judgments of Life Satisfaction. *Psychological Science*, 9 (5), 340-346.

Prevalence of Seasonal Affective Disorder:

Cox, D. (2017, October 30). The science of Sad: understanding the causes of 'winter depression'. *The Guardian*.

Royal College of Psychiatrists. (2015, April). Seasonal Affective Disorder (SAD). https://www.rcpsych.ac.uk/mental-health/mental-illnesses-and-mental-health-problems/seasonal-affective-disorder-(sad)

Work and commuting:

Longhi, S., Nandi, A., Bryan, M., Connolly, S., & Gedikli, C. (2017). *Gender and Unemployment: Analysis of Understanding Society: the UK Household Longitudinal Survey Summary Report*. What Works Wellbeing.

Jobs and Recovery Monitor. (2023, May 26). *Unemployment rate over twice as high for BME workers than white workers*. Trades Union Congress.

Roberts, J., Hodgson, R., & Dolan, P. (2011). "It's driving her mad": gender differences in the effects of commuting on psychological health. *Journal of Health Economics*, 30, 1064-76.

Office for National Statistics. (2022). *Is Hybrid Working Here to Stay? Three quarters of hybrid workers reported improved work-life balance and nearly 50% reported improved well-being.*

Mutebi, N., & Hobbs, A. (2022). *The impact of hybrid and remote working on workers and organisations.* UK Parliament Research Briefings.

Happiness and free time:

Sharif, M. A., Mogilner, C., & Hershfield, H. E. (2021). Having too little or too much time is linked to lower subjective well-being. *Journal of Personality and Social Psychology,* 121 (4), 933–947.

Giurge, L.M., Whillans, A.V., & West, C. (2020). Why Time Poverty Matters for Individuals, Organisations and Nations. *Nature Human Behaviour*, 4, 993-1003.

Religion and spirituality:

Inglehart, R. (2010). Faith and Freedom: Traditional and Modern Ways to Happiness. In Diener, E., Kahneman, D., & Helliwell, J. (Eds.), *International Differences in Well-Being.* Oxford University Press.

Happy behaviours:

King, V. (2016). *10 Keys to Happier Living: A Practical Handbook for Happiness.* Headline Home.

Chatterjee, R. (2019). *Feel Better In 5: Your Daily Plan to Feel Great for Life.* Penguin.

Peters, S. (2012). *The Chimp Paradox: The Mind Management Program for Confidence, Success and Happiness.* Vermilion.

Attia, P (2023). *Outlive: The Science and Art of Longevity.* Vermilion.

Vaillant, G., McArthur, C., & Bock, A. (2010). Grant Study of Adult Development, 1938-2000. *Harvard Dataverse,* V4.

Sandstrom, G. M., & Dunn, E. W. (2014). Social interactions and well-being: the surprising power of weak ties. *Personality and Social Psychology Bulletin,* 40 (7), 910–922.

Dweck, C. (2017). *Mindset: Changing the Way You Think to Fulfil Your Potential.* Robinson Publishing.

Berge, J. M., Larson, N., Bauer, K. W., & Neumark-Sztainer, D. (2011). Are parents of young children practicing healthy nutrition and physical activity behaviors? *Pediatrics,* 127 (5), 881-887.

Hongwei, J. (2024). Sex differences in association of physical activity with all-cause and cardiovascular mortality. *Journal of the American College of Cardiology,* 83 (8), 783-793.

Kraft, T. L., & Pressman, S.D. (2012). Grin and bear it: The influence of manipulated facial expression on the stress response. *Psychological Science,* 23 (11), 1372-1378.

Langer, E. J. (2023). *The Mindful Body.* Robinson Publishing.

Moran, C. (2021). *More Than a Woman.* Ebury Press.

Agarwal, P. (2023). *Hysterical: Exploding the Myth of Gendered Emotions.* Canongate Books.

Four significant things women need for happiness:

Grant, A. (2014). *Give and Take: Why Helping Others Drives Our Success.* Orion Publishing.

Housman, J., & Dorman, S. (2005). The Alameda County study: a systematic, chronological review. *Journal of Health Education,* 36 (5), 302-308.

Taylor, S. E., Klein, L. C., Lewis, B. P., Gruenewald, T. L., Gurung, R. A., & Updegraff, J. A. (2000). Biobehavioural Responses to Stress in Females: Tend-And-Befriend, Not Fight-Or-Flight. *Psychological Review,* 107 (4), 411-429.

Jones, L. (2023). *Matrescence: On the Metamorphosis of Pregnancy, Childbirth and Motherhood.* Allen Lane Publishing.

Hogenboom, M. (2021). *The Motherhood Complex: The Story of Our Changing Selves.* Piatkus.

Salary.com. (2019). *How Much is a Mother Really Worth?* Mom Salary Survey.

Zakrewski, A., Reeves, K, Kahlich, M., Klein, M., Mattar, A., & Knobel, S. (2020). *Managing the Next Decade of Women's Wealth.* Boston Consulting Group.

Villa, M. (2017). *Women own less than 20% of the world's land, it's time to give them equal property rights.* World Economic Forum.

Hughes, B. (2021). *The Hidden Harm of Financial Abuse.* Insight. The Financial Conduct Authority.

Fidelity. (2015). *Women Fit Money Study.* Fidelity Investments.

White, N. (2022). *The Gender Pay Gap in the UK: 2022.* Office for National Statistics.

Greyson, D., & Baker, S. (2022). *Ethnicity Pay Gap Campaign.* Equilibrium Mediation Consulting.

Brown, M. (2024, January 8). Women of Bangladeshi and Pakistani Heritage Earn Almost a Third Less Than White Men. *The Guardian.*

Prospect. (2024). *What is the Gender Pension Gap?* https://prospect.org.uk/article/what-is-the-gender-pension-gap/

Murray-West, R. (2022). There is a Gender Investment Gap and the Numbers are Shocking. *Metro News.*

Philogene, H. (23rd July, 2023). Things to know for 2023 Black Women's Equal Pay Day. *The Grio.*

Fidelity Investments. (2021). *Women and Investing Study.* https://www.fidelity.com/bin-public/060_www_fidelity_com/documents/about-fidelity/FidelityInvestmentsWomen&InvestingStudy2021.pdf

Beauvoir, S. de. (1949, c2015). *The Second Sex.* Vintage Random House.

Hirsch, P., Koch, I., & Karbach, J. (2019) Multitasking is not good for either men or women: Putting a stereotype to the test: The case of gender differences in multitasking costs in task-switching and dual-task situations. *PloS ONE,* 14 (8), e0220150.

Murphy, R., Dennes, M., & Harris, B. (2022). *Families and the Labour Market, UK.* Office for National Statistics.

United Nations. (2015). *The World's Women: Women's Work.* https://unstats.un.org/unsd/gender/chapter4/chapter4.html

Gershuny, J., & Kan. M. Y. (2012). Halfway to gender equality in paid and unpaid work? Evidence from the multinational time-use study. In Scott, J. L., Dex, S., & Plagnol, A. C. (Eds.), *Gendered Lives: Gender Inequalities in Production and Reproduction* (pp.74-94). Edward Elgar Publishing.

Organisation for Economic Cooperation and Development. (2020), *"Executive summary", in How's Life? 2020: Measuring Well-being.* OECD Publishing.

Action Aid. (September, 2016). *Not Ready, Still Waiting.* https://actionaid.org/publications/2016/not-ready-still-waiting

Hogenboom, M. (2021, May 18). The Hidden Load: How 'Thinking of Everything' Holds Mums Back. *BBC News.*

Etheridge, B., & Spantig, L. (2022). The gender gap in mental well-being at the onset of the Covid-19 pandemic: Evidence from the UK. *European Economic Review,* 145, 104114.

Thorsteinsen, K., Parks-Stamm, E. J., Kvalø, M. et al. (2022). Mothers' Domestic Responsibilities and Well-Being During the COVID-19 Lockdown: The Moderating Role of Gender Essentialist Beliefs About Parenthood. *Sex Roles,* 87, 85–98.

Helliwell, J. F., Layard, R., Sachs, J. D., De Neve, J.-E., Aknin, L. B., & Wang, S. (Eds.) (2024). *World Happiness Report 2024.* New York: Sustainable Development Solutions Network.

United Nations Women (2020). *Whose Time to Care? Unpaid Care and Domestic Work During COVID-19.* https://data.unwomen.org/publications/whose-time-care-unpaid-care-and-domestic-work-during-covid-19

World Economic Forum. (2020). *Gender Gap Report.* https://www.weforum.org/publications/gender-gap-2020-report-100-years-pay-equality/

Guterres, A. (2023, March 6). *Secretary General's Remarks to the Commission on the Status of Women.* United Nations General Assembly.

Bjornskov, C., Dreher, A., & Fischer, J. A. (2007). On gender inequality and life satisfaction: Does discrimination matter? *Working Paper Series in Economics and Finance,* 657.

Inglehart, R., Foa, R., Peterson, C., & Welzel, C. (2008). Development. Freedom, and rising happiness. *Perspectives on Psychological Science*, 3 (4), 264-85.

Jorm, A. F., & Ryan, S. M. (2014). Cross-national and historical differences in subjective well-being. *International Journal of Epidemiology*, 43 (2), 330-340.

Ruth, L., & Napier, J. (2014). *Gender inequality and subjective well-being.* In Encyclopedia of quality of life and well-being research, 2446-2451. Springer.

Chapter 4

Over(under)whelmed:

Brown, B. (2004). *Women and Shame: Reaching Out, Speaking Truths and Building Connection.* 3CPr.

O'Meara, M. (2022). *Girly Drinks: A World History of Women and Alcohol.* Hurst Publishers.

Lenz, L. (2024, February 28). Women are Divorcing and Finally Finding Happiness. *The Washington Post.*

Work, choice and happiness:

Gash, V. (2008). Preference or constraint? Part-time workers' transitions in Denmark, France and the United Kingdom. *Work, Employment and Society*, 22 (4), 655-674.

Leahy, M., & Doughney, J. (2006). Women, Work and Preference Formation: A Critique of Catherine Hakim's Preference Theory. *Journal of Business Systems, Governance and Ethics,* 1 (1), 37-48.

Women's happiness in paid employment:

Boye, K. (2009). Relatively Different? How do Gender Differences in Well-Being Depend on Paid and Unpaid Work in Europe? *Social Indicators Research*, 93, 509–525.

Gregory, M., & Connolly, S. (2008). The Price of Reconciliation: Part-Time Work, Families and Women's Satisfaction. *Economic Journal*, 118, F1-F7.

Della Giusta, M., Jewell, S., & Kambhampati, U. (2011). Gender and Life Satisfaction in the UK. *Feminist Economics,* 17 (3), 1-34.

Mendes, E., Saad, L., & McGeeney, K. (2012). *Stay-at-Home Moms Report More Depression, Sadness, Anger.* Gallup.

The enrichment model:

Greehaus, J. H., & Powell, G.N. (2006). When work and family are allies: A theory of work-family enrichment. *Academy of Management Review,* 31 (1), 72-92.

Carlson, D. S., Kacmar, K. M., Wayne, J. H., & Grzywacz, J. G. (2006). Measuring the positive side of the work-family interface: Development and validation of a work-family enrichment scale. *Journal of Vocational Behaviour,* 68 (1), 131- 164.

Postpartum depression:

Wang, Z., Liu, J., Shuai, H., Cai, Z., Fu, X., Liu, Y., Xiao, X., Zhang, W., Krabbendam, E., Liu, S., Liu, Z., Li, Z., & Yang, B. X. (2021). Mapping global prevalence of depression among postpartum women. *Translational Psychiatry,* 11 (1), 543.

Adams, C. (2021, August 8). The motherhood dilemma: When does ambivalence tip into regret? *The Independent.*

Housework and happiness:

Offer, S., & Schneider, B. (2011). Revisiting the gender gap in time-use patterns: Multitasking and well-being among mothers and fathers in dual-earner families. *American Sociological Review,* 76 (6), 809-833.

Mencarini, L., & Sironi, M. (2012). Happiness, housework and gender inequality in Europe. *European Sociological Review,* 28 (2), 203-219.

McMunn, A., Bird, L., Webb, E., & Sacker, A. (2020). Gender divisions of paid and unpaid work in contemporary UK couples. *Work, Employment and Society,* 34 (2), 155-173.

Freud:

Cherry, K. (2022, August 29). *Freud's Perspective on Women.* Very Well Mind.

Motherhood penalty:

Brearley, J. (2022). *The Motherhood Penalty: How to Stop Motherhood Being the Kiss of Death for Your Career.* Simon and Schuster.

Shevinsky, E., (2015). *Lean Out: The Struggle for Gender Equality in Tech and Start-Up Culture.* OR Books.

Imposter syndrome:

Sandberg, S. (2013). *Lean In: Women, Work and the Will to Lead.* Random House.

Amatulli, J. (2017, March 13). What Happened When a Man Signed Work Emails Using a Female Name for 2 Weeks. *Huffington Post*.

Harassment:

The Fawcett Society (2022). *Tackling Sexual Harassment in the Workplace: Recommendations for Employers.*

United Nations Women National Committee. (2021). *Safe Spaces Now*. UN Women.

The work of caring:

Brekke, I., & Alecu, A. (2023). The health of mothers caring for a child with a disability: a longitudinal study. *BMC Women's Health*, 23, 639.

Mutschler, P. (2015). *Women and Caregiving: Facts and Figures*. The National Centre on Caregiving at Family Caregiver Alliance.

Marçal, K. (2015). *Who Cooked Adam Smith's Dinner? A Story About Women and Economics*. Granta Books.

De Henau, J., & Himmelweit, S. (June 2020). *A Care-Led Recovery from Coronavirus. The case for investment in care as a better post-pandemic economic stimulus than investment in construction.* Women's Budget Group.

Chavez, D. (2018, June 28). *ILO calls for urgent action to prevent looming global care crisis.* International Labour Organization.

Fathering:

Statista. (2022). *Number of stay-at-home dads in the United Kingdom (UK) in 3rd quarter 2019 and 3rd quarter 2022.*

Childcare and children's outcomes:

Herbst, C. (2017). Universal Child Care, Maternal Employment, and Children's Long-run Outcomes: Evidence from the US Langham Act of 1940. *Journal of Labor Economics*, 35, 2.

Havnes, T., & Mogstad, M. (2011). No Child Left Behind: Subsidized child care and children's long-run outcomes. *American Economic Journal: Economic Policy*, 3 (2), 97-129.

Felfe, C., Nollenberger, N., & Rodriguez-Planas, N. (2015). Can't buy mommy's love? Universal childcare and children's long-term cognitive development. *Journal of Population Economics*, 28, 393-422.

Domestic load:

Cox, T. (2023, May 24). The biggest marriage killer is NOT what you think, says Tracey Cox – as she shares a warning to men who don't pull their weight. *Daily Mail*.

Action Aid. (2016, September). *Not Ready, Still Waiting.* https://actionaid.org/publications/2016/not-ready-still-waiting

Part-time work:

Francis-Devine, B., & Hutton, G. (2024, March 4). *Women and the UK Economy.* House of Commons Library. https://researchbriefings.files.parliament.uk/documents/SN06838/SN06838.pdf

U.S. Bureau of Labor Statistics. (2022, March). *Women in the labor force: a databook. Division of Information and Marketing Services, Report 1097.*

Weston, G., Zilanawala, A., Webb, E., et al. (2019). Long work hours, weekend working and depressive symptoms in men and women: findings from a UK population-based study. *Journal of Epidemiology and Community Health*, 73, 465-474.

Hill, E. J., Martinson, V., & Ferris, M. (2004). New concept part time employment as a work family adaptive strategy for women professionals with small children. *Family Relations,* 53 (3).

Booth, A., & van Ours, J. C. (2013). Part-time jobs: what women want? *Journal of Population Economics,* 26, 263-283.

Booth, A., & Van Ours, J. C. (2008). Job Satisfaction and Family Happiness: The Part-Time Work Puzzle. *The Economic Journal,* 118, 526, F77–F99.

Chung, H., & van der Lippe, T. (2020). Flexible Working, Work-Life Balance, and Gender Equality: Introduction. *Social Indicators Research,* 151 (2), 365-381.

PwC UK. (2023). *Women and Work Index.* https://www.pwc.co.uk/services/economics/insights/women-in-work-index.html

Schuller, T. (2017). *The Paula Principle: How and Why Women Work Below Their Level of Competence.* Penguin Random House.

Cunha, M., André, S., Aparício, G., Santos, E., & Nunes, C. (2016). Organization of Housework in Heterosexual Couples: Systematic Review of the Literature. *Social and Behavioral Sciences*, 217, 459-468.

Gattuso, R. (2021, March 11). Why LGBTQ couples split household tasks more equally. *BBC Equality Matters.*

Lyttelton, T., Zang, E., & Musick, K. (2022). Telecommuting and gender inequalities in parents' paid and unpaid work before and during the COVID-19 pandemic. *Journal of Marriage and Family,* 84 (1), 230–249.

Javed, U. (2019). Combining career and care-giving: The impact of family-friendly policies on the well-being of working mothers in the United Kingdom. *Global Business and Organizational Excellence,* 38, 5, 44-52.

Noda, H. (2020). Work–Life Balance and Life Satisfaction in OECD Countries: A Cross-Sectional Analysis. *Journal of Happiness Studies,* 21, 1325–1348.

Jobs which make you happy:

Goodwin, G. (2021). *An exploration of the eudaimonic well-being of UK women entrepreneurs.* The British Library.

Portfolio career:

Honderich, H. (2021, April 14). Why 'stay at home parent' is a job title. *BBC News.*

Chapter 5

Gender:

Bower-Brown S. (2022). Beyond Mum and Dad: Gendered Assumptions about Parenting and the Experiences of Trans and/or Non-Binary Parents in the UK. *LGBTQ+ Family*, 18 (3), 223-240.

Butler, J. (1990). *Gender Trouble: Gender and the Subversion of Identity.* Routledge.

Stock, K. (2022). *Material Girls: Why Reality Matters for Feminism.* Fleet.

Shaw, D. (2023) A tale of two feminisms: gender critical feminism, trans inclusive feminism and the case of Kathleen Stock. *Women's History Review*, 32 (5), 768-780.

Fausto-Sterling, A. (2020). *Sexing the Body: Gender Politics and the Construction of Sexuality. Revised Edition.* Basic Books.

Joyce, H. (2021). *Trans: When Ideology Meets Reality.* Oneworld Publications.

Serano, J. (2016). *Whipping Girl: A Transsexual Woman on Sexism and the Scapegoating of Femininity.* Seal Press

Arnaud, L., & Trottmann, M. (2019). Genetics of disorders of sex development: The DSD-TRN experience. *Nature Reviews Endocrinology*, 15 (7), 453-471.

Aguera y Aracs, B. (2023). *Who Are We Now?* Hat and Beard Publishing.

Neuroplasticity:

Fuchs, E., & Flugge, G. (2014). Adult Neuroplasticity: More Than 40 Years of Research. *Neural Plasticity*, Vol. 2014, 541870.

Grossman, S. (2014, November 13). Here's a Picture of the World's Tallest Man and the World's Shortest Man Shaking Hands. *Time Magazine.*

Roser, M., Appel, C., & Ritchie, H. (2024). *Human Height. Our World in Data.*

Emotional intelligence:

Mattingly, V., & Kraiger, K. (2019). Can emotional intelligence be trained? A meta-analytical investigation. *Human Resource Management Review,* 29 (2), 140-155.

Fischer, A. H., Kret, M. E., & Broekens, J. (2018). Gender differences in emotion perception and self-reported emotional intelligence: A test of the emotion sensitivity hypothesis. *PloS ONE,* 13 (1), e0190712.

Warrier, V., Toro, R., Chakrabarti, B. et al. (2018). Genome-wide analyses of self-reported empathy: correlations with autism, schizophrenia, and anorexia nervosa. *Translational Psychiatry*, 8, 35.

Maths:

Betz, D., Ramsey, L., & Sekaquaptewa, D. (2014). Gender stereotype threat among women and girls. *The SAGE Handbook of Gender and Psychology* (428-449). SAGE Publications, Ltd.

Shapiro, J., & Williams, A. M. (2011). The Role of Stereotype Threats in Undermining Girls' and Women's Performance and Interest in STEM fields. *Sex Roles,* 66 (3-4), 175-183.

Eagly, A. (2017, August 16). *Does biology explain why men outnumber women in tech?* The Conversation.

Shih, M., Pittinsky, T. L., & Ambady, N. (1999). Stereotype Susceptibility: Identity Salience and Shifts in Quantitative Performance. *Psychological Science,* 10 (1), 80-83.

Hyde, J. S. et al. (2008). Gender Similarities Characterize Math Performance. *Science,* 321, 494-495.

Risk-taking:

Fine, C, (2017). *Testosterone Rex: Unmaking the Myths of our Gendered Minds*. Icon Books.

Weber, E. U., Blais, A. R., & Betz, N. E. (2002). A domain-specific risk-attitude scale: Measuring risk perceptions and risk behaviors. *Journal of Behavioral Decision Making*, 15 (4), 263–290.

Croson, R., & Gneezy, U. (2009). Gender differences in preferences. *Journal of Economic Literature*, 47 (2), 448–474.

Niederle, M., & Vesterlund, L. (2007). Do women shy away from competition? Do men compete too much? *The Quarterly Journal of Economics*, 122 (3), 1067–1101.

Leadership:

Adams, R. B., & Ferreira, D. (2009). Women in the boardroom and their impact on governance and performance. *Journal of Financial Economics*, 94 (2), 291-309.

Eagly, A. H., Johannesen-Schmidt, M. C., & van Engen, M. L. (2003). Transformational, transactional, and laissez-faire leadership styles: A meta-analysis comparing women and men. *Psychological Bulletin,* 129 (4), 569-591.

United Nations Development Programme. (2020). *The Social Norms and Beliefs that Underpin Women's and Men's Lives.*

Gillard, J., & Okonjo-Iweala, N. (2020). *Women and Leadership: Lessons From Some of the World's Most Powerful Women.* Penguin Random House.

Heilman, M. E., & Okimoto, T. G. (2007). Why are women penalized for success at male tasks? The implied communality deficit. *Journal of Applied Psychology*, 92 (1), 81-92.

Field, E., Krivkovich, A., Kugele, S., Robinson, N., & Yee. L. (2023). *Women in the Workplace.* McKinsey & Company.

Catalyst. (2021). *Quick Take: Women in Management.*
https://www.catalyst.org/research/women-in-management/

Anger:

Hooven, C. (2021). *Testosterone: The Story of the Hormone that Dominates and Divides Us.* Cassell.

Turner, J. (2013, May 18). Why do men commit almost all the crime? *The Times.*

Biology:

Tiller, N. B., Elliott-Sale, K. J., Knechtle, B. et al. (2021). Do Sex Differences in Physiology Confer a Female Advantage in Ultra-Endurance Sport? *Sports Medicine,* 51, 895–915.

Sanger, M. (1938). *An Autobiography.* (Reprint 2024). True Sign Publishing House.

Macfarlane, A., & Dorkenoo E. (2015). *Prevalence of Female Genital Mutilation in England and Wales: National and Local Estimates.* City University London and Equality Now.

Frederick, D. A., St. John, H. K., Garcia, J. R., & Lloyd, E. A. (2018). Differences in Orgasm Frequency Among Gay, Lesbian, Bisexual, and Heterosexual Men and Women in a U.S. National Sample. *The Archives of Sexual Behavior*, 47 (1), 273-288.

World Health Organisation. (2021). *Abortion Factsheet.*
https://www.who.int/news-room/fact-sheets/detail/abortion

Miscarriage Association UK. (2024). *Miscarriage Association: The Knowledge to Help.* https://www.miscarriageassociation.org.uk

Houston, M. (2019, November 4). The contraceptive pill: is the one-week break a relic of the past? *The Irish Times.*

Gupta, A. (2023, October 17). More than a third of women under the age of 50 are iron deficient. *New York Times.*

Stedeford, H. (2020, July 12). *Periods and Pandemics.* Bloody Good Period.

Tidwell, S. (2023, December 7). Wimbledon dress code change, explained: Women allowed to wear dark-coloured undershorts amid period anxieties. *The Sporting News.*

MacSwan, A. (2022, July 9). Protesters at Wimbledon urge end to all-white dress code due to period concerns. *The Guardian.*

Barnett, E. (2019). *It's About Bloody Time. Period.* Harper Collins.

Williams, J. (2003). *A Game for Rough Girls: A History of Women's Football in England.* Routledge.

British Fertility Society. (2024). *A Guide to Fertility: What is Infertility?* https://www.britishfertilitysociety.org.uk/fei/what-is-infertility/

Gregory, A. (2023, December 6). A third of new mothers worldwide 'have lasting health issues after childbirth'. *The Guardian.*

Sherman, C., Witherspoon, A., Glenza, J., & Noor, P. (2024, January 12). Abortion rights across the US: we track where laws stand in every state. *The Guardian.*

Castleman, T. (2022, June 24). 5 justices overturned Roe. 91% of senators confirming them were men. *Los Angeles Times.*

Cosslett, R. (2017, January 24). This photo sums up Trump's assault on women's rights. *The Guardian.*

Rodrigues, M. (2021, September 4). The absurd pregnancy math behind the 'six-week' abortion ban. *Scientific American.*

BBC Woman's Hour. (2023, May 30). *Childcare Debt, Big Boobs, Succession.* BBC Sounds. https://www.bbc.co.uk/programmes/m001mbwj

Kowal, M. et al. (2022). Predictors of enhancing human physical attractiveness: Data from 93 countries. *Evolution and Human Behavior,* 43, 6, 455-474.

Elsesser, K. (2019, October 28). The Link Between Beauty and the Gender Gap. *Forbes.*

Safety:

Stripe, N. (2021). *Perceptions of personal safety and experiences of harassment, Great Britain.* Office for National Statistics.

Stripe, N. (2021). *Nature of sexual assault by rape or penetration*. Office for National Statistics.

United Nations Women National Committee. (2021). *Safe Spaces Now*. UN Women.

Home Office. (2019, March 7). *Violence Against Women and Girls and Male Position Fact Sheet.* https://homeofficemedia.blog.gov.uk/2019/03/07/violence-against-women-and-girls-and-male-position-factsheets/

BBC Verify Reality Check Team. (2022, March 27). Why do so few rape cases go to court? *BBC News*.

Lee, G. (2018, October 12). Men are more likely to be raped than be falsely accused of rape. *Channel Four News Fact Check*.

Walker, A. (2020, July 17). Transgender people twice as likely to be victims of crime in England and Wales. *The Guardian*.

Bradley, A., & Potter, A. (2018). *Women most at risk of experiencing partner abuse in England and Wales.* Office for National Statistics.

Fleming, P. J., Gruskin, S., Rojo, F., & Dworkin, S. L. (2015). Men's violence against women and men are inter-related: Recommendations for simultaneous intervention. *Social Science and Medicine,* 146, 249-56.

Gregory, P. (2023). *Normal Women: 900 Years of Women Making History*. William Collins.

Wolfe-Robinson, M., & Dodd, V. (2021, March 16). Institutional misogyny erodes women's trust in UK police. *The Guardian.*

Kay, K., & Shipman, C. (2014). *The Confidence Code*. Harper Business.

Women's Aid. (2023). *Domestic abuse is a gendered crime.* https://www.womensaid.org.uk/information-support/what-is-domestic-abuse/domestic-abuse-is-a-gendered-crime/

Walby, S., & Towers, J. (2018). Untangling the concept of coercive control: Theorizing domestic violent crime. *Criminology & Criminal Justice,* 18 (1), 7-28.

Sweet, P. (2019). Sociology of Gaslighting. *American Sociological Review,* 84 (5), 851–875.

United Nations Development Programme. (2023). *2023 Gender Social Norms Index: Breaking down gender biases: Shifting social norms towards gender equality.* New York.

Girls in crisis:

Gregory, A. (2020, February 28). Thousands of girls as young as 11 in England hiding signs of 'deep distress'. *The Guardian*.

Benner, A. D., Wang, Y., Shen, Y., Boyle, A. E., Polk, R., & Cheng, Y. P. (2018). Racial/ethnic discrimination and well-being during adolescence: A meta-analytic review. *American Psychologist,* 73 (7), 855-883.

Girlguiding Girls' Attitudes Survey. (2023). *Girls' happiness hits an all-time low.* Girlguiding UK.

Women and Equalities Committee. (2020). *Body Image Survey.* UK House of Commons. https://publications.parliament.uk/pa/cm5801/cmselect/cmwomeq/805/80502.htm

Ball, J. (2013, March 28). Men, you're bigger than you think! (But women - you're thinner). *The Guardian.*

Mental Health Foundation. (2023). *Body image in childhood.* https://www.mentalhealth.org.uk/explore-mental-health/articles/body-image-report-executive-summary/body-image-childhood

World Economic Forum. (2023). *Global Gender Gap Report 2023.* https://www.weforum.org/publications/global-gender-gap-report-2023/in-full/benchmarking-gender-gaps-2023/#global-results

Ritchie, H., & Roser, M. (2019). *Gender Ratio. How does the ratio of men and women differ between countries? And why?* Our World in Data.

Porsche, D., & Giorgianni, S. J. (2020). The Crisis in Male Mental Health: A Call to Action. *American Journal of Men's Health,* 14 (4).

Helliwell, J. F., Layard, R., Sachs, J. D., Aknin, L. B., De Neve, J.-E., & Wang, S. (Eds.) (2023). *World Happiness Report 2023.* Sustainable Development Solutions Network.

Stevenson, J., & Rao, M. (2014). *Explaining levels of wellbeing in Black and Minority Ethnic populations in England.* Institute for Health and Human Development.

Oppenheim, M. (2021, May 20). Women with disabilities 'more like to suffer domestic abuse'. *The Independent.*

Sex:

Vera-Gray, F. (2024). *Women on Porn: One hundred stories. One vital conversation.* Transworld Digital.

Smith, M., & Mac, J. (2018). *Revolting Prostitutes: The Fight for Sex Workers Rights.* Verso Books.

Global Network of Sex work Projects. (2021) *Consensus Statement on Sex Work, Human Rights and the Law.*

Vandepitte, J., Lyerla, R., Dallabetta, G., Crabbé, F., Alary, M., & Buvé, A. (2006). Estimates of the number of female sex workers in different regions of the world. *Sexually Transmitted Infections,* 82 (3),18-25.

Matolcsi, A., Mulvihill, N., Lilley-Walker, S. J. et al. (2021). The Current Landscape of Prostitution and Sex Work in England and Wales. *Sexuality & Culture*, 25, 39–57.

Bullock, C. (2020, November 17). Covid: Second lockdown 'will deepen sex work crisis'. *BBC News*.

Bryant, M. (2023, April 29). Vulnerable UK Women Forced into 'Sex for Rent' by cost of living crisis. *The Guardian*.

Walter, N. (2009). *The Return of Sexism*. Virago.

Shallcross, R., Dickson, J. M., Nunns, D., Mackenzie, C., & Kiemle, G. (2018). Women's Subjective Experiences of Living with Vulvodynia: A Systematic Review and Meta-Ethnography. *Archives of Sexual Behavior*, 47 (3), 577-595.

Nolsoe, E. (2022, June 16). *Only a third of sexually active women say they never experience pain during sex*. YouGov UK.

Coppard, H. (2024). *Vulval and Vaginal Pain: A practical guide to treatment options, self-management strategies and pain management techniques*.

Newsbeat. (2021, June 21). Porn: The 'incredible' number of UK adults watching content. *BBC News*.

Kirby, M. (2021), Pornography and its impact on the sexual health of men. *Trends Urology & Men Health*, 12, 6-10.

Ofcom. (2023). *Online Nation 2023 Report*. https://www.ofcom.org.uk/__data/assets/pdf_file/0029/272288/online-nation-2023-report.pdf

Lindner, J. (2024, January 9). *Pornography Industry Statistics*. Gitnux Market Data Report.

Fritz, N., Malic, V., Paul, B., & Zhou, Y. (2020). A Descriptive Analysis of the Types, Targets, and Relative Frequency of Aggression in Mainstream Pornography. *Archives of sexual behavior*, 49 (8), 3041–3053.

De Sousa, R. (2023, January). *Young People and Pornography: 'A lot of it is actually just abuse'*. Children's Commissioner.

Refuge. (2017). *What is Domestic Abuse, The Facts*. Refuge: For Women and Children. Against Domestic Violence.

Schrager, A., Groskopf, C., & Cunningham, S. (2017, November 5). *How the internet changed the market for sex*. Quartz.

Boseley, M. (2020, December 22). 'Everyone and their mum is on it': OnlyFans booms in popularity during the pandemic. *The Guardian*.

Friday, N. (1973). *My Secret Garden*. Pocket.

Chapter 6

Striving for more:

Ngozi Adichie, C. (2014). *We Should all Be Feminists*. Fourth Estate.

History of women in medicine:

Sylvester, R., & Lay, K. (2023, September 12). One in three female surgeons have been assaulted by a colleague. Today they speak. *The Times.*

BBC News. (2019, July 6). First female medical students get degrees at last. *BBC News.*

Maudsley, H. (1873). *Body and mind: An inquiry into their connection and mutual influence, specially in reference to mental disorders*. (Enlarged and revised edition). Macmillan.

Jefferson, L., Bloor, K., & Maynard, A. (2015). Women in medicine: historical perspectives and recent trends. *British Medical Bulletin,* 114 (1), 5–15.

DiFranco, J. T., & Curl, M. (2014). Healthy Birth Practice #5: Avoid Giving Birth on Your Back and Follow Your Body's Urge to Push. *Journal of Perinatal Education,* 23 (4), 207-10.

Women's healthcare:

Criado Perez, C. (2019). *Invisible Women: Exposing Data Bias in a World Designed for Men*. Vintage.

University of California - Berkeley. (2020, August 12). *Lack of females in drug dose trials leads to overmedicated women*. ScienceDaily.

Billock, J. (2018, May 22). Pain bias: The health inequality rarely discussed. *BBC Future.*

Mitchell, J. (2021, May 28). *Report calls out unequal treatment for women with heart disease across the world*. British Heart Foundation.

Caulfield, M. (2022, February 23). *New taskforce to level-up maternity care and tackle disparities*. UK Government Department of Health and Social Care.

NHS England News. (2021, June 13). *NHS pelvic health clinics to help tens of thousands of women across the country*. National Health Service, England.

Progress and backlash:

IPSOS. (2024, March). *International Women's Day 2024*. King's Global Institute for Women's Leadership.

IPSOS. (2022, March). *International Women's Day 2022*. King's Global Institute for Women's Leadership.

Bartholomew, J. (2022, February 22). Number of women in FTSE 100 boardrooms up to 39% in a decade. *The Guardian*.

Arguedas, A. R., Mukherjee, M., & Kleis Nielse, R. (2024, March). *Women and Leadership in the News Media 2024: Evidence from 12 Markets*. Reuters Institute.

Adu, A., & Goodier, M. (2024, July 5). Keir Starmer's cabinet will have most female ministers in history. *The Guardian*.

Harman, H. (2017). *A Woman's Work*. Allen Lane

Clarke, M. (2015). Dual Careers: The New Norm for Gen Y Professionals. *Career Development International*, 20 (6), 563-582.

Organisation for Economic Cooperation and Development. (2021, November). *Employment, Labour and Social Affairs Policy Briefs. Can pay transparency tools close the gender wage gap?*

Francis, A. (2022, June 14). Gen Z: The workers who want it all. *BBC Worklife*.

Powell, C. (2012). *It Worked For Me: In Life and Leadership*. Harper.

Gavett, G. (2021, September 28). *The Problem with 'Greedy Work'. Why high-salary jobs with long, inflexible hours exacerbate the gender pay gap – and what to do about it.* Harvard Business Review.

Giattino, C., Ortiz-Ospina, E., & Roser, M. (2020, December). *Working Hours*. Our World in Data.

Grosse, R. (2018). *The Four-Day Workweek*. Routledge.

Campbell, T. T. (2023). The four-day work week: a chronological, systematic review of the academic literature. *Management Review Quarterly*.

Broom. D. (2023, October 25). *Four-day work week trial in Spain leads to healthier workers, less pollution.* World Economic Forum.

Sandberg, S. (2013). *Lean In: Women, Work and the Will to Lead*. Random House.

Societal solutions:

Bartley, P. (2022). The Selfish Seventies?: 1970–1979. In *Women's Activism in Twentieth-Century Britain. Gender and History.* Palgrave Macmillan.

Gillard, J. (2023). *Annie Lennox on anthems, activism and global feminism*. A Podcast of One's Own. https://podcasts.apple.com/au/podcast/annie-lennox-on-anthems-activism-global-feminism/id1466658814?i=1000631006202

Blaffer Hrdy, S. (2023, November 7). *The Life Scientific: Human Evolution and Parenthood*. BBC Radio 4. https://www.bbc.co.uk/programmes/m001s5ff

Korkodilos, M. (2015, August 10). *Ensuring all children have the best start in life*. UK Health Security Agency. Gov.UK.

Brearley, J. (2021, September 13). *Parliamentary briefing: the case for an independent review of the early years sector.* Pregnant Then Screwed and The Fawcett Society.

Brearley, J. (2024, March 24). *Childcare cost crisis persists despite new government funding.* Pregnant Then Screwed.

Ashdown, M., & Hooker, L. (2023, November 6). One in 10 mothers with under-fours quit work over childcare, says charity. *BBC News.*

Skopeliti, C. (2023, November 8).'Major anxiety': parents describe nightmare of England's childcare crisis. *The Guardian.*

Shine, I. (2023, July 19). *These countries have the highest childcare costs in the world.* World Economic Foundation.

Topping, A. (2021, September 12). How do UK childcare costs stack up against the best. *The Guardian.*

Arneson, K. (2021, June 29). Why doesn't the US have mandated paid maternity leave? *BBC Equality Matters.*

Peaker, H. (2017). *Women's Equality Party Manifesto.* UK Women's Equality Party.

Chzhen, Y., Gromada, A., & Rees, G. (2019). *Are the world's richest countries family friendly? Policy in the OECD and EU.* UNICEF.

Kan, M. Y., & Gershuny, J. (2010). Gender segregation and bargaining in domestic labour, in Scott, J., Crompton, R., & Lyonette, C. (Eds.) *Gender Inequalities in the 21st Century: New Barriers and Continuing Constraints.* Edward Elgar Publishing.

Pregnant Then Screwed. (2022). *March of The Mummies Demands.* https://pregnantthenscrewed.com/march-of-the-mummies-demands/

Winchester, N. (2021, July 1). *Women's health outcomes: Is there a gender gap?* House of Lords Library. UK Parliament. https://lordslibrary.parliament.uk/womens-health-outcomes-is-there-a-gender-gap/

Campbell, O. M. R., Cegolon, L., Macleod, D., & Benova, L. (2016). Length of Stay After Childbirth in 92 Countries and Associated Factors in 30 Low- and Middle-Income Countries: Compilation of Reported Data and a Cross-sectional Analysis from Nationally Representative Surveys. *PLOS Medicine*, 13 (3), e1001972.

InfoFinland. (2024, February 8). *Holidays and Leave.* City of Helsinki.

Fortin, P. (2017). *What have been the effects of Quebec's Universal Childcare System on Women's Economic Security?* Brief Submitted to the Standing Committee on the Status of Women (FEWO) of the House of Commons, Ottawa.

Campbell, D. (2023, December 5). Huge delays to access maternal mental healthcare in England called a scandal. *The Guardian.*

Berrisford, G., & Dunkley-Bent, J. (2023, March 17). *Perinatal mental health services - supporting pregnant women and new mothers.* NHS England.

Laborde, S. (2024, May 27). *The Latest Women in Tech Statistics to Know in 2023.* Tech Report.

Duffy, C. (2024, May 23). Meta created an advisory council that's composed of entirely White men. *CNN News.*

Bethune, S., & Lewan, E. (2017). *APA's Survey Finds Constantly Checking Electronic Devices Linked to Significant Stress for Most Americans.* American Psychological Association.

Cibean, T. (2022, June 5). *Adults in the U.S. check their phones 352 times a day on average, 4x more often than in 2019.* TechSpot.

Rao, D. (2024, February 8). The ideological gap between younger men and women is becoming a chasm. *The Week US.*

Asher, S. (2019, December 16). Barack Obama: Women are better leaders than men. *BBC News.*

Chan, V. (2010, January 25). *Western Women Can Come to the Rescue of the World.* The Dalai Lama Centre for Peace and Education.

Our World in Data. (2024). *Share of women in parliament. Data adapted from Inter-Parliamentary Union (via World Bank).* https://ourworldindata.org/grapher/share-of-women-in-parliament-ipu

Collignon, S., & Cowper-Coles, M. (2022). *Women's Political Careers.* King's Global Institute for Women's Leadership.

Hinsliff, G. (2022, June 18). How to get a better class of MP? Help mothers stand for parliament. *The Guardian.*

Individual solutions:

Indian Opinion. (1913, August 9). *The Collected Works of Mahatma Gandhi,* 13 (153), 241.

Holmes, C. (2024). *Happier Hour: How to Spend Your Time for a Happier, More Meaningful Life.* Penguin.

Rodsky, E. (2019). *Fair Play: Share the mental load, rebalance your relationship and transform your life.* Hachette.

Lakshmin, P. (2023). *Real Self-Care: A Transforming Programme for Redefining Wellness.* Penguin.

Slaughter, A. M. (2012, July). Why Women Still Can't Have it All. *The Atlantic.* https://www.theatlantic.com/magazine/archive/2012/07/why-women-still-cant-have-it-all/309020/

Aswell, S. (2019, February 13). Viral Comic Shows All the Literal Hurdles Working Women Face. *Scary Mommy.*

Crenshaw, K. (1991). Mapping the Margins: Intersectionality, Identity Politics, and Violence against Women of Color. *Stanford Law Review*, 43 (6), 1241-1299.

Cox, B. (2017). *Jo Cox, More in Common.* Two Roads.

Lucy Delap. (2000). The Freewoman, Periodical Communities, and the Feminist Reading Public. *The Princeton University Library Chronicle*, 61 (2), 233–276.

Index

5-HTT gene 77

abortion 20, 21–2, 21n3, 171n55, 175, 218
   see also female bodies
acceptance of life and self 100, 101–3
Action for Happiness (charity) 88n27, 98
adversity, and developing life purpose 103–4
age and happiness 82, 117
ageing
   elderly parent care 138
   and kindness to others 91
   longevity 107–8
AI (Artificial Intelligence) 215–16
'Alexa,' risks of using 218
alloparenting 24, 141, 210
altruism (kindness) 90–2, 91n29
ambition 47–8, 55–6, 58, 70–1
American Declaration of Independence 74–5
Anderson, Elizabeth Garrett 199, 200
anger, gender differences 168–9
animals, gendered behaviour 59–61
Aristotle 3, 74
   assertiveness, and gender 133–4, 167
Astor, Nancy 40n7
attachment theory 107
Attenborough, David 103
Attia, Dr Peter 102–3
attractiveness
   see also beauty
   recognition of 45
   requirement to maintain 15, 35, 36–7, 38, 45, 53, 194
authenticity of self 101–2
autism spectrum disorder 164n48
autoimmune disease, gender differences 81n24
autonomy at work 125–6, 152–3

beauty
   see also attractiveness
   and self-worth 17, 83, 176–9
beauty premium 15, 83
Beauvoir, Simone de 112
behavioural science, happiness interventions 76, 88–106
Belam, Martin 175
biological determinism 62
   see also nature and nurture
biological differences 169–76, 194
   and gender 161–3
   impact on women's workload 113

birth control 20, 170–1
birth-rate decline 40–1
Black Women's Equal Pay Day 111n34
blue colour gendering 62–3
body hating and shaming 15, 177–8
body-mind relationship 93
bonobos, social behaviours 61
boundary setting for guilt 228
Bowlby, John 107
boys, mental health issues 186n64
brain
   intelligence 83–4, 162, 163, 199
   neurochemicals for reward 77, 85, 90, 91
   neuroplasticity 99, 164
Brearley, Joeli 214
British Social Attitudes Surveys 39, 53
Brown, Dr Dorothy Lavinia 40n7
Brown, Professor Brené 119, 229–30
Burke, Tarana 134
Burton, Frances 61

cancer, gender differences 81n24
careers
   ambition 47–8, 55–6, 58, 70–1
   beauty premium 83
   dropout from high level positions 57, 58
   effect of part-time working for women 147
   kaleidoscope model 205
   portfolio careers 153–6, 157, 223–4
   pros and cons 43, 45
caregiving
   alloparenting 24, 141
   in animals 59, 61
   avoiding fatigue 91–2
   childcare 141–2, 209–12
   of children with disabilities 123
   economic bias against 139–40
   elderly parents 138
   in friendships 108
   government failings 58
   privileges and benefits 136–7
   and self-confidence loss 122–3
   time commitment 23–4, 50
   by women compared to men 37–8, 70, 71
'catfishing' (social media) 186
change, adapting to 99–100
Chatterjee, Dr Rangan 89
child marriage 4
childbearing see motherhood
childbirth
   complications 174–5
   male doctors 200n72
   male fear of 201
   maternal mortality 63n19, 166, 202
   postnatal care 212–13
childcare 139–40, 141–2, 209–12
   see also alloparenting; caregiving
children with disabilities, impact of caregiving 123
chimpanzees, social behaviours 61
choice
   and happiness 26, 110, 152–3
   limited choices for work 124–5
climate, impact on women 58, 85
Clinton, Hillary 56
coercive control 5n1, 110
commuting to work 86
confidence vs assertiveness 133–4
Confucius 150
constrained choice 26, 125
contraception 20, 170–1
Cooper, Daisy May 188
COVID-19 pandemic 114, 144, 186, 187, 190, 206
Cox, Jo 233
Cox, Tracey 142
Crenshaw, Kimberlé 232n74
Criado Perez, Caroline 201
critical voice (inner voice) 102–3
cultural difference 54n15, 138

cultural feminism 67–8, 69, 69–70
cyber misogyny 136

Dalai Lama XIV 75, 100
Darwin, Charles, opinion of women 59, 199n71
Day, Elizabeth 227
Delevingne, Cara 160
depression 149
Desiderata (poem) (Ehrmann) 156
Diener, Ed 83
discretionary time 87, 225
divorce 46, 79–80, 124n36, 143, 147, 148–9
DNA
  and ageing 91
  comparisons of animals and humans 60
doctors, women as 198–203
Dolan, Paul 74
domestic abuse 4–5, 110, 184
  legislation 5n1, 21
domestic load 225
  see also caregiving; emotional labour; mental labour
  deprioritising 223
  inequality in relationships 53, 58, 125, 129, 136, 142–4
  part time working mothers 148
  shared with partner 46, 148, 225–6
  and work factors 86
dopamine 90, 91
Doyle, Glennon 119
Dufu, Tiffany 49–50
Dweck, Carol 99

early years care
  see also childcare
  benefits and provision 210–11
earnings
  equal incomes 45–6
  high incomes 144
  main factors 84
  part-time incomes 146
  power of main breadwinner 53
economy, value of childcare 139–40
education
  gender inequalities 4, 20, 21
  and happiness 84
emotional intelligence 164, 164–5
  see also emotional labour
emotional labour
  see also attractiveness; caregiving; mental labour
  in marriage 79
  role of women 10, 33–4, 35, 37–8, 53, 113, 114, 143
  at work 36
  worthiness work 160, 183–4
emotions
  see also emotional intelligence; happiness
  anger 168–9
  depression 149
  gratitude 101
  resentment 228
empathy 164
employment *see* work; working mothers
EMPOWER LIFE mnemonic 221–32
endometriosis 81n24
enrichment model of multiple roles 89–90, 157
equal pay 20, 111
  historically 42n10, 43n11
Equal Pay Act 1970 20
ethnicity, and inequalities 81, 111, 165, 166, 202
eudaimonia (happiness) 74n20
eustress 97
Everard, Sarah, fatal attack 182n62
exercise, benefits 93–5

Faludi, Susan 203
families
  fathers' involvement 13, 58, 140–1
  single parents 5, 23, 124, 125,

141, 147, 187
types of family 5
fathers
   being a good parent 24
   caregiving 13–14, 58, 140–1
   and employment 5–6, 51–2, 131
   importance for children's development 13
Fausto-Sterling, Anne 199
Fawcett Society 134, 211
female bodies
   beauty 17, 83, 160, 176–9, 194 (*see also* attractiveness)
   female biology 159–60, 169–76, 194
   safety issues 160, 179–86, 194–5 (*see also* domestic abuse)
   sex and sexuality 160, 187–94, 195 (*see also* sex and sexuality)
female genital mutilation (FMG) 4, 170n52
feminised industries 132n39
feminism
   first wave 19–20
   second wave 8–9, 20–1, 43, 200
   third wave 21, 232n74
   fourth wave 216
   attitudes towards women 203–4
   definition 65
   historical perspective 19–21, 71, 197–8
   repercussions of 35
   types 66–8, 69–70, 232
fertility 173–4
financial abuse 110, 110n33
financial independence 34, 39–40, 43, 109–10, 116, 125–6, 147
financial issues 78–9, 120, 123
   gender inequalities 109–12, 111
Fine, Cordelia 166
first wave feminism 19–20
fixed mindset 99
flexible working 86, 144, 206, 214–15, 226

four-day workweek 206
Frances-White, Deborah 43
Frankl, Viktor 103–4
free time, and happiness 87
Freud, Sigmund
   on women 130n38
   work/life balance 130
Friday, Nancy 192n69
Friedan, Betty 43, 223
friendship, protective factor for women 107–8
full-time work 58, 121–2, 142, 145, 148, 149–50

Gandhi 223
Gates, Melinda 57, 231
Gawdat, Mo 28–9
gender
   see also gender equality; gender identity; gender inequalities
   and biological differences 68–9, 81n24, 107–8, 161–3, 199
   and social conditioning 163–5, 166, 194
   social construct 161
   societal attitudes 10, 161–2, 205
   stereotypes 163–4
gender equality
   see also gender inequalities
   correlation with happiness 114–15, 117
   effect on relationships 46n12
   encouraging in families 227
   and feminism 65–6, 68–9, 69–70
   global comparisons 114–15
   legislation 20
   and paternal leave 213
   pay 20
   timeline target 115
   views on 203–4
   women in professions 204–5
gender identity
   see also LGBTQ+
   colour association 62–3
   gender identity and economics

54n14
transgender and intersex persons 162n46, 181n60
gender inequalities
see also domestic load; emotional labour; gender equality
  assertiveness 133–4, 167
  in caregiving 37–8, 70, 71
  due to social conditioning 162–9
  education 4, 20, 21
  effect on women in society 57
  and happiness 27–9
  health and healthcare 80–1, 149, 201, 231
  OECD statement 29
  pay 111, 131, 146, 205, 206
  in relationships 53n, 54, 58, 143–4, 149
  time poverty of women 87, 112–14
  wealth ownership 57, 110
  work 124–5, 131–6, 156–7
gender investment gap 111, 146
gender pay gap 111, 131, 146, 205, 206
gender pension gap 111, 146
Generation Z 48, 151, 205
genetics
  see also nature and nurture
  predisposition to happiness 76–7, 116
girls in crisis, teenage sexual challenges 185–6, 195
giving 90–2, 91n29
Glick, Patrick 79
goals, importance 97–8, 126–7, 149–50
Goldin, Claudia 226
good enough parenting 23
government
  abolition of tax on sanitary products 172
  failings 57, 58, 209
  gender health gap report 81n24
  paternal leave policies 213
  women in government 205, 219–20
Grant, Adam 107
gratitude 101–2
GREAT DREAM mnemonic 88
Gregory, Philippa 16, 181n61, 208n73
growth mindset 99
guilt of mothers
  causes 25–6, 71, 93, 119–20
  conditioning of working mothers 48–50
  exploited at work 36
  inadequacy 122, 128–9
  letting go 227–8
Guterres, António 115

habits for happiness 76, 88–106
Hamilton, Dr David 91
happiness
  and age 82, 117
  and beauty 83
  and choice/autonomy 26, 110, 124–6, 151–2, 197–8
  concept and definitions 73–4, 75, 116
  and education 84
  and employment 86, 108–9, 126, 127–8, 130–1, 150–2, 151–2, 157
  and exercise 93–5
  and gender equality/inequality 27–9, 114–15, 117
  habits and behaviours 88–106, 117
  happiness equation 28–9
  and health 80–2
  and housework 129–30
  and intelligence 83–4
  life circumstances 78–88
  and location 84–6, 117
  and marriage 79–80, 116
  mindset 99
  negative impact of 104–6
  and parenting 74
  and practising kindness 90–2
  and relationships 92

and single status 79–80
spiritual practices 87–8, 117
spreading 91
and wealth 78–9, 116
happiness dip
  parents 74n21
  unemployed 86
happiness solutions 88–104, 106–16
happy genes 77
Harari, Yuval N. 16–17
Harman, Harriet 205
Harvard Grant Study (happiness) 92
Hatmaker, Jen 183
having it all, experience and challenges 34–5, 53, 58
health and healthcare
  and happiness 80–2, 84n25
  mental health 95–6, 123, 185–6, 186n64, 212, 216
  women 63n19, 80–1, 149, 201, 202, 231
heart disease, gendered healthcare 202
hedonia (happiness) 74n20
helicopter parenting 23, 50, 71
higher education of women 20, 21, 84
Hillingdon, Alice Marion, Baroness, Victorian view of sex 188n67
Hines, Melissa 62–3
Hochschild, Arlie 53n13
Holmes, Professor Cassie 224–5
home working 215
  see also flexible working
housework
  see also domestic load
  gender division 46, 125, 129, 142–3
  and happiness 129–30
  and sex 46
Hrdy, Sarah Blaffer 24, 210
hunter-gatherer societies 64

ikigai 151n45

intelligence
  factor in happiness 83–4
  and gender 162, 163, 199
intensive parenting 23, 50, 71
internet *see* online *entries*; social media
intersectional feminism 232
intersex gender 162n46

Japan, birth-rate decline 40n8
Jefferson, Thomas, President 74–5
Jex-Blake, Sophia 199, 200
job satisfaction 151–2
Johnson, Dr Sue 107
Johnson, Spencer 99
Jong, Erica 48

Keltner, Dr Dacher 90
Kennedy, Dr Becky 222
kindness (altruism) 90–2, 91n29
King, Vanessa 88

Lakshmin, Dr Pooja 230
Langer, Professor Ellen 95–6
Lao Tzu (Chinese philosopher) 95
Layard, Richard 83–4
leadership, and gender 167
learning new things 96–7
legislation for women's rights 19, 20, 21
LGBTQ+
  rights 20, 21
  same-sex couples 5, 21, 148
  transgender and intersex persons 162n46, 181n60
liberal feminism 67, 68, 69–70
life circumstances, effect on happiness 76, 78–88
lion analogy 59
location, and happiness 84–6, 117
London School of Medicine for Women 200
longevity 107–8, 111
Luxemburg, Rosa 227

macaque monkeys, caregiving patterns 61
make-up 177–8, 179
Marçal, Katrine 139
marginalised groups
 gender pay gap 111
 healthcare 81, 202
 sexual harassment and attacks 134, 182n62
marriage 79–80, 107–8, 116
Maté, Dr Gabor 168n50
maternal ambivalence 128–9
maternal care 212–13
 see also childbirth
maternal mortality 63n19, 166, 202
mathematics, gender gap 165–6
matrilineal societies 64
Maudsley, Sir Henry 199
McCarthy, Helen 41, 148
McKinsey Report: *Women in the Workplace* 54n15, 80, 167
Me Too movement 134, 182, 216
meaning in life 103–4
medical research, gender inequalities 201
medicine, women in 198–203
men
 domestic abuse victims 184n63
 effect of marriage 79, 107–8, 116
 emotional response 81–2
 employment after fatherhood 131
 employment rights assumed 184
 expectations of sex 187–8
 family role 45–6, 52
 Peter Principle 147
 suicide 82
 violence 21, 168–9, 180–1
 violent crime victims 181n60
 work-life pressures 51–2
menopause 174
 see also female bodies
menstruation 172
 see also female bodies

mental health
 addictive technology 216
 during and after pregnancy 212–13
 depression 149
 healthcare 186n64, 212, 216
 mindfulness 95–6
 mothers of children with disabilities 123
 teenagers 185–6
mental labour 112–13
 see also emotional labour
millennial generation 47–8, 205
mind-body connection 93, 95–6
mindfulness 89, 95–6
mindset for happiness 99
miscarriages 171n54
misogynist attitudes 59, 74n22, 130n38, 136, 163–4, 186, 199, 199n71
mobile phones 216, 217–18
money *see* financial independence; financial issues
Moran, Caitlin 104–5, 171
mortality rates 63n19, 166, 202
motherhood
 see also mothers
 effect on career ambition 48, 70–1
 societal attitudes 34, 42–3, 71
motherhood penalty 131–2
mothers
 see also motherhood; working mothers
 being a good parent 24
 'giving' role 90–1 (*see also* caregiving)
 guilt 25–6, 36, 48–50, 49–50, 71, 93, 119–20, 128–9
 mental health problems 212
 responsibilities 37–8
 self-care 94–5, 130–1, 222, 228, 229, 230
 effect of smiling 93
 time poverty 87, 89n28, 112–14
 unemployment due to lack of childcare 211, 214

nature and nurture 161–4, 164–5, 168
see also biological determinism
negative visualisation 100
neurochemicals 77, 85, 90, 91
neuroplasticity 99, 164
Ngozi Adichie, Chimamanda 71–2, 197, 232
NHS (National Health Service) 11n2, 95, 203, 212
nurture and nature 161–4, 164–5, 168

Obama, Barack 219–20
Obama, Michelle 55, 94
obesity 35
O'Meara, Mallory 119
online abuse 136
online pornography 191–4
online safety and awareness 217–18, 219
online sex work 189–90
OnlyFans 189–90
optimism 104
Orgad, Shani 27
orgasm gap 160, 170n52
oxytocin 13–14, 91

parental leave 212–14
parenting
  see also caregiving; fathers; intensive parenting; mothers
  alloparenting 24, 141, 210
  being a good parent 24, 52, 141
  challenges of working mothers 14–15, 25–6, 33–4
  encouraging equality in children 227
  gender inequalities 71
  'good enough' parenting 23
  maternal ambivalence 128–9
  parental leave 212–14
  privileges and benefits 74, 136–7
  single parents 5, 23, 124, 125, 141, 187
  stay-at-home parents 52, 109, 122–3, 125, 141, 145
part-time work 15, 132, 144, 145–9, 157
partners 45, 46n12, 96
  see also housework; relationships; sex and sexuality
paternal leave 213
patriarchal society 16–17, 17–19, 45, 53, 63–4, 66, 71
  see also misogynist attitudes
Paula Principle 125, 147
pay inequality 111, 131, 146, 205 206
  see also equal pay
people pleasing 183, 228–9
Peter Principle 147
Peters, Steve 102
pink colour gendering 62–3
politics
  see also government
  polarisation 218–19
  political change 207–8, 219–20
  women in government 205, 219–20
pornography 191–4, 195
portfolio careers 153–6, 157, 223–4
positive thinking 96
postnatal care 212–13
poverty
  effect on women 56–7, 78, 110
  from part-time working 146
pregnancy 166, 170, 174
  see also female bodies
Pregnant Then Screwed campaigns 211, 214
primates, species differences 60–1

Quebec childcare system 211

rape 21, 181–2
relationships
  see also housework; partners
  attraction 46n12
  benefit of new activities 96

benefits of connection 92
divorce 46, 79–80, 124n36, 143, 148–9
domestic task-sharing 46, 148, 225–6
effect of financial independence 109–10
fitting in vs belonging 229–30
impact of kindness 91
marriage 79–80, 107–8, 116
and self-acceptance 102–3
and sex 46, 190
and women's health 107–9
women's proportion of total labour 129n37, 143–4, 149
at work 108–9
religion, and happiness 87, 117
resentment, avoiding 228
residential location *see* location
resilience 84, 98–100
risk taking 166
Roberts, Kevin (Saatchi & Saatchi) 30, 47
Rodman, Frances 100
Rodsky, Eve 225–6
Rohn, Jim 107
rural locations 85–6

safety of women 160, 179–86, 180–3, 194–5
same-sex couples 5, 21, 148
Sandberg, Sheryl 207
sandwich generation 138
Sanger, Margaret 170–1
sanitary products 172
Saroyan, William 96
Schneider, Martin 133
Schuller, Tom 147
seasonal affective disorder (SAD) 85
'second shift' of domestic load 53n13
second wave feminism 8–9, 20–1, 43, 200
self-acceptance 101–3
self-care 94–5, 130–1, 222, 228, 229, 230

self-esteem 102
Seligman, Martin 75
Sellers, Pattie 154
serotonin 77, 85
sex and sexuality
  see also sex work; sexual assault; sexual harassment
  female bodies 160, 187–94, 195
  men's expectations 187–8
  in relationships 46, 190
  teenagers 185–6, 195
  used in bargaining 187
  Victorian view of sex 188n67
  women's experience 46, 160, 187–9
sex differences *see* biological differences
Sex Discrimination Act 1975 20
sex positivity movement 189
sex work 187–91
sexism 59, 72n22, 130n38, 134, 150n43, 163–4, 186, 199, 227
sexual assault 21, 180–3, 195, 198
sexual contract 23–4, 39–40, 55, 70
sexual harassment 134–5, 181, 186
sexual violence in young people 193
single mothers 23, 125, 147
single parents 5, 23, 124, 125, 141, 147, 187
single status, and happiness 79–80
smiling
  effect on happiness 93
  requirement for women 106n32
social class, and women working 41–2
social comparison theory 27
social connection 92, 107–8
social contract 156
social identity theory 26–7
social media 71, 105, 185, 186, 217, 218, 220
socialisation

of gender 163–5, 166, 194
gender inequalities 81–2
societal attitudes
 cyber misogyny 136
 historical misogyny 59, 130n38, 186, 199, 199n71
 sexual contract 39–40, 70
 towards motherhood 34
 towards women working 39, 42–3, 145
societal solutions 232
 childcare 209–12
 flexible working 214–15
 online safety and awareness 218, 219
 parental leave 212–14
 political change 207–8, 219–20
 women in technology 215
society models 63–4
spiritual practices 87–8, 117
stay-at-home parents 52, 109, 122–3, 125, 141, 145
Steinem, Gloria 21n3
Streep, Meryl 223
stress, working mothers 38, 149, 157
Swift, Taylor 178

Tall Poppy Syndrome 54–6, 70
task prioritisation 224–5
technology, challenges and regulation 215–16
teenagers *see* young people
'third shift' of beauty tasks 53n13, 194
third wave feminism 21, 232n74
time poverty 87, 112–14, 117, 120, 224–5
To-do lists 98
transgender persons 162n46, 181n60

unemployment
 due to poor childcare provision 211, 214
 effect on happiness 86
United Nations reports 140, 167, 184
urinary tract infections, gender differences 81n24

vagus nerve 93
Vera-Gray, Dr Fiona 191
violence 168–9
 see also domestic abuse
 crimes against women 180–1
 sexual violence 192, 193
vision boards 98

walking, health benefits 93, 94
wealth
 and happiness 78–9, 116
 inequalities 57, 110
weather, impact on women 58, 85
Winnicott, Donald 23
witch trials 200, 201
women
 see also gender equality; gender inequalities
 assertiveness 167
 autonomy in society 26, 125–6, 151–2, 197–8 (*see also* feminism; women's suffrage)
 impact of biology 169–76, 194
 in business 25, 54–6, 133–4, 135–6, 147, 204–5
 deference to men 183–4
 as doctors 199–203
 domestic abuse 4–5, 5n1, 21, 110, 184 (*see also* sexual assault; sexual harassment)
 emotional response 81–2
 as family breadwinners 23, 41, 57, 124
 friendships with other women 107–8
 global bias against 184
 global challenges and issues 4–5
 in government 205, 219–20, 233
 and happiness 71, 79–80, 106–16

health and healthcare 63n19, 80–1, 149, 201, 202, 231
historical perspective 19–22, 64, 197–8
as investors 111n35
need for women leaders 55, 57–8, 219–20
Paula Principle 125, 147
and pornography 191–2
poverty 56–7, 78, 110, 146
professional status 199–203, 204–5, 207
relationships 79, 107–8, 116 (*see also* partners)
safety from danger 160, 179–86, 180–3, 194–5
sex and sexuality 46, 160, 187–9
sexual assault and harassment 21, 134–5, 180–3, 186, 195, 198
societal expectations 105–6
total labour in partnerships 129n37, 143–4, 149
victims of sexual abuse 180–1
voting rights *see* women's suffrage
workforce dropout 56–7, 58
workload *see* emotional labour; mental labour; time poverty
women in technology 215
Women's Budget Group 139
Women's Liberation Movement Conference 1970 209
women's suffrage 19–20, 203, 207
Wong, Wang Ivy 62–3
Woolf, Virginia, on women writers' needs 112
work
  assertiveness in women 133–4, 167
  flexible and part-time working 86, 144, 206, 214–15, 226
  gender inequalities 124–5, 131–6, 156–7 (*see also* caregiving; domestic load; emotional labour)
  goals 97–8, 126–7, 149–50
  and happiness 86, 126, 127–8, 130–1, 151–2, 157, 266, 271
  high earning jobs 144
  job satisfaction 151–2
  limited choice for mothers 70, 124–5
  making connections 92
  motherhood penalty 131–2
  relationships and happiness 108–9
  requirements from women 36–7, 105–6
  sexism and sexual harassment 134–5, 227
work culture change 226
work-life balance
  conflict for women 44–5
  men 51–2
working-class women, historical employment 41–2
working from home 215
  see also flexible working
  drawbacks 144
working hours, reduction 203, 206
working mothers
  see also motherhood; mothers; women
  challenges of motherhood 14–15, 25–6, 33–4
  and divorce 147
  domestic load *see* domestic load; housework
  guilt 25–6, 36, 71
  historical perspective 41–2
  mid-life challenges 82
  motherhood penalty 131–2
  preference for part-time work 145
  sexual contract 23–4, 39–40, 55, 70
  social isolation 108
  societal attitudes 15, 145
  solutions 221–32
  statistics 5, 11n2, 23, 25, 38,

56, 111, 124, 131, 145, 146,
   174, 187, 204–5, 215, 220
  stress 38, 149, 157
  work not a choice 124–5
World Happiness Report 114–15
World Health Organisation
   (WHO)
  happiness definitions 75
  physical activity
     recommendations 93
worthiness work 160

young people
  impact of online pornography
     193
  impact of social media 105,
     185, 186
  teenage sexuality 186

Giselle lives in Cheshire, England, with her husband and two teenage daughters, but spent her childhood in Canada. Her accent can be placed somewhere in the middle of the Atlantic Ocean, and she has no idea how to pronounce the words 'tomato' or 'water'.

A writer of self-help specifically aimed at women, she is passionately interested in all causes relating to equality and social justice. If you are too and would like to connect with her, she would love to hear from you. You can reach out to Giselle through her website, gisellegoodwin.com, where you can also download a free companion guide to this book to help you create your own happiness manifesto.